Julie Dash: Interviews

Conversations with Filmmakers Series

JULIE DASH INTERVIEWS

Edited by Kameelah L. Martin

University Press of Mississippi / Jackson

The University Press of Mississippi is the scholarly publishing agency of
the Mississippi Institutions of Higher Learning: Alcorn State University,
Delta State University, Jackson State University, Mississippi State University,
Mississippi University for Women, Mississippi Valley State University,
University of Mississippi, and University of Southern Mississippi.

www.upress.state.ms.us

The University Press of Mississippi is a member
of the Association of University Presses.

Any discriminatory or derogatory language or hate speech regarding race,
ethnicity, religion, sex, gender, class, national origin, age, or disability
that has been retained or appears in elided form is in no way an endorsement
of the use of such language outside a scholarly context.

Copyright © 2025 by University Press of Mississippi
All rights reserved
Manufactured in the United States of America
∞

Publisher: University Press of Mississippi, Jackson, USA
Authorised GPSR Safety Representative: Easy Access System Europe -
Mustamäe tee 50, 10621 Tallinn, Estonia, *gpsr.requests@easproject.com*

Library of Congress Cataloging-in-Publication Data

Names: Martin, Kameelah L., 1978– editor.
Title: Julie Dash : interviews / Kameelah L. Martin.
Other titles: Conversations with filmmakers series.
Description: Jackson : University Press of Mississippi, 2025. | Series: Conversations with
 filmmakers series | Includes bibliographical references and index.
Identifiers: LCCN 2025023103 (print) | LCCN 2025023104 (ebook) | ISBN 9781496859327
 (hardback) | ISBN 9781496859310 (trade paperback) | ISBN 9781496859334 (epub) |
 ISBN 9781496859341 (epub) | ISBN 9781496859358 (pdf) | ISBN 9781496859365 (pdf)
Subjects: LCSH: Dash, Julie—Interviews. | African American women motion picture producers
 and directors—United States—Interviews. | Independent filmmakers—United States—
 Interviews. | African American women screenwriters—United States—Interviews. |
 African American women television producers and directors—United States—Interviews. |
 African American women novelists—United States—Interviews. | African American
 women authors—United States—Interviews.
Classification: LCC PS3554.A823 D37 2025 (print) | LCC PS3554.A823 (ebook)
LC record available at https://lccn.loc.gov/2025023103
LC ebook record available at https://lccn.loc.gov/2025023104

British Library Cataloging-in-Publication Data available

Contents

Introduction   vii

Chronology   xvii

Filmography   xxiii

An Interview with Julie Dash   3
   Zeinabu irene Davis / 1991

Not Without My Daughters: A Conversation with Julie Dash and Houston A. Baker Jr.   13
   Houston A. Baker Jr. / 1992

"I Do Exist": From "Black Insurgent" to Negotiating the Hollywood Divide—A Conversation with Julie Dash   28
   Michael T. Martin / 2010

6° of Geechee   45
   Stephanie Hunt / 2015

Interview: Julie Dash   50
   Cassie da Costa / 2016

Audio Story: *Daughters of the Dust*—Julie Dash Interview   57
   Andrea Chase / 2016

Interview: Julie Dash   63
   So Mayer / 2016

The "Daughter" Returns: Julie Dash Speaks About Her Triumphant Revival—And Where She's Been   67
   Bilge Ebiri / 2016

Filmmaker Interview: Julie Dash   74
    Michael Glover Smith / 2016

Daughters of the Dust Director Julie Dash Talks Filmmaking and Shaping the Black Female Image   79
    Carlos Valladares / 2016

Julie Dash on the Coming of Age of *Daughters of the Dust*   88
    Stephen Saito / 2016

Invisible Scratch Lines: An Interview with Julie Dash   95
    Maori Karmel Holmes / 2016

Filmmaker Julie Dash: "#OscarsSoWhite Worked!"   106
    Simran Hans / 2017

Controlling the World Within the Frame: Julie Dash and Ayoka Chenzira Reflect on New York and Filmmaking   109
    Michele Prettyman / 2019

An Interview with Julie Dash   120
    Carina del Valle Schorske / 2020

Without Living in the Folds of Our Wounds: A Conversation with Julie Dash   133
    A. E. Hunt / 2020

In the Director's Chair with Frances-Anne Solomon and Julie Dash   142
    Frances-Anne Solomon / 2020

Race, Rebellion, and Resilience: In Conversation with Julie Dash   154
    Kameelah L. Martin / 2023

Additional Sources   177

Index   183

Introduction

Julie Dash is a pioneering African American filmmaker whose groundbreaking work has significantly impacted both Black independent cinema and the broader landscape of American filmmaking. If #BlackGirlMagic could be defined by a person, Dash would be a strong contender for the cultural weight of that title. Her visual artistry and commitment to privileging the narrative arts of Africa and its diaspora inscribe her as cultural royalty within Black feminist creative production. The visibility and veracity with which she deploys the lived experiences of Black women in film have unequivocally altered the trajectory of their representation in the contemporary moment. The southern gothic aesthetic recognizable in Kasi Lemmons's *Eve's Bayou* (1997) and Beyoncé's *Lemonade* (2016) would not be possible without the marshlands and Spanish moss-laden trees of the Georgia Sea Islands captured through Dash's vision. Dash is a cultural treasure; her work a testament to the quintessence of Black life and orature. This collection seeks to contextualize the longevity of her career, provide a view of her full body of work, and offer a comprehensive resource on this iconic filmmaker.

In the words of another famous New Yorker, "it was all dream." Julie Ethel Dash stumbled into cinematography by pure accident. Born in 1952 in Queens, New York, to Rhudine Henderson and Charles Edward Dash, migrants from South Carolina, Dash's sensibility was influenced by her parents' Gullah Geechee roots. Where her neighborhood friends had "cold cereal" for breakfast, the Dash household served "fish roe . . . and grits" as a breakfast staple (Solomon 2020, 143). Each summer she would travel to Charleston and be immersed in the melodious sounds of her relatives' Gullah tongue, "without knowing that was what she was hearing" (del Valle Schorske 2020, 120). She tells *The Believer*, "Nobody explained it to me"; she came to understand the beauty and difference of her familial heritage (del Valle Schorske 2020, 120). It was a cultural distinction Dash would come to appreciate and leverage as part of her creative process.

As an adolescent growing up in the Queensbridge Projects, she sought a productive way to spend her after-school and weekend hours. She and a friend signed up for a photography class with Omar Mubarak (Randy Abbott) at the nearby Studio Museum of Harlem. As it turned out, the class was about moving images rather than still photography. Dash hadn't even known that being a filmmaker was a dream a little Black girl from Long Island, New York, could dare to dream. The early immersion into the craft made an indelible impression on her, and the Studio Museum of Harlem became a launchpad for success. She went on to complete an undergraduate degree in film and television production from the Leonard Davis Center for Performing Arts at the City College of New York in 1973. As a student there, she was hired as film crew for St. Clair Bourne, and she directed her first documentary, *Working Models for Success*, for the New York City Housing and Development Administration. Driven by a need to move beyond the documentary genre, Dash headed west to Los Angeles by 1974.

She enrolled in the American Film Institute's Conservatory Fellowship Program in Producing and Writing. Dash began to establish her own aesthetic as she adapted "Four Women," a song written and performed by Nina Simone, for the screen. Influenced by the Black Arts Movement and creatively drawn to the stories of Black women, Dash produced the short film *Four Women* (1975), which would later win a Director's Guild Award. It was also awarded Best Film by a Woman at the Miami International Film Festival in 1978. She also began drafting a story about her father's Gullah Geechee heritage around this time, which evolved into the screenplay for her first feature film. Dash's time in Los Angeles was productive. After earning her masters of fine arts from AFI, she fell in with a new cadre of African and African American students at the University of California Los Angeles.

In the realm of Black independent film, Dash is a key figure of the LA Rebellion, a movement of African American filmmakers who emerged from UCLA in the 1970s and 1980s. Billy Woodberry, Charles Burnett, Haile Gerima, Barbara McCullough, and Larry Clark were among the unofficially dubbed LA School of Black Filmmakers. Their innovative style and cultural awareness in independent film, however, caused them to be known more popularly as the LA Rebellion. Dash's work exemplifies the movement's commitment to creating authentic, nuanced representations of Black life and challenging the stereotypes perpetuated by Hollywood. Their "postsoul" or Black Arts Movement sensibility ushered in a generational shift in what is possible for Black images in the media.

Dash worked with her peers to create and agitate for more space for independent Black film. She also took her studies seriously, learning and working in every part of film production. She did sound work for fellow student Larry Clark's *Passing Through* (1977) and earned script and continuity credit for *A Different Image* (1982) by Alile Sharon Larkin, also an UCLA film school student. She worked as first assistant director with classmate Charles Burnett on his film *My Brother's Wedding* (1983). She and classmate Barbara McCullough attended the Cannes International Film Festival for the first time, intent on showcasing films by their young Black filmmaking colleagues. They leave the festival having called more attention to Black independent cinema internationally.

The impression of Black women writers on Dash's filmic vision reared its head when she adapted Alice Walker's short story "Diary of an African Nun" to short film as a student in 1977. Her approach to storytelling—which often incorporates elements of oral tradition, folklore, and historical research—places her firmly within the tradition of Black women's narrative practices specifically and Black narrative traditions more generally. Dash's films, like the novels of Toni Morrison, Toni Cade Bambara, and Alice Walker, seek to disinter and reimagine African American histories that have been overlooked or misrepresented in mainstream narratives. As Dash herself has noted, her approach is heavily influenced by historical research and a desire to excavate and visualize the stories of Black women that have been relegated to the margins. In an interview with Carina del Valle Schorske (2020), Dash remarked, "History is all there: I just dig it up, unearth it, make it available. It's in the books; it's in the journals and oral histories from primary sources" (122).

Also in 1977, *Diary of an African Nun* was screened at the Los Angeles Film Exposition; it went on to earn Best Film by a Woman at the Miami International Film Festival the following year. Dash earned a Director's Guild Award for *Four Women* in 1977 as well. Soon after, in 1981, Dash earned two national awards—a Guggenheim Fellowship and a National Endowment for the Arts grant—to support her filmmaking odyssey. By 1982 she was writing and directing her second short film, *Illusions*, which she also submitted as her thesis at UCLA. The film, which earned First Prize from the Black American Cinema Society and Best Film of the Decade from the Black Filmmaker Foundation, conveys the phenomenon of African Americans "passing" for white. The influence of stories like Nella Larsen's *Passing* (1929) and the film *Imitation of Life* (1959) can be seen as creative predecessors of Dash's film, but *Illusions* specifically calls out the lack of diversity in the film industry without subtlety. Dash's commitment to such realism and cultural specificity has made her work a touchstone for discussions on Black identity and representation in cinema. Dash then returned to her work in documentary film, directing *Breaking the Silence* (1988) for the National Black Women's Health Project in Atlanta, Georgia. The following year she earned a Rockefeller Fellowship and worked with performance artist Ishmael Houston-Jones to direct the short film *Relatives* (1990).

Most notably, in 1990, she began production on her first feature-length film, *Daughters of the Dust*. Much of the filming took place on Sapelo Island, one of the last undeveloped barrier islands off the coast of Georgia. Dash employed her friend Gloria Naylor, author of *The Women of Brewster Place* (1982) and *Mama Day* (1988), as a production assistant. She also borrowed her central character

Eula's monologue about Ibo Landing from author Paule Marshall, whose novel *Praisesong for the Widow* (1983) is partly set in the fictional Sea Island community of Tatem, South Carolina, where one of the characters recalls the tale of the Ibo Landing as told by the elders. Dash masterfully incorporates Marshall's eloquent rendition of the folktale into *Daughters*, forever linking the two narratives—her film and Marshall's novel—in a legacy of Black women's literary and filmic craft. In a conversation with bell hooks (not included in this collection), Dash describes the film in literary terms: "*Daughters of the Dust* is like speculative fiction, like a *what if* situation" captured in moving images (Dash 1992, 29).

At her core, Dash is committed to telling stories about Black life and culture in unconventional ways. She intentionally decenters Western linear narrative and tired tropes of Blackness. "I also want to do something very different, and that's where we get into the poetic thing," she says of her depictions in *Daughters*. She confides to hooks, "I want to show black families, particularly black women, as we have never seen them before. I want to touch something inside of each black person that sees [my film], some part of them that's never been touched before" (Dash 1992, 32). *Daughters* premiered at the prestigious Sundance Film Festival in 1991 and was nominated for the Grand Jury Prize. It earned the Excellence in Cinematography award before going on to become the first film by an African American woman to be released theatrically in 1992.

In the years since its release, the film has become a staple resource in academic disciplines such as English, film studies, women's and gender studies, African American studies, and the like. It has a cultlike following across the globe, a nod to the foreign film aesthetic with which it has been compared. In *Daughters of the Dust: The Making of an African American Women's Film* (1992), Dash, with Black feminist scholars Toni Cade Bambara and bell hooks, documents the tedious detail and copious research that went into her creative process. Explaining the girls' and women's hairstyles as a sign of social hierarchy, the Kongo cosmogram impressed upon the turtle shell, the rhythmic counting game played in an African tongue, and the visage of the glass bottle tree, Dash provides a deeper context for the film's message and representation of a different type of pre-emancipation legacy. The book, if not the film on its own merit, squarely situates Dash among the most prolific artistic innovators of African American life and culture and establishes her film as a visual classroom.

Throughout her career, Dash has consistently pushed boundaries and challenged conventional narratives, particularly in her portrayal of African American women. Her early short films, including *Four Women* (1975) and *Illusions* (1982), showcased her innovative approach to storytelling and her commitment to exploring complex themes of identity, history, and culture. *Daughters of the Dust*, considered her magnus opus, stands as a landmark in American cinema, to be sure. As the first feature film directed by an African American woman to receive wide theatrical release in the United States, it broke the tough terrain of the film industry in terms of both representation and artistic concept. The film's lyrical, nonlinear narrative and rich visual style drew attention to Gullah Geechee culture, offering a distinct perspective on African American history and identity. In the present age in which Gullah Geechee culture is more widely recognized and celebrated, *Daughters* is often cited as a signature representation responsible for bringing more awareness to the region and culture. Such positive images of Black life were hardly accessible at the time of the film's release. I recall the late 1990s, when securing a VHS copy from my campus library for my own educational viewing was no easy feat. My Black professor guarded the single library edition for entire semesters, afraid it would be lost or damaged.

Dash offered the world a very different representation of what it can mean to be African American and southern in *Daughters*. Her film redirects the visual symbols of enslavement away from the trite motifs of cotton fields, whips, and chains to more subtle, though no less insidious, indicators of a life enslaved. The story of the Peazants continues in Dash's first published novel, *Daughters of the Dust: A Novel* (1997). The care and masterful symbolism with which she weaves the saga of second and third generations of Peazants is reminiscent of Zora Neale Hurston. It is an underappreciated gem that has rarely been discussed in interviews. (I broach the subject with Dash in a new interview published exclusively in this collection.) The audiobook (2021), in a sweet twist of fate, is narrated by Bahni Turpin, the screen actress who played Iona in the iconic film and who has successfully pivoted from the stage and screen to a vibrant career as an acclaimed voice actor.

Daughters of the Dust has earned numerous awards over its more than thirty-year life, and it was added to the National Registry of Films maintained by the Library of Congress in 2004. Though it is easily the film for which Dash is best known, it is not the culminating achievement of her career. Despite the many challenges she has faced in actualizing her dream to make films, she is a living, breathing, and *actively* working filmmaker. Her filmography is likely to be out of date by the time this collection is published, in fact.

Dash's credits in the film industry include music videos, television films, short films, television advertisements, documentary films, television serial episodes, and webisodes. She is a writer, producer, and director. Yet much of the scholarship and many interviews, with their singular focus on *Daughters*, imply that Dash is a one-hit wonder of the film genre. A review of her filmic portfolio indicates otherwise. She has done the work. She *has* the range. But the film industry has made this reality nearly impossible to perceive. The initial release of *Daughters* did not lead to a surge of opportunities for Dash; instead, she had to continue fighting for visibility and resources in an industry that remained largely indifferent to her vision. Dash has faced numerous challenges in the film industry as a Black woman, navigating a landscape that historically has been exclusionary and biased against both women and people of color. Hollywood has long been dominated by white male directors, making it difficult for other filmmakers to gain recognition and opportunities. Dash's experience reflects the broader issues of racism and misogyny (or, more aptly, *misogynoir*, to use Moya Bailey's terminology) that have plagued the industry since its inception.

Despite the critical acclaim for her work, Dash struggled to secure financing and support for her projects beyond *Daughters*, as Hollywood executives were typically uninterested in narratives that deviated from traditional racial stereotypes. She pitched various unique stories, such as those about African American women serving overseas during World War II and Black magicians, but found little interest from studio executives who preferred more conventional racial narratives or who simply wanted to work with other filmmakers. In our 2023 interview, Dash told me unabashedly that she gets attached to projects because other stakeholders have asked for her specifically. Many of these stakeholders are other Black women. They make space for her when others do not. This resistance to greenlighting Dash's screenplays underscores the industry's reluctance to embrace stories that challenge prevailing stereotypes and offer nuanced portrayals of Black existence. Because Dash faced ongoing challenges in securing funding for her feature-length projects, she turned to television, directing films such as *Funny Valentines* (1999), *The Rosa Parks Story* (2002), and serial episodes of TV shows like *Queen Sugar* (2017), *Our Kind of People* (2021), and *Reasonable Doubt* (2022). This shift to television allowed her to continue working and telling important stories, but it also reflected the limitations imposed by the film industry on Black female directors.

Notwithstanding these impediments, Dash's work has had a lasting impact on Black independent cinema and the representation of Black women in film. She is also cementing her impact on the future of Black independent cinema through her instruction at institutions of higher learning—many of which have been historically Black colleges and universities. In our 2023 interview, we discussed her role as Professor Dash and what legacy she wants to impart to her students. Her oeuvre is celebrated for its poetic storytelling and laser focus on the resilience and complexity of Black women. She doesn't describe herself or her work as Black or feminist, per se, but the correlations are ever present. Dash's legacy is one of perseverance and innovation, paving the way for future generations of Black female filmmakers to tell their stories on their own terms.

The significance of Dash's work extends beyond her role as a filmmaker. As a scholar whose work sits at the crossroads of literary studies of the African

Diaspora and folklore studies, I can attest that Dash is among the foundational storytellers embedded in my research and teaching. The intertextuality of *Daughters of the Dust* (both the film and novel), for instance, with the Black literary archetype of the conjure woman cannot be understated. Scholars have extensively analyzed Dash's narrative style and artistic vision. For instance, hooks, in *Reel to Real: Race, Sex, and Class at the Movies* (1996) praises Dash for her ability to "create a visual narrative that is both politically and aesthetically radical" (hooks 1996, 107). Similarly, in *Black American Cinema*, edited by Manthia Diawara, Dash's work is highlighted for its "innovative use of visual and narrative techniques to convey the complexities of Black women's experiences" (1993, 17). Dash's use of Black feminist narrative and her ability to supplant the status quo of Black women's representation in cinema aligns with the evolution of Black women's writing and visual arts that exploded in the late 1970s. She is as much a part of Black feminist narrative tradition as Toni Cade Bambara and Ntozake Shange.

This collection of interviews celebrates the genius of Julie Dash's filmmaking career and is much overdue as we approach the thirty-fifth anniversary of *Daughters of the Dust*. While a plethora of scholarship exists on the impact and politics of her films, this collection satisfies a need for a more holistic approach to studying her body of work, presenting a well-structured history of her career captured in the chronology and filmography. It addresses her films and directorial work through multifaceted, interdisciplinary approaches (academic, journalistic, and otherwise) to engaging Dash in her own words; it makes every attempt not to repeat ideas or oversaturate the audience with myopic interpretations. The interviews collected here will put students, scholars, and admirers of Dash's oeuvre in closer proximity to her creative thought process and filmic influences, as well as make accessible an archive of conversations in which she discusses the longevity and challenges of her career, intergenerational shifts, and the reception of her work across the globe. Starting with conversations about her debut film, *Illusions* (1982), and touching upon other works such as *Praise House* (1991) and the series *Queen Sugar* (2016–2022), the interviews weave together the stylistic integrity and unconventional model of storytelling that Dash cogently midwives into existence. The breadth of the conversations captured in this collection showcases the diversity of Dash's portfolio and underlines why she is one of the most recognized Black women in cinema.

The interviews provide firsthand accounts of Dash's experiences and challenges in the film industry, offering valuable context for understanding her work and its significance. Through these interviews, readers gain insight into Dash's creative process, her influences, and her approach to storytelling, which are essential for appreciating the depth and complexity of her films. The collection highlights Dash's contributions to Black independent cinema and the broader cultural landscape, showcasing her role in shaping the representation of Black women in media. For students and researchers, the interviews serve as primary sources that can be used to study and analyze Dash's work, her impact on the film industry, and her place within the tradition of Black women's narrative practices.

The interviews are but a small sample of those she has granted over the course of her decades-long career. Currently, interviews and conversations with Dash are in disparate publications, making a holistic view of Dash's thoughts in her own words a rather taxing exercise. There are a bevy of interviews that take place around 2016, noting the twenty-fifth anniversary digital remastering and rerelease of *Daughters* in theaters. This milestone coincided with a renewed interest in Dash's work, partly sparked by Beyoncé's visual album *Lemonade* (2016), which drew inspiration from *Daughters*. The rerelease brought Dash's groundbreaking film to a new demographic of viewers and reignited discussions about its enduring impact on cinema and cultural representation. Dash's renewed cultural cache ("street cred," we jokingly called it in our interview) and sway on a new cohort of filmmakers and artists signal that this is the right moment to anthologize her words for the future study of her visual style and cinematic aesthetic. Finally, Dash is the first and only Black woman filmmaker in the Conversations with Filmmakers Series, making this collection an important contribution to the series as well as to scholarship about filmmaking.

Dash's legacy is a testament to her groundbreaking contributions to Black cinema and her influence on filmmakers such as Ava DuVernay, Ryan Coogler, and Dee Rees. The 2020 interview with her colleague Frances-Anne Solomon is one example of the esteem in which her peers hold Dash and her work. The Academy of Motion Picture Arts curated a wonderful, filmed exchange between Dash, Euzhan Palcy, and DuVernay—an interview for which I was unable to secure permission to include here but that conveys a second contemporary example of Dash's place and import among other Black women who make cinema. (Rest assured the reference can be found in the Additional Resources section, along with many others that illustrate the incredibly robust scholarship that treats Dash's films and places them in context and in conversion with Black feminist theory.) Her peers and admirers continue to celebrate her work, and this edited collection of her interviews provides an essential resource for understanding her enduring legacy and impact on the moving Black image.

Julie Dash's films and her influence on the film industry are vast. Her work not only broke barriers for Black female filmmakers but also enriched the cinematic landscape with narratives that celebrate and explore the intricacies of Black life and culture. An edited collection of her interviews would have been an invaluable resource for me as a young scholar daring to enfold her film into my burgeoning research. It is my hope that by offering this collection, I provide deep insights into her artistic vision and the enduring significance of her work to those whose projects are incomplete without a thorough analysis of Dash's characteristic films. The collection situates Dash's work within the broader cultural and historical context of Black cinema. It highlights her role in the LA Rebellion and her contributions to the representation of Black women in media. The collection amplifies Dash's perseverance and dedication to her craft, underscores the importance of telling diverse and authentic stories, and highlights the effect such narratives can have on "the culture."

KLM

Chronology

1952–69 Julie Ethel Dash is born in Queens, New York, in 1952 to Rhudine Henderson and Charles Edward Dash. She grows up in the Queensbridge Housing Project in Long Island City and attends Jamaica High School.

1968 Enrolls in her first cinematography workshop with Omar Mubarak (Randy Abbott) at the Studio Museum of Harlem and begins editing using upright Movieola and shooting with a 16mm Bolex camera.

1969–73 Attends City College of New York, where she studies psychology until she is accepted into the film school at the Leonard Davis Center for the Performing Arts, David Picker Film Institute. As a student, she is hired as film crew to work with St. Clair Bourne. She writes and directs her first documentary film, *Working Models of Success*, for Dr. Eugene S. Callender, deputy director of the New York City Housing and Development Administration. She earns a bachelor of arts degree in film and television production in 1973.

1974–76 Moves to Los Angeles, California, to attend the American Film Institute's Conservatory Fellowship Program in Producing and Writing. She produces the short film *Four Women* based on the song written and performed by Nina Simone. Begins working on a story about her father's Gullah Geechee background in 1975, which evolves into the screenplay for her first feature film.

1977–80 Enrolls in the University of California Los Angeles's graduate program in film and television production as part of a new cadre of African and African American students that includes Billy Woodberry, Charles Burnett, Haile Gerima, Barbara McCullough, and Larry Clark. They come to be known unofficially as the LA School of Black Filmmakers and are colloquially referred to as the LA Rebellion. Her student film *Diary of an African Nun* is screened at the Los Angeles Film Exposition, and she earns the Director's Guild Award for her film *Four Women*, which is also named Best Film by a Woman at the 1978 Miami International Film Festival. She works for the Motion Picture Association of America as a member of the Classifications and Ratings Administration. She is credited for sound work on *Passing Through* (1977), directed by fellow UCLA student Larry Clark. Dash and McCullough attend the Cannes International Film Festival to showcase films by young Black filmmakers, a move that calls more attention to Black independent cinema globally.

1981   Receives a Guggenheim Fellowship and National Endowment for the Arts grant.

1982   Writes and directs her second short film, *Illusions*. Earns script and continuity credit for *A Different Image*, directed by fellow UCLA student Alile Sharon Larkin.

1983   Works as first assistant director on *My Brother's Wedding*, directed by her UCLA classmate Charles Burnett.

1985–89   Earns her MFA in motion picture and television production from the University of California Los Angeles. *Illusions* receives First Prize, Black American Cinema Society Award (1985), and the Black Filmmaker Foundation's Jury Prize for Best Film of the Decade (1989). Directs short documentary *Breaking the Silence* for the National Black Women's Health Project. Receives a Rockefeller Fellowship (1989).

1990   Directs performance artist Ishmael Houston-Jones in the short film *Relatives* and begins production on her first feature film, *Daughters of the Dust*.

1991   *Daughters of the Dust* premieres at the Sundance Film Festival. It is nominated for the Grand Jury Prize and wins the Excellence in Cinematography award. Dash receives a second Rockefeller Fellowship and a Fulbright Fellowship.

1992   In collaboration with Jawole Willa Jo Zollar, founder and choreographer of Urban Bush Women, adapts and directs the short film *Praise House*. Directs music video for "Lost in the Night" by Peabo Bryson. *Daughters of the Dust* is released theatrically. Becomes the first African American woman to have a feature film theatrically released in the United States. Publishes *Daughters of the Dust: The Making of an African American Women's Film*, with the assistance of Toni Cade Bambara and bell hooks. She is awarded the Candace Award by the National Coalition of 100 Black Women.

1994   Directs video of Sweet Honey in the Rock's "Breaths" for inclusion in short AIDSFILM music video for PBS.

1996–97   Directs music videos "More Than One Way Home" by artist Keb' Mo', Tracy Chapman's "Give Me One Reason," Tony! Toni! Toné!'s "Thinking of You," and Adriana Evans's "Love is All Around." Chapman's video is nominated for an MTV Music Video Award. Writes and directs the episode "Grip Till it Hurts" of the Showtime Network series *Women: Stories of Passion*, as well as the segment "Sax Cantor Riff" of the ten-part television movie *Subway Stories: Tales from the Underground* for HBO. Writes and publishes *Daughters of the Dust: A Novel*, which follows the narrative of the film twenty years into the future.

1998–99   Directs the original features *Funny Valentines* and *Incognito*. Directs a public service announcement commercial, "My Brother's Jersey," for Health Watch. Receives Delta Sigma Theta Sorority, Inc. Lillian Award (1998), the American Film Institute's Maya Deren Award (1998), and the National Foundation for Women Legislators Leadership in Women's Filmmaking Award (1999). *Illusions* receives Best of 20th Century Black Cinema Award from the Newark Black Film Festival.

2000   Commissioned to direct the print campaign and commercial spot for GMC Yukon, *Make That Move*. Directs MTV film *Love Song*.

2002   Directs *The Rosa Parks Story*. The film is awarded a NAACP Image Award for Best Television Movie and a Family Television Award (Television Movies and Mini-Series category). Dash is nominated for Outstanding Directorial Achievement in the category of Primetime Movies Made for Television at the 55th Annual Directors Guild Awards.

2003   *The Rosa Parks Story* is awarded the Black Reel Award for Outstanding Television Film and a New York Christopher Award.

2004   Commissioned by the National Underground Railroad Freedom Center to direct the short film *Brothers of the Borderland* as part of an immersive exhibit shown in the Harriet Tubman Theater. The short film is narrated by Oprah Winfrey. *Daughters of the Dust* is added to the National Film Registry by the Library of Congress.

2005   *Daughters of the Dust* is awarded the Excellence in Cinematography Award at the 15th Cascade Festival of African Films in Portland, Oregon.

2007   Receives a USA Artists Fellowship.

2008   Works as an interview producer for the *American Masters* documentary series, *Zora Neale Hurston: Jump at the Sun* (season 22, episode 2).

2009   Named Resident Artist in Film Production at Indianapolis Museum of Art. Collaborates with the Indianapolis Museum of Art's Museum Apprentice Program to mentor and direct high school students through the filmmaking process. Directs and edits *Smuggling Daydreams into Reality*, a short film about the students' creative process, as part of the exhibit.

2010	Receives the Paul Robeson Award from the Department of Radio, Television, and Film at Howard University.
2011	Directs short documentary *My Marlton Square* for Community Build, Inc. The Director's Guild of America recognizes the twentieth anniversary of the release of *Daughters of the Dust* with a special ceremony. The Avery Research Center for African American History and Culture at the College of Charleston hosts a 20th Anniversary Symposium for *Daughters of the Dust*.
2012	Sundance Film Festival screens *Daughters of the Dust* as part of its "From the Collection" screenings, which bring awareness to the importance of film preservation and pays tribute to groundbreaking films. Dash is named UCLA Alumni of the Year.
2013	Serves as Bob Allison Endowed Chair, Department of Media at Wayne State University in Detroit, Michigan.
2014	Serves as Visiting Professor of African American Studies at the College of Charleston.
2015	Directs a webisode of *The Kitchen Table Series: New Orleans Edition* for the Coca-Cola Company. Joins faculty at Morehouse College as Distinguished Professor of Cinema, Television and Emerging Media (2015–2017).
2016	Writes, directs, and produces short documentary *Standing at the Scratch Line* for the Philadelphia Museum of African America History. *Daughters of the Dust* is digitally remastered and distributed for theatrical release at the Toronto Film Festival to mark its twenty-fifth anniversary. Other screenings to commemorate the occasion take place at the Honolulu Museum of Art, the American Film Institute, and the Theater at Ace Hotel. Beyoncé pays homage to the film in her visual album *Lemonade*. Elected as an honorary member of Alpha Kappa Alpha Sorority, Inc. Earns the New York Film Critics Circle Special Award for the restoration of *Daughters of the Dust*. Serves as the Time-Warner Visiting Professor in the Cathy Hughes School of Communications at Howard University. Receives the Richard Nichols Luminary Award at the BlackStar Film Festival and the Legendary Award by the Peachtree Village Film Festival.
2017	Directs two episodes of the second season of the television series *Queen Sugar* (episode 9, "Yet Do I Marvel," and episode 10, "Drums at Dusk"), created and produced by Ava DuVernay for the Oprah Winfrey Network. Begins preproduction on the feature-length documentary *Travel Notes of a Geechee Girl*. Dash earns the New York Women in Film and Television MUSE Award, the Robert Smalls Merit and

CHRONOLOGY xxi

Achievement Award at the Beaufort International Film Festival, Hollywood Women in Film and Television Trailblazer Award, and the Women in Film and Video's Women of Vision Award. Receives the Spirit of Queens Award at the 7th Annual Queens World Film Festival. Joins faculty of Spelman College as Distinguished Professor in the Arts to develop a major in filmmaking in the Department of Art and Visual Culture.

2018 Serves as Governor of the Toronto International Film Festival Filmmaker Lab. Inducted into the Penn Cultural Center's 1862 Circle (St. Helena's Island, South Carolina). Receives the Gold Thumb Award at the 20th Ebert Film Festival.

2019 Receives a grant from the National Endowment of the Humanities to support *Travel Notes of a Geechee Girl*. Produces short film (with Nefertitie Nguvu) *Bride Price*, directed by Chuckwunonso Dureke. Receives UCLA Distinguished Alumni Award in Film, Television, and Digital Media.

2020 Lionsgate Entertainment announces that Dash will direct the forthcoming biopic on scholar and activist Angela Y. Davis. Flavor Unit announces Dash is attached to direct forthcoming biopic on Mahalia Jackson. Scholar Patricia Williams Lessane publishes *Teaching Daughters of the Dust as a Womanist Film and the Black Arts Aesthetic of Filmmaker Julie Dash*.

2021 Directs "The Miseducation of the Negro" on the Fox network series *Our Kind of People* (season 1, episode 5). Writes and directs the experimental short *Why the Sun and the Moon Live in the Sky*, featuring Chloe and Halle Bailey.

2022 Directs two episodes of the ABC anthology series *Women of the Movement*, which retells the civil rights movement from the perspective of the Black women who led from the margins (episode 1, "Mothers and Sons," and episode 4, "Man Hunt"). Directs "Renegade," an episode of the drama series "*Reasonable Doubt* (season 1, episode 4)." The mayor of Charleston, South Carolina, John J. Tecklenburg, presents Julie Dash with the Joseph R. Biden President's Lifetime Achievement Award for a lifelong commitment to building a stronger nation through volunteer service. Dash is invited to design two rooms for the Metropolitan Museum of Art and *Vogue*.

2023 The International African American Museum in Charleston, South Carolina, has its grand opening in June. One of the inaugural exhibits includes the short film *Seeking: Mapping a Gullah Geechee Story*, written and directed by Dash.

2024 International African American Museum hosts a conversation with Dash in honor of Women's History Month. Dash formally presents the rerelease and restoration of *Naked Acts* (1996), an independent film by Bridgett M. Davis, at the Film Forum in New York City. Directs "Primetime" (*Reasonable Doubt*, season 2, episode 4).

Filmography

WORKING MODELS OF SUCCESS (1973)
Documentary
Director: **Julie Dash**
Producer: Julie Dash
Color, 50 minutes

FOUR WOMEN (1975)
Short student film
Ethos Film
Executive Producer: Winfred Tennison
Director: **Julie Dash**
Cinematography: Robert Maxwell
Editing: Julie Dash
Cast: Linda Martina Young
Color, 7 minutes
Best Short Film Made by a Woman (1974), Miami International Film Festival

DIARY OF AN AFRICAN NUN (1977)
Short student film
Producer: Julie Dash
Director: **Julie Dash**
Writers: Alice Walker (short story), adaptation by Julie Dash
Cinematography: Orin Mitchell
Editing: Julie Dash
Cast: Barbara O., Marnita Caraway, Makini Price, and Barbara Young
Black & White, 13 minutes

ILLUSIONS (1982)
Short
Executive Producer: Brenda Y. Shockley
Producer: Julie Dash

Director: **Julie Dash**
Writer: Julie Dash
Cinematography: Ahmed El Maanouni
Editing: Charles Burnett & Julie Dash
Cast: Lonette McKee, Rosanne Katon, Ned Bellamy, Jack Lundi Faust, Lisa Henke, Laddy Ashley, Rita Crafts, Sandy Brooke, and Johnny Crear
Black & White, 30 minutes

DAUGHTERS OF THE DUST (1991)
Feature film
Geechee Girls Productions, American Playhouse, WMG Film
Executive Producer: Lindsey Law
Producers: Julie Dash, Arthur Jafa
Director: **Julie Dash**
Cinematography: Arthur Jafa
Writer: Julie Dash
Editing: Joseph Burton and Amy Carey
Cast: Alva Rogers, Adisa Anderson, Tommy Redmond Hicks, Barbara O., Cora Lee Day, Cheryl Lynn Bruce, Kaycee Moore, and Trula Hoosier
Color, 113 minutes

PRAISE HOUSE (1991)
Short
Geechee Girl Productions, Inc., Twin Cities Public Television, Inc.
Producer: Julie Dash and Gina Harrell
Director: **Julie Dash**
Writers: Angelyn DeBord, adaptation by Julie Dash
Cinematography: Arthur Jafa
Editing: Amy Carey
Cast: Urban Bush Women, Laurie Carlos, Viola Sheely, and Terri Cousar
Color, 25 minutes

"GIVE ME ONE REASON" BY TRACY CHAPMAN (1996)
Music video
Director: **Julie Dash**
Cinematography: Matthew Libatique
Cast: Tracy Chapman, Diane Reeves
Color, 4 minutes
Nominated for an MTV Music Video Award

WOMEN: STORIES OF PASSION (1997)
TV series
Episode: "Grip Till It Hurts"
Showtime Networks, Playboy Entertainment Group
Executive Producer: Elisa M. Rothstein
Producer: Maricel Pagulayan
Director: **Julie Dash**
Writer: Julie Dash
Cinematography: Matthew Libatique
Editing: Amy Carey
Cast: Siena Goines, Lawrence LeJohn, Bahni Turpin, Scott B. Smith, Courtney Delancy, and Elisa M. Rothstein
Color, 26 minutes

SUBWAY STORIES: TALES FROM THE UNDERGROUND (1997)
TV movie
Segment: "Sax, Cantor, Riff"
Clinica Estetico, HBO NYC Productions, and Ten in a Car Productions
Executive Producers: Jonathan Demme, Rosie Perez, Edward Saxon
Producers: Richard Guay and Valerie Thomas
Director: **Julie Dash**
Writer: Julie Dash
Cinematography: Ken Kelsch
Editing: Elizabeth Kling
Cast: Kenny Garrett, Sam Rockwell, Sol Frieder, Tammi Cubilette, Kavi Ladnier, Bruklin Harris, Taral Hicks, Daniel Rous, and Will Hare
Color, 10 minutes

"THINKING OF YOU" BY TONY! TONI! TONÉ! (1997)
Music video
Mercury Records
Director: **Julie Dash**
Cast: Tony! Toni! Toné!
Color, 4 minutes

FUNNY VALENTINES (1999)
TV movie
Black Entertainment Television, Chelsey Avenue Productions, Starz! Pictures
Executive Producers: Ashley Tyler and Ron Stacker Thompson

Producer: Scott White
Director: **Julie Dash**
Writers: J. California Cooper (short story), adaptation by Amy Ferris, Ron Stacker Thompson, and Ashley Tyler
Cinematography: Karl Herrmann
Editing: Hibah Schweitzer
Cast: Alfre Woodard, Loretta Devine, CCH Pounder, Tom Wright, Peter Jay Fernandez, Megalyn Echikunwoke, Kajauana S. Marie, Denise Burse, Chris Dunn, Debra Terry, Van Coulter, Afemo Omilami, Christopher Ryan Dunn, Ruth Beckford, Saycon Sengbloh, Chandler Parker, Marty Terry, Elizabeth Omilami, and Yolanda King
Color, 108 minutes

INCOGNITO (1999)
TV movie
Directors' Circle Filmworks
Producer: Roy Campanella II
Director: **Julie Dash**
Writers: Francis Ray (novel), adaptation by Shirley Pierce
Cinematography: David E. West
Editing: Hibah Schweitzer
Cast: Allision Dean, Richard T. Jones, Phil Morris, Vanessa Williams, Roger Guenveur Smith, Ron Glass, Joan Pringle and Bonita Brisker
Color, 100 minutes

LOVE SONG (2000)
TV movie
Handprint Entertainment, Taurus 7 Film Corporation, and Viacom Productions
Producers: Claudio Castravelli, Jean Guy, Despres, Kimberly Ogletree
Director: **Julie Dash**
Writer: Josslyn Luckett
Cinematography: David Claessen
Editing: Pamela Malouf-Cundy
Cast: Monica, Christian Kane, Essence Atkins, Rachel True, Vanessa Bell Calloway, Tyrese Gibson, and Peter Francis James
Color, 90 minutes

THE ROSA PARKS STORY (2002)
TV movie
CBS, Chotzen/Jenner Productions, Come Sunday, and Jaffe/Braunstein Films

Executive Producers: Angela Bassett, Howard Braunstein, Yvonne Chotzen, Willis Edwards, Michael Jaffe, and William Jenner.
Producers: Pearl Devers, Christine A. Sacani, and Elaine Steel
Director: **Julie Dash**
Writer: Paris Qualles
Cinematographer: David Claessen
Editing: Wendy Hallam Martin
Cast: Angela Bassett, Peter Francis James, Tonea Stewart, Von Coulter, Dexter King, Sonny Shroyer, Mike Pniewski, Chardé Manzy, Cicely Tyson, and Charles Black
Color, 97 minutes

BROTHERS OF THE BORDERLAND (2004)
Short
ZoMotion
Producers: Theresa Anne Mathews and Alphonzo Wesson
Director: **Julie Dash**
Writer: Ronald Taylor
Cinematography: David Claessen
Editing: Terry Lukemire
Cast: Oprah Winfrey, Barrett Clark, Dan Davidson, Christopher Dressler, Camille Gaston, Steve Holm, Giselle Jones, Christopher Kelly, and Ken Strunk
Color, 25 minutes

STANDING AT THE SCRATCH LINE (2016)
Short
Scribe Video Center
Executive Producer: Louis J. Massiah
Producer: Julie Dash
Director: **Julie Dash**
Writer: Julie Dash
Cinematography: David Claessen
Editing: Matteo Marchisano-Adamo
Color, 10 minutes

QUEEN SUGAR (2017)
TV series
Season 2, Episode 9 "Yet Do I Marvel"
Warner Horizon Television
Executive Producers: Oprah Winfrey, Ava DuVernay, and Monica Macer

Producers: Kat Chandler, Carla Gardini, Dana Greenblatt, and Mimi Won Techentin
Director: **Julie Dash**
Writers: Natalie Baszile (novel), adaptation by Ava DuVernay and Jason Wilborn
Cinematography: Kira Kelly
Cast: Rutina Wesley, Dawn-Lyen Gardner, Kofi Siriboe, Omar J. Dorsey, Nicholas L. Ashe, Dondré T. Whitfield, and Tina Lifford
Color, 43 minutes

QUEEN SUGAR (2017)
TV series
Season 2, Episode 10 "Drums at Dusk"
Warner Horizon Television
Executive Producers: Oprah Winfrey, Ava DuVernay, and Monica Macer
Producers: Kat Chandler, Carla Gardini, Dana Greenblatt, and Mimi Won Techentin
Director: **Julie Dash**
Writers: Natalie Baszile (novel), adaptation by Ava DuVernay and Jason Wilborn
Cinematography: Kira Kelly
Cast: Rutina Wesley, Dawn-Lyen Gardner, Kofi Siriboe, Omar J. Dorsey, Nicholas L. Ashe, Dondré T. Whitfield, and Tina Lifford
Color, 43 minutes

TRAVEL NOTES OF A GEECHEE GIRL (2017)
Documentary
Producers: Juanita Anderson, Julie Dash, Bernard Gourley, Patricia Williams Lessane, and Rachel Watanabe-Batton.
Director: **Julie Dash**
Writer: Julie Dash
Cinematography: David Claessen
Cast: Mashall Allen, Olu Dara, Manthia Diawara, and Danny Glover
Color

WHY THE SUN AND THE MOON LIVE IN THE SKY (2021)
Short
Karat Entertainment International
Producer: Kimberly Ogletree
Director: **Julie Dash**
Writer: Julie Dash

Cinematography: Edward Beckfort (drone operator) and Alexxiss Jackson
Cast: Chloe Bailey and Halle Bailey
Color, 6 minutes

OUR KIND OF PEOPLE (2021)
TV series
Season 1, Episode 5 "The Miseducation of the Negro"
Lee Daniels Entertainment and Fox Entertainment
Executive Producers: Gretchen Berg, Claire Brown, Rodney Ferrell, Karin Gist, Aaron Harberts, Lee Daniels, Montrel Key, Ben Silverman, Marc Velez, and Pamela Oas Williams.
Producers: Jahil Fisher, Lawrence Otis Graham, Mike Gray, Rebecca Boss, and Michelle Fowler
Director: **Julie Dash**
Writer: Karin Gist, Nambi Kelley, and Lauren Goodman.
Cinematography: Roger Chingirian
Cast: Yaya DaCosta, Nadine Ellis, Lance Gross, Rhyon Nicole Brown, Alana Bright, Morris Chestnutt, and Joe Morton
Color, 43 minutes

MOTHERS OF THE MOVEMENT (2022)
TV series
Season 1, Episode 5 "Mothers and Sons"
Two Drifters, Westbrook Studios, Roc Nation, and Kapital Entertainment
Executive Producers: Marissa Jo Cerar and Michael Lohmann
Producers: Jessi Clark and John McCoy
Director: **Julie Dash**
Writers: Mamie Till Mobley, Christopher Benson, Devery Anderson, Marissa Jo Cerar, and Hayley Tyler
Cinematography: Tommy Lohmann
Cast: Adrienne Warren, Cedric Joe, and Julie McDermott
Color, 45 minutes

MOTHERS OF THE MOVEMENT (2022)
TV series
Season 1, Episode 4 "Manhunt"
Two Drifters, Westbrook Studios, Roc Nation, and Kapital Entertainment
Executive Producers: Marissa Jo Cerar and Michael Lohmann
Producers: Jessi Clark and John McCoy

Director: **Julie Dash**
Writers: Mamie Till Mobley, Christopher Benson, Devery Anderson, Marissa Jo Cerar, Cristian Martinez, and Sylvia Franklin
Cinematography: Tommy Lohmann
Cast: Adrienne Warren, Cedric Joe, and Julie McDermott
Color, 46 minutes

REASONABLE DOUBT (2022)
TV series
Season 1, Episode 6 "Renegade"
ABC Signature and Onyx Collective
Executive Producers: Pete Chatmon and Roger Bobb
Director: **Julie Dash**
Writer: Raamla Mohamed, Loy A. Webb, Natalia Temesgen
Cinematography: Michael Negrin
Cast: Emayatzy Corinealdi, Natalie Britton, Eugene Byrd, and Christopher Cassarino
Color; 47 minutes

SEEKING: MAPPING A GULLAH GEECHEE STORY (2023)
Short
International African American Museum, Charleston, South Carolina
Producers: Mishka Brown, Nanette Nelms, and Rachel Watanabe-Batton
Director: **Julie Dash**
Writer: Julie Dash
Cinematographer: Bradford Young
Cast: Brady Carpenter, Michael Alvarado, Toochukwu Anyachonkeya
Color, 15 minutes

REASONABLE DOUBT (2024)
TV series
Season 2, Episode 4 "Primetime"
ABC Signature and Onyx Collective
Executive Producers: Raamla Mohamed, Kerry Washington, and Larry Wilmore
Director: **Julie Dash**
Writers: Raamla Mohamed, Zahir McGhee, Michelle Flowers, Ryan Richmond, and Dallas Rico
Cinematography: Robert E. Arnold
Cast: Emayatzy Corinealdi, McKinley Freeman, Tim Jo
Color, 47 minutes

Julie Dash: Interviews

An Interview with Julie Dash

Zeinabu irene Davis / 1991

From *Wide Angle: A Film Quarterly of Theory, Criticism, and Practice* 13, nos. 3–4 (July 1991): 110–18.
Reprinted by permission of Steven Ross, Director of Ohio University School of Film.

A graduate of American Film Institute (AFI) and University of California (UCLA) film programs, Julie Dash is one of the most prolific Black women independent filmmakers working today. *Illusions*, her 1982 short [film], won Best Film of the Decade from the Black Filmmaker Foundation and numerous other national and international awards.

Despite the usual setbacks of financial difficulties, Dash's spirit stands unbroken and optimistic. In the midst of postproduction in her own living room, where she had two huge flatbeds and thousands of feet of film in editing bins, Dash took the time to talk to *Black Film Review* about the inspiration and production of her new film, her first feature, *Daughters of the Dust*. Her other works include the award-winning *For Women, Relatives*, and *Diary of an African Nun*, an adaptation of a short story by Alice Walker.

Black Film Review: I want to start with a genesis of *Daughters of the Dust*. How did you first come up with the idea?

Julie Dash: The genesis of the idea came from always hearing my father being called a Geechee and then wanting to do something. On Geechee culture, which is also called Gullah. I was also inspired by reading Melville Herskovitz's *The Myth of the Negro Past* and Robert Farris Thompson's *Flash and the Spirit*. I wanted to do something on African retentions and survivals, because the Sea Islands had remained culturally isolated and insulated from Western cultural experiences for a long time. To this day, the people of the Sea Islands maintain and preserve a wealth of West African tradition, mores, and religion. So it was an area which was ripe for discovering. Usually, when we see films and television productions on early African Americans, they deal with African Americans living in Alabama and Mississippi.

BFR: When you were living in Los Angeles, I remember you talking about a triptych or a series of films. Is *Daughters of the Dust* a part of that?

JD: Yes, it is a part of a series of films that I am doing on the experiences of Black women in the United States from the turn of the century up to and beyond the year 2000. *Illusions* is the section that took place in the 1940s. I hope to do a section in the 1920s and something in the '60s, and then something beyond the year 2000 because you usually don't see futuristic films with Black people involved in them.

BFR: Yeah, that's right. We don't exist past the year 2000.

JD: The whole series is trying to show Black women at pivotal moments in their lives and to incorporate historical events and issues. I focus on and depict experiences that have never been shown on the screen before. Specifically, I focus on intragroup relationships rather than on images of Black women as victims of the outside world that's impacting on them.

BFR: How about the title *Daughters of the Dust*, does it have any special significance?

JD: Yes, it does. It goes way, way, way back. It's kind of paraphrasing a passage in the Bible, in Ezekiel, which goes "O ye sons of the dust," and I changed it to "daughters of the dust." Dust also implies the past and something that's grown old and crumbling. The whole film is about memories, and the scraps of memories, that these women carry around in tin cans and little private boxes. Everyone's grandparents or old aunts and uncles have scraps of memories—like when you go to an old relative's house and you find boxes with all these little bits of this and that, that have to do with your family. "Scraps of memory" is also taken from a paper W. E. B. Du Bois wrote about the fact that African Americans don't have a solid lineage that they can trace. All they have are scraps of memories remaining from the past. I wanted memory to be a central focus of the story.

BFR: Can you give us a brief synopsis of the story of *Daughters of the Dust*?

JD: It's about a family that's preparing to migrate north, and the great-grandmother is trying to get them to remain on the island. The story is concerned with conflict and struggle as the family prepares to migrate north at the turn of the century. That's not a great synopsis. It's such a dense script. . . . There are so many subplots that it's hard to say that it is any one thing. To really make it simple, it's about a family of women who carry their cultural traditions into the future. These women carried scraps of memory from the past, and then they carry these same scraps of memory into the future.

BFR: Over the years, how did the script change for you? Did your life experience affect the story?

JD: Having my daughter had a great impact on the script and the storyline because it made me think a lot about what it would be like to have a child and then have that child taken away, sold away in slavery. I mean, exactly how would that feel? What kind of impact would that have on the rest of your life? How do you maintain? What happens to you? I think we all take slavery for granted. Sometimes we say, "Yeah, there was slavery, and people were sold away." But what did it do to an individual when that sort of personal tragedy occurred?

BFR: How and when did you begin writing the script?

JD: I began writing it in 1976 when I was at AFI. I wrote it as a thirty-page script, and it was funded originally by the National Endowment for the Arts as a short. It kept growing as I was doing more research on it; it kept getting longer and longer, and I realized it was a feature. It was funded in 1981 by the Guggenheim Foundation for Research; that was how I was able to do intensive research on it. I had historical advisers working on the project, like Margaret Washington Creel and Oscar Sims at UCLA. I realized that I would need more money to make it into a feature, and we went to the islands in 1987, shot for two weeks, and made a trailer out of it.

BFR: Was the initial intent to make a trailer?

JD: No, it wasn't; it was to make a short film. When I realized it was a much longer piece, I got money from the Rockefeller Fellowship, from the Fulton County Arts Council here in Georgia, then from the Georgia Humanities and the Appalshop Southeast fellowships. All these fellowships and grants I got, for the most part, after I came to Georgia. When I was in LA, I couldn't get practically any funding for the project except from the NEA. I couldn't get any studio development money. At one point Universal Studios called me up after seeing *Illusions*; they wanted to hear my idea. I went and spoke to them, but they said no; I spoke to Warner Brothers, and they said no; and then I spoke to some people at Columbia, and they passed on it, too. They said to bring it back to them when I had finished the film. Who needs to do that at that point? I came to Georgia and shot the trailer, and from the trailer I went to the PBS weekend retreat at Sundance, and Lynn Holst from American Playhouse was there. She saw the trailer, liked it, and told me to send her the screenplay. I did, and American Playhouse agreed to do it; the Corporation for Public Broadcasting [CPB] put some money into it, too. Prior to that CPB had rejected it. That was while I was in California; they said that the script wasn't very "interesting." So we went and shot it in '89.

BFR: From when to when?

JD: From October 16 to November 19. We finished right before Thanksgiving. We've been in postproduction ever since. The final budget from American Playhouse was $800,000.

BFR: Did they ever tell you why it was so low? I thought their rate was supposed to be $1.5 million for a picture.

JD: They told me that it was high, that normal budgets were $500,000.

BFR: Could you go back a little more into your research process? I think its interesting, and people don't realize that filmmakers do research about a subject. I think most people think all ideas just come out of your head. But I know that you took a long time to carefully uncover your story.

JD: Yes, it came from intensive research at UCLA's University Research Library, the Schomberg Center for [Research in Black Culture] in New York, the National Archives in Washington, DC, and from Margaret Washington Creel, who is an expert on the Sea Islands' culture, religions, etc. There was a five-year period of research and writing. I also collected stories from relatives who came from the area. I included some of [my mother's] recollections of folklore and things like that. I included lots of my father's stories, and my grandmother's on my father's side, and my aunts'. Things that they used to say, I used as dialogue.

BFR: Would you like to talk at all about the restrictions that were placed on you by American Playhouse, in terms of the script?

JD: Well, actually, it was a very good experience working with American Playhouse. I couldn't think of a better situation in which to give voice to a story. They did not put any restrictions on me; in fact, what I did and what they wanted me to do was to expand the story. I expanded the story, the dialogue, and the locations; so I just made it a bigger story.

BFR: Could you tell us who some of the actors are and what their roles are?

JD: I really tried to use actresses who had worked previously in other Black independent films. The great-grandmother, Nana Peazant, is played by Cora Lee Day, who was in Haile Gerima's *Bush Mama*. Kaycee Moore plays the part of Haagar Peazant. She, of course, was in *Killer of Sheep* [Charles Burnett] and *Bless Their Little Hearts* [Billy Woodberry]. Then, of course, Barbara O. plays Yellow Mary and was previously in *Diary of an African Nun* and Saundra Sharp's *Back Inside Herself*. I also used Alva Rogers, who was in *School Daze* (she's the female lead, Eula); Adisa Anderson as the male lead, Eli, who was in Alile Sharon Larkin's *A Different Image*, Geraldine Dunston from Iverson White's *Dark Exodus*, and also Trula Hoosier from *Sidewalk Stories*.

The whole thing was to hire actors and actresses who you know are good and who have also supported Black filmmakers in the past. These people worked months on films for little or no pay at all; so, now that I was finally able to pay them for their work, why look somewhere else? Of course, there are many other people who were in it, but the main characters I wanted to be these people.

BFR: Can you talk a little about your crew?

JD: I had a great crew! The director of photography was A. J. Rogobodiyan; second camera operator was N'gai Kai. She just recently married one of the actors in the film, Cornell Royal, who plays the part of Daddy Mac. They met on the set and married about a month later.

Then we had the wonderful and fabulous Nandi Bowe as first assistant director. She worked on *Cry Freedom* and *Do the Right Thing*. I tried to hire Black women in key positions.

BFR: I see. That was going to be my next question. Most people don't think there are Black women film technicians. Is there anyone else you would like to mention?

JD: Veda Campbell did sound; she also did sound for Charles Burnett on *To Sleep with Anger* and *My Brother's Wedding*. The whole production design and set was real interesting, too. They were done by fine artists as opposed to so-called experienced film production designers. I had Kerry Marshall, who is an artist in his own right, as production designer. The art director was Michael Kelly Williams. Their work usually shows at the Studio Museum of Harlem and many other galleries. Martha Jones Jarvis was a production artist on the set, and David Hammon was also a production artist whose work can be seen in the film. I wanted to the look of the film to come from a rich African base. All the artists I just mentioned are nationally known African American artists.

I would also like to mention Butch Morris for the music he has been composing for the project for the last two years. I used some music on the soundtrack in the trailer, and some people went off on it. Butch is Black and is composing original music for the film that will incorporate South Carolina field cries and calls. There will also be strings and large orchestral sounds. We've been experimenting with a lot of things.

BFR: Was any of Butch's music on the trailer's soundtrack?

JD: No, because it would cost about $30,000 to have the music recorded—with the musicians and rental of the studio time. The music that's on the trailer came from a record.

BFR: Were there any other Black independent filmmakers who were on your set?

JD: Yes, William Hudson was an assistant camera person. Nandi Bowe is an independent filmmaker. Pam Jackson is an independent producer who worked on *She's Gotta Have It* and *School Daze*. Floyd Webb worked with us as unit publicist. There are others I'd like to mention who helped so much. Steven Jones was production manager, line producer, and now he's postproduction supervisor. He is possibly the best feature film production manager that I have ever worked with.

Gloria Naylor also worked with us from the beginning to the end as a swing production assistant. She worked in the art department, costumes, and all over the place for us.

BFR: How did you get her?

JD: She came to us. She has a house there, and she's going to be shooting *Mama Day*. She heard that we were in preproduction down there, so she came and volunteered her services. She was a tremendous help.

BFR: Could you tell us about your production period? Did you shoot with any special cameras?

JD: We shot in Super 35, which is similar to Super 16. So the film will have to go through a reduction process. We required a special camera and special editing equipment and all that.

BFR: Why was that done?

JD: We did it so it would look better. When you go to a reduction process, the grain will be even smaller. And, of course, we used Agfa-Gevaert film instead of Kodak because Black people look better on Agfa.

BFR: Any other aspects of the production that were unique?

JD: We used this prototype piece of machinery called a speed-aperture control—it's the only one that exists in the United States. It's a computer-operated speed control where you can have a character speaking at twenty-four-frames-a-second sync and you can click off and go into slow motion right in the middle of the scene without stopping and starting and vice-versa.

We used it throughout the film, but one specific scene is when Viola, the Christian missionary, is talking to the photographer that she brought to the island to document the family's crossing over to the mainland. She talking about the old souls and how the children are the most important members of the family. While she's talking, the camera pushes forward, and we see two children near in slow motion. After they practice hand signals, the camera pulls back out to the scene encompassing Viola and Steve watching them, and their dialogue continues at twenty-four frames.

BFR: Can you talk about some of the differences for you as a director–writer on a feature as opposed to short films?

JD: Actually, I think it is more difficult to do a short because you have less time as a writer to develop characters. You have to introduce them, develop them, and resolve the story all within thirty minutes. But in a longer form like the feature, you have a chance to develop, to embellish, and to have lots of nuances and really stretch out creativity without falling into stereotypes on certain characters.

BFR: Would you go back to doing short films after this?

JD: Oh, sure I would. In fact, I've been talking to a dancer, Jawole Willa Zollar from *Urban Bush Women*, about doing a thirty-minute dance film based on a piece called *Praise House*.

I'm not locked into features. For me, it's about making films and showing Black women in ways that have never been seen before. It's about moving people, about disseminating information.

BFR: It was a long process to get *Daughters of the Dust* from the script to celluloid. What other kinds of things did you do in the interim?

JD: I did quite a few videotapes for an organization in Atlanta called the National Black Women's Health Project. They were doing things on adolescent pregnancy in the Black community; I did some medical films for them on preventing cancer and things like that. I also did a piece for *Alive from Off Center* called *Relatives*, a dance film with Ishmael Houston-Jones. Ishmael danced in *The Brothers from Another Planet* (he was the one who was throwing himself up against the wall). He's a great dancer. So I've been working, even though it hasn't been in film. I've worked a lot in videotape.

BFR: What kinds of things are you trying to do aesthetically with *Daughters of the Dust*?

JD: I think viewers will see the film as a foreign film. It will be something very different to most people because we came from an Afrocentric approach to everything, from the hair to the way the makeup was put on. You know, the way Black women put on makeup: They put liner on the inside of their eye—that comes from wearing kohl in the desert regions of Africa.

BFR: When you say you approached the film from an Afrocentric point of view and way of doing things, what makes that different from Western or Hollywood standards?

JD: Like the "doo-rag" on the hair and how it's tied and all that kind of stuff. The way we approached it was to do as your mother did—and as did her mother before her. So it would be tied in a much different way than what popular American culture would allow us to see. The manners in which African women tie their heads with scarves have different meanings. Everything means something; there's a source for everything. You just don't put a scarf up on someone's head. You just don't put jewelry on someone; you put it on in a certain way. People's motor habits—the way they stand and the way they walk, the way they laugh—I tried to maintain the integrity of West African motor habits. An example would be of turning the head slightly to the left when listening to an elder and putting a hand over your mouth when you laugh.

All this is approached from an Afrocentric perspective. I wanted to have a connection to the past. The men have these hand signals that they give to each other from across the sand dunes; they communicate with one another in hand signals. These were derived from secret societies in West Africa, like the Poro for men, and Sande, which was a women's secret society.

BFR: I think that gives people a deeper understanding of what you mean, because people use the term Afrocentric quite loosely. Then there are also different camps of opinion on Afrocentrism. Some people look at Afrocentrism in strict political terms of Black Nationalism, and that's supposed to be what Afrocentrism is.

JD: No, Afrocentrism, as I'm applying to this film, is that your actions are derived from West African culture rather than from hinterlands of Europe.

BFR: What would you like *Daughters* to do in terms of distribution?

JD: I'm looking for a wide and general distribution. We already have several distribution companies set up that are interested in the film. American Playhouse is pleased with what we shot.

BFR: How come they're not distributing?

JD: They don't distribute, not theatrically. They just deal with PBS. After two years of theatrical release, they then put it on television, and they own all the PBS rights.

BFR: Do you feel hopeful about the recent attention to Black filmmakers? Because some people feel like it's just lip service and that it won't last.

JD: Well, we have to make sure that it's not. I'm very optimistic about it. We need films financed by Hollywood. We deserve them, and it's long overdue. Filmmaking is a business, not a charity. We have stories to be told, and studios have money to be made.

BFR: So you don't think that Hollywood will try to rip us off like they did with the Black exploitation era?

JD: No, I don't think so. I don't think that's going to be the case this time. There are so many filmmakers just ready to go with product, and they're certainly competent. Their films have been winning awards in film festivals and getting critical acclaim worldwide. I think there's a possibility of a rash of Black films that will also be made by white Hollywood filmmakers, but I think we're in a much better position right now than we were twenty years ago.

BFR: But with *Daughters*, by choosing a style . . .

JD: Yes, that was the problem with *Daughters*. The studios looked at the idea and said, "It doesn't seem commercial." But now they're interested in it because it's already been done. The films Black filmmakers want to do . . . we're just going to have to start them and not worry about what someone else may think about commercial viability or lack of it.

Black people want to see what Black people are doing, thinking, and seeing. It's time for Black businesses to start supporting African American independent filmmakers.

BFR: In what way?

JD: Financially. There are these large Black insurance and hair care companies. They should start investing in Black independent film. It's as simple as that. They will be making just as much money on their hair care products, and our stories will be getting told—and their stories will be getting told.

BFR: Do you prefer a particular aspect of filmmaking?

JD: I think the writing and research is exciting, but I like it all. As Black independent filmmakers we've always had to write, direct, and edit our films in total, and I think we have an advantage over some other directors who only direct. They don't know the whole process like we do, and they can't incorporate that knowledge into each phase of their project because they don't have that experience. When we're writing something, we know how much money we have or will have to do our films, and we know how we can write it, and that we can't have the rocket ship in it. We know what our constraints are, so we're cutting it as we're shooting it.

BFR: From your example, if you write a scene or film and you have a rocket ship in it, then as a Black independent filmmaker you can't have a rocket in it . . .

JD: But you can have the smoke of the rocket ship taking off. . . . That's how you can pull that one off.

BFR: . . . But some people say that's self-censorship.

JD: I don't think it's censorship; I think it's knowing what your parameters are. Censorship would be saying, "Well, I can't have a scene in here at all about people taking off in a rocket ship because it's not economically possible; the budget won't be able to withstand that." You have to get creative, more creative than someone who *does* have a budget for a rocket ship.

BFR: I'm going to play devil's advocate. I'm going back to Clyde's [Taylor, *BFR* 4, no. 4] argument that if Black filmmakers continue to be auteurs, it won't be productive for the movement as a whole. Do you think that it's a good idea that Black filmmakers write, direct, produce, and edit their own films?

JD: I think we do that out of necessity rather than desire to do it all. I mean, it's better to write, direct, produce, edit, and dip it in the developing solution to have a film than not to do it at all. But if it's possible to have someone else produce for you who can pull together everything that you need and require, then get them. If you can locate an editor that works with you and if you can hook up with a writer who expresses things that you never even thought of and better than you ever thought possible, then I think that's great. You can work together. But if you can't, then I don't suggest that you just sit home and rent a tape.

Some people might *prefer* to do it all and be the auteur, but I would like to write from scripts that have already been written. I don't know anyone who would give me a script right now; I can't afford to option a script or a book. I don't have that kind of clout or money yet. Hopefully, after *Daughters* I will. But for now, I'll keep writing and doing all the things that I need to do in order to get the visions that I want on the screen rather than sit back and complain about it.

BFR: Would you like to address yourself to the position of Black women filmmakers?

JD: In the 1990s we are going to start seeing a lot of work by Black women independent filmmakers, and I think it's going to open up a whole new world of dreams, desires, and aspirations. It's going to make a lot of young Black women happy and inspire them and address their needs. I think it's a good thing, and I think we've all been out here for a long time. It's all going to come together in the 1990s.

Not Without My Daughters: A Conversation with Julie Dash and Houston A. Baker Jr.

Houston A. Baker Jr. / 1992

From *Transition*, no. 57 (1992): 150–66. Reprinted by permission.

Julie Dash's *Daughters of the Dust* creates a magically historical world midway between revelation and cultural memory. Occupying both real and mythical Sea Island territories off the coast of South Carolina and Georgia, *Daughters of the Dust* refigures Gullah history in brilliant ways. The film's plot is cross-generational, its geographies global. Both are almost unimaginably enriched by the film's extraordinary cinematography, which makes *Daughters* a richly textured work of art. A work ten years in the making, *Daughters* arrives as a minutely detailed and carefully researched product of an incredible talent.

Houston A. Baker Jr.: Let's begin by looking at the present moment of cultural production in the United States. Cultural products are currently available that could not have been dreamed of a decade ago. It's the 1990s. People are talking about film in ways that many of us were discussing poetry, drama, and fiction in the 1960s and 1970s. Back then, you couldn't enter a conversation with Black people without someone asking, "Have you seen *What the Wine-Sellers Buy*, brother? Have you checked out the latest thing by Baraka? Are you reading John A. Williams's new novel? Have you checked out Toni Morrison?" Certainly, all of those traditional forms of writing that have "gone Black" were cultural productions of record during the 1960s and '70s. Have Black filmmakers and their productions taken the place of this earlier Black writing?

Julie Dash: As photojournalists, I think we have. At the same time, I remember when I was in college in the early 1970s, and was first exposed to writers like Ton Morrison, Toni Cade Bambara, John Williams, and all the poets from the '60s. And I believe I was very much influenced and informed by their work. In our dormitory we used to perform the poetry. We'd act out the poetry of Sonia

Sanchez, let's say, or we would act out—we used to almost remember by heart Toni Cade Bambara's work. I can't express how much her book *Gorilla, My Love* influenced my whole generation. The way Toni Cade takes a thought, weaves it for many paragraphs, and then brings it back around, it was just like regular conversation. It was the way your mother used to talk to you, the way your grandparents would speak to you. I would go so far as to say her work even had an influence on *Daughters of the Dust*. It was later that I found out about African griots and the way they would recount a family's history over a period of days, perhaps even a week's length of time, and how the stories would expand outward and then come back inward, and that, yes, that was a viable way of telling a story, as opposed to sticking to the male Western narrative, which stems from the tall tale or the book. With *Daughters of the Dust*, I decided I was not going to stay with the usual approach of Western narrative. Instead, my narrative structure is based upon the way an African griot would recount a story's history, would recount a tale based upon African deities, West African deities, like Ogun, Osun, Yemoja. And so of course, yes, I think that contemporary filmmaking by African American artists is very much part of the continuum of the past and the writers from the 1960s.

HB: So, in narrative terms, Toni Cade Bambara had, in your patterns of expectation and what you encountered before, broken out. She and you are artists of the break, aren't you? You've created patterns of expectation that are different, by refiguring New World African patterns. Does Toni Morrison's influence appear in your life soon after Bambara?

JD: Yes. Toni Morrison came soon after and went on a different road because she gave me the depth of character that I had not seen before. The strangeness of character, the uniqueness of character, that the tall tale.... That tall tale you could only see in your own family, but you wouldn't tell anybody about, because it's like, "Whoa."

HB: Now what would you say if some "unlearned" and "unkind" person said, "But Morrison is just an alternative Black womanist New World African formula. I mean, hasn't her mode been played out, exhausted, in the books that we've all read now?"

JD: Well, it's only been around twenty years! That's too short for formula, especially the ancient history of Africa versus the tall tale. That tall tale has been around for how long?

HB: So you're suggesting that Black women's New World African aesthetics have much longer to live and remain vital and surprising. But you began, of course, working in the mode of the documentary. Is the documentary form always what's recommended for young filmmakers? Is it a filmic given that the documentary is more accessible than other "creative" modes or forms of cinema?

JD: Because of the political climate of the times, it was something that was much in demand, and it was easier to get people to teach you the format. You could just grab a camera and shoot, shoot, shoot. There was so much stuff on the street happening, and you could just shoot it and then come back and edit it into story. We had a goal, at one point, of doing newsreels for the community. Everything was community oriented. There were lots and lots of speakers on the streets. And so we had access to political dialogue going on every weekend, and we did film those people and come back and try to make a little documentary newsreel film about them.

HB: Did you and your fellow apprentices all feel the imperatives of the Black Arts Movement then?

JD: It was around, we were exposed to it, but to be honest we weren't a part of it. We didn't have an understanding of it, but I'm sure some of it seeped through.

HB: Was your moment of awakening and the realization that you wanted to be in the arts something that came early?

JD: No, it did not come early. At the time, the Studio Museum of Harlem's film workshop was just a place to go, to hang out. I've always been fascinated by a lot of mechanical things. When I was a child, I wanted electric trains. We didn't have any brothers in my family, so we never got mechanical things, and I wanted those things in my house. So coming into the Studio Museum of Harlem for the first time, I come across all this equipment, these moviolas, audiotape recorders, microphones, 16mm cameras, and, I think, one Arriflex camera. All this equipment, and I was allowed to touch it, play with it, and be confused by it, and then make the decision to master it. We used to have games, contests on who could thread a leader through an editing machine faster than the next, because it seemed like something very complex. I was very proud that I was able to do it after the first time someone showed me. I was hooked on film not for the art, but for the mechanics of it. I was hungry to touch and work with video equipment. Now, today, twenty years later, it's no big deal for girls to have mechanical things. But it was then.

HB: Well, what happened when you came home and said, "I think I know what I want to do"?

JD: But see, that was an after-school program, it was considered a hobby. And it wasn't called a "film workshop"; it was called cinematography workshop. So I came home and said I was in a cinematography workshop, and they said, "That's nice." Weeks later I found out that they didn't know what a cinematography workshop was—not my father, my mother, nobody. Now, when I first entered college, I told everyone I was going to be a clinical psychologist. I found that very interesting, the study of what people later developed into; or maybe I would rather be an anthropologist or something like that. I like to study people and cultures in depth. But when I was in my junior year, I switched to a film major. I think my mother and my sister felt as long as it was at the Studio Museum of Harlem, it was a hobby, and it was a safe hobby. But at the point when I switched my major to film production, then it became like, "Are you crazy?" Because there was no precedent for it—no other role models to point to.

HB: Well, I was going to ask you exactly that: Who did you look to? I mean, you were a Black woman at City College saying, "I want to be a filmmaker."

JD: St. Clair Bourne, who was a filmmaker at the time, became a model for me. He had a company called Chamba Productions. It was the Chamba Brothers, as a matter of fact, Charles Hopson, Stan Wakeman; this was around 1971. Also, I think the most important thing that summer of '71 was my meeting Kathleen Collins. Kathleen Collins is one of the first African American women film directors of narrative film. She was a playwright, and she was a film editor. So Kathleen was editing a film for St. Clair Bourne, and she was very young at the time too, and she was very, very kind and very, very open, and she would teach me about editing. I'd come in and watch her, and she would be editing with Delores Eliott, who was her assistant and who is another African American woman who is now a producer and an editor.

HB: What was the film that he and Kathleen were working on?

JD: It was a documentary about a Baptist preacher. They went down south to shoot it. And I remember I was so disappointed because he wouldn't take me along with him. He said I was too young and told me to go back to school. I said, "I'll take a leave of absence." He said, "No, you need to go back to school." And then he said something shocking: "Well, you don't need to be around all these older men." That was my first realization that I was different, and because I wanted to be a technician, I was going to have problems.

HB: This was where "gender" and professional "roles" collided, then?

JD: Yes. Because I wasn't even thinking about it in those terms. I just wanted to go travel with them on this long documentary production. And he didn't want to be bothered with that. After that I went back to school, to a pilot program in film at City College. In the class, I got a job during the summer with the New York Urban Coalition to produce a film for them, a promotional film. The Reverend Eugene S. Calendar took a look at some of my Super 8 films and said, "I'm going to let her do it." And it sent shock waves through the New York Urban Coalition because of my age. Everybody was saying, "Well, who is she? Why her?"

HB: What kind of feedback did you get? Did people approach you in the industry and in the arts in New York once they had seen the film?

JD: The feedback was very good, but by that time I had decided I didn't want to do documentary film anymore. And a lot of that came from the response of my own family, who came to the premiere of the film. I called them up and said,

"I'm having a premiere of my film. Would you like to come?" There would be a pause, and then they would say, "Is it a documentary?" And I'd say, "Yes." And then it would be, "Okay, honey, we'll try to make it." And I'd say, "What's wrong?" "Well, can't you tell a story?" Then I realized that people in the community want to see a story. It was a growing concern. You could give them the same information that you can in documentary and put it in a story form. And it's a little more relaxing for them, a little less of an imposition. So I decided I wanted to learn how to make narrative film, and I had already started taking some courses in screenplay writing. But of course, there was no one at City College at the time who could really teach me how to write a screenplay. So I knew then that I was going to have to head to the West Coast. Part of it was that I could not get a job in New York. If you were someone's secretary-slash-girlfriend, you were more likely to get a producing job than someone who had a film background and a bunch of films under her arm. That's the way it was. So I decided to go to the West Coast and see what was happening there because people were making narrative films, and on the East Coast it was mostly documentary that was going on among Black folks.

HB: Had you thought through the gender issues?

JD: I didn't want to think about it. I felt that I was not free to make the kind of films that I wanted to. I was not free to explore the possibilities of filmmaking because the early 1970s, of course, were very much the same in thought and in action as the 1960s. And as students, we would submit ideas of what we would like to do. And one of mine was of the four women that I drew from Nina Simone's ["Four Women"], and which I eventually did as a dance piece. I wanted to do that as early as '69, and at the Studio Museum of Harlem and at City College I was discouraged because it was considered "fluff." "Why would you do that? Why would you waste the people's film stock for something like that? Someone jumping around? . . . Four women? It's a great song, but, sister, you need to get out there and do something."

HB: Well, you mentioned the connection to the "community," but this translated as "the only viable subject matter for the Black filmmaker was. . . ."

JD: *Do something* . . . about the rent control. Do something . . . about the hungry children, the rats in the tenement, and so on, which was certainly necessary. Certainly someone needed to do it. But after a while, I was not interested in doing that. Even had I wanted to, I didn't even know how. It's not easy; you can't just grab a camera and say, "I'm going to do a narrative story about a hungry single mother with kids and rats in the apartment." You don't even know where to attack the story from, much less write it down. With my first attempt at writing a narrative piece, I remember one of my professors writing at the top of the script, "Talk, talk, talk! This is not radio!" Because I had one character saying,

"Well, you know, this and that," and the other one saying, "That's right, honey." And they would just sit there and talk, saying things like "I remember the day when I saw that pimp out on the street. . . ." Just two people sitting there.

HB: So you were going to be a social activist-slash-narrative person, and your characters just sat and talked? Tell me, how did people think of the relation of film to the other arts?

JD: Film was not—at least the way I perceived it—really something hip. If you wanted to be a hip person in the arts, having anything to do with film, you would be a photojournalist.

HB: So it would have seemed fairly impossible to do what you wanted to do in New York. And you had heard about filmmaking group at UCLA. Were they being called the "LA Rebellion" then?

JD: Not at all. They were just young folks out in LA. So I applied to UCLA, and I went out there, knowing that I was going to get in. I had the films under my arm. Everything was fine, but there was one problem. You need three recommendations to get into film school, and one of my recommendations had not been sent in. One of my teachers, a Black man, who I had hired to shoot one of my films, didn't send the letter. I was devastated. Two white professors had sent their recommendations in, and then a Black one, Doug Harris, didn't send his in. So I had to begin looking for ways of getting grants in LA. I ended up going to the American Film Institute, which was located within this huge sprawling mansion. And we went into this huge hall, and I was very nervous. There's this sprawling staircase, and here's this Black guy walking down the stairs; I assumed he was the janitor. It was the character from *The Love Boat*, Ted Lange. You know, I'm a Black person, and I see another Black person, so he must be the janitor. And it was Ted Lange, and he says, "My sister, why are you here?" And I said, "Application for a grant." And he said, "Application for a grant? You should apply to be here. Larry Clarke told me about you. Go on upstairs and get an application." I went upstairs, got an application, filled it out, sent my film work with it, and I was accepted into the American Film Institute within several weeks. And people were saying, "Boy, are you lucky! They don't let people in there."

HB: And by this time you are twenty-two. Within a couple of weeks, this all happens, in LA.

JD: I had never heard of the American Film Institute before. I had no idea where I was or the opportunity that I had being at the American Film Institute at that time when it was a conservatory. Because in my class, there were only eighteen people. It was very intimate, and we worked there fifteen hours a day. I think one of the most remarkable things about my being there, was my having these classes with this legendary [Serbian] montagist, Slavko Vorkapich. He was in his late nineties at the time, and he had to walk around with a microphone because his voice was so weak. Because that was a turning point for me; film aesthetics really wasn't clicking in at that time until I had seen his presentations and what you could do with film—in terms of movement of the frame, movement within the frame, binary polarity. All of that just wasn't clicking. You need to have someone do a demonstration.

HB: What type of visuals was he using?

JD: Slides, photographs. He worked for Hollywood like in the 1920s and '30s, just doing montage scenes. And so I decided to do *Four Women* finally, the Nina Simone song, using some of his principles. He died in Spain while we were still at the American Film Institute. He used to invite us over to his house, and I didn't go again, simply because I'm a Black girl from the projects and didn't know what to make of this ninety-year-old [Serbian] inviting me: "I ain't going over there." I think that was my loss. I had no idea who he was in the world.

HB: The thing that strikes me here is that here's a tradition of aesthetics coming out of a specific culture. Here's a person who is teaching it. And your access to what you passionately wanted to do as a narrative filmmaker is through a ninety-year-old [Serbian] montagist. In terms of what our children, Black young men and women, should do these days who want to be filmmakers, there is an assumption that the route is a credit card—a little bit of chutzpah, and that's it. They seem to reject the formalist or craft implications of the story that you've just told. Whereas you're saying, "I found aesthetics. I discovered the filmic form of my story through a [Serbian] aesthetic." Do you believe your own mode of discovery is a desirable route for young Blacks today?

JD: I think my instruction in Los Angeles was a matter of growth in layers. After I was able to understand what aesthetics mean, then I could just turn my focus to Afrocentric aesthetics rather than the [Serbian] way. I think cognition set in with the [Serbian] experience, and then I was able to turn it back on to where I came from and express and use it.

HB: Who could you talk to about this? I mean, as you were making this discovery, what was your community of shared vision?

JD: The wonderful thing about the American Film Institute at that time was that half of the students came from other countries. There was a cinematographer from Tunisia, from Guyana, Germany, and Turkey. And so I shared their films and saw how they pursued their work. Our work was so different. Theirs was non-Western, and it was bold, and the shots were more dynamic. They weren't formula, the way I was used to seeing it. Because of course, coming out of New York and struggling to find a way to work within a narrative form, I was copying what was on television. I mean, that's why I had the two women sitting there talking to one another and telling each other what they each should have already known.

HB: That's a word that I see constantly repeated by people like Donald Bogle, for example: *formula*. Is this the taboo category in any filmmaker's vocabulary these days?

JD: I think *formula* should be taboo, because I think that names what we've exhausted—what we all know and we're all comfortable with. I remember when my child was two years old and just beginning to speak, the television was on one day, and some kind of drama came on. The music went duh-duh-duh, and she turned to me and said, "Oh, he gonna get it now!" Here's a two-year-old and she can tell. She knows the formulaic setup, the shots, the musical cue on the soundtrack.

HB: What other artists do you admire in terms of pushing alternative modes of narration, mining depth of character?

JD: Camille Billops is a fascinating woman artist and personality. She has a new film out called *Finding Christa*. It's a new form of documentary. Documentaries don't have to be that didactic little thing. She includes dramatic moments and reenactments. It's basically about her daughter, whom she gave up to an adoption agency in the 1960s because she wanted to be an artist. And years later her daughter finds her. The film is about what they each have to go through and what they have gone through during their lives. And I remember when Camille was telling me about the story she was going to do, my daughter was four—the same age Camille's was when she put her up for adoption—and I just looked over and said, "God, Camille."

HB: You're thinking, "God, she's a hard woman," right?

JD: Yes. How could you do that? How could you give up a child that you have a relationship with already? A child that you've been talking to? And she gave up the child and went to Egypt. You have to see the film and see what a celebration of life it is and how it worked out for the best, for Christa and for Camille. And they came together, and Christa had a wonderful mother in Oakland, an adoptive mother and family. But you have to see it to believe it because it sounds too cold-blooded.

HB: Let's ask the question. To be a Black American woman artist now that the 1990s are in effect, live, and brought to you by Japanese corporations, can a single Black mother be an artist? Let's talk about the category itself. I mean, what does existence as a Black woman artist feel like in the 1990s?

JD: It's very hard. And that's why it's very hard to watch *Finding Christa* because those are the things that you think about, but you keep pushing them aside. You think about when you were single, and you think about when you didn't have the children. It's extremely hard, and I'm not going to pretend that it's not. I often think of kind of giving up and teaching just to have the benefits, just to have the security for my daughter—not for myself, but for her.

HB: Are Black male artists more contemptuous of the work of Black women artists today than they were, say, in the 1970s?

JD: I think, gosh, six months ago I would have said, "It's not so bad." But I'm seeing a whole new thing happening now. I can only speak directly to the Black film experience, but in the 1970s, Black filmmakers traveled together doing different European festivals. Everything was very nice, and we worked together. But now I'm seeing something new: There's so much competition. I can't say it's happening with the people that I have known for years, like Billy Woodbury, Charles Burnett, and Haile [Gerima], but it is with some of the newer filmmakers. You see them in another country, and they won't even speak to you. You'll be standing in an elevator with them, and they will avert their eyes. I think it's a harder age and it's very competitive. We don't even see ourselves right now as a movement. I don't think these filmmakers are thinking in terms of history, of movement and progression. I think they're thinking in terms of what I'm doing, and where I'm going, and how much money I am making . . . alone. And I think there lies the problem.

HB: Do these people feel they have any responsibility, any relationship to something that your parents called "the people"?

JD: I don't think they feel any responsibility. I was on a show with a young filmmaker, and someone from the audience asked him, "Do you have any responsibility for this, for my kids who go out and see this film and there's a lot of cussing and this and that?" And he said to her, "I can't raise your kids." You see, the way I was raised, you can't talk to an older person like that. They'll jump across and slap you. And he wasn't even nervous. He just said, "I can't raise your kids. That's your job." I was going crazy. My heart was beating fast.

HB: What accounts for the New Jack, no-responsibility, Black competition today? Is it because the potential payoff is, first, available and, second, so big?

JD: I think it's because some of these young filmmakers, men and women both, have no memory. They weren't born in the 1960s. They weren't born until 1970-something. They don't have the same background.

HB: What's a young person going to do? I mean, if you've got a dedicated person—and I'm sure there are literally thousands of them across this country—if you have a community-oriented, young, Black aspiring filmmaker, how can she avoid the current drive to avarice?

JD: I think there are a lot of young women who are entering film schools now but who are on a mission to eradicate this whole "Yo, ho!" mentality. I think they have had enough. Everyone has had enough of it. So I think we're going to be seeing a lot of responses to that. A lot of Black women are like, "Hey, I'm going to make a film now. If I have to watch this, I'll make my own film." And I think that's good.

HB: Is there any film that you feel has social and filmic merit that has been produced by such emergent artists as the Hudlins, Robert Townsend and John Singleton, Matty Rich, and Spike Lee? Is there any good in their work?

JD: Yes. I see good and bad in all of them. I see *Boyz n the Hood*, John Singleton's film, as really an extension of Charles Burnett's *Killer of Sheep*. I see it as being a contemporary, color version with rap artists, of Burnett's work. I see it also as an extension of Billy Woodbury's *Bless Their Little Hearts*, which, of course, featured Billy and Charles collaborating on the writing. At the time Billy and Charles started, they did not have Hollywood studios behind them saying, "This is great!" But their films would have had the same impact on America as *Boyz n the Hood* had Hollywood studios released them. And I think Singleton should understand that. But I think he does not.

HB: We can't do a Black film interview without bringing up the guru, can we? The sneaker-wearing Spike Lee!

JD: Do you want to go back to when Spike became "Spike"? Spike changed the face of Black independent filmmaking in a single stroke with *She's Gotta Have It*. He totally eclipsed all the other filmmakers out here, and I think that was a good thing. He gave it boldness, a shot in the arm, all of that. Of course, we can debate from now on about the narrative, what was inside of *She's Gotta Have It*. . . .

HB: Somebody told me it was a postmodern Black woman's autobiography.

JD: I think Spike wanted it to be. But I think he needed to have more sensitivity, more input from a woman who knew something. Because if it was a woman's point of view, it was a woman's point of view "as told to." It didn't work. And the stakes were set higher; the stakes were set for a broader audience. Now, we knew that we should be reaching a broader audience because we were still dragging on, carrying the luggage of the 1960s. But we weren't thinking of a wider audience. And the wider audience wants to see and experience the films, not just a select small group, and film festivals and all of that. Plus, I think one of the most magnificent things that Spike reintroduced into Black film was sex. Because the rest of us were making these righteous films, like, no sex, none of that. And he introduced all this sex and sensuality and eroticism, and it's just like, "Oh yeah, we have a sex life, too. Why can't we show . . . ?" I think most of the filmmakers were so afraid to depict anything sexual because we were trying to stay away from the Black exploitation films of the early 1970s. And so our films became very dry and very didactic and so on. Then here comes *She's Gotta Have It*. We've laughed, we've watched it, we've argued over it. And I think he brought life back into the Black independent film movement.

HB: Nola Darling seems to be an entirely new creation in Afro-American expressive culture. Is that right?

JD: Well, we knew she existed. We know her. Some of us have been her. But we had not dared to show her because I think we were too full of ourselves.

HB: This is a transgressive woman on the scene as she is presented. She moves against our familiar figures who we see on the streets. Sure, some people may have seen them in various galleries at one time or another. Some may, in actuality, have only fantasized that they could be them. But here's Nola, playing against this surrounding cast. She is there as a transgressive figure. From the point of view of a person who has been in the Black arts for a long time, where do you think Spike went wrong?

JD: I think it's in the writing. I think he comes up with great provocative ideas for a story. But we can't be everything. I look forward to putting on the screen works by Toni Morrison, Toni Cade, and other people. The reason that Black filmmakers write their own screenplays is because we can't afford to option the "classics." So we just got in the habit of writing our own things. But I think we still should start moving toward collaboration. You can't be expected to be a great storyteller and a great visual artist, too. You start off with something that is a little weak, and it gets weaker.

HB: Is *She's Gotta Have It* Spike Lee's best film?

JD: It's the one I like best.

HB: What would be your forecast for his Malcolm X project?

JD: I think it's just going to be one Malcolm X film. I think, of course, it will be one film that makes other people get off their butts and make some Malcolm X films. And Malcolm will be approached from different angles—the poetry of Malcolm, the politics of Malcolm, Malcolm the man, Malcolm the family man. I mean, he was a huge person. There's just so much to tell by any one person in only one film. I mean, there could be a whole film on Malcolm in Mecca. I'm glad Spike is doing it, rather than Norman Jewison.

HB: What can one take from Spike Lee? I mean, if there was only one thing young people could draw from him, what would you point them to?

JD: Tenacity. Spirit. He's a little fighter. You have to view him in the big picture. He's outspoken. He says what he says. Sometimes I think he says too much. But that's Spike. He called Eddie Murphy on when he thought Eddie Murphy should speak out to Paramount about—all the millions that Eddie's made and that he should help place a Black exec at Paramount. Spike was absolutely right. No one else had said it, and he said it. He had this public feud going on with Eddie for several years, and now they have patched that up. Spike has made his place in history. I don't think we need to spend a lot of time trying to "Spike bash" or second guess him or whatever. Spike had a major impact on American filmmaking, and if we have problems with his work or his philosophy, we need to go on and spend that energy doing what we think should be done rather than turning toward him. He's already done it.

HB: It sounds just right to me. Black folks have a hard time with successful members of their community, don't they?

JD: The man has made five films in a row.

HB: Juxtaposition is always great for that surprising narrative turn. If Spike has "done it" in the USA, tell me what you think of Isaac Julien and the development of Black independents in Great Britain.

JD: I think Isaac Julien has had a tremendous impact on the film world, not just the UK, within both theory and practice. I'm interested to see how *Young Soul Rebels* is received in this country, especially by Black men. A lot of Black men tend to be homophobic in a major way. Professor [Charlotte] Pierce-Baker was telling me yesterday in her class that one of her students would not see *Paris Is Burning* because he did not want anyone to see him going in to see it. I was like, "Wow! it never even crossed my mind that such a thing would be a consideration." To be a Black woman is to be a lot freer in this society. Man, I can go see anything and never care what anyone said. So *Young Soul Rebels* is deep, because of its subject matter and its graphic depiction of homosexual relations. But that's one of the things I like. That it's not just the homosexual relationship that's strong. The strongest relationship is the relationship between a heterosexual male and a homosexual male, and they are just buddies. And that aspect just never comes up. I really found that to be quite inspiring in a way.

HB: Do Black British intellectuals, artists, filmmakers, academics work more collaboratively, in your view, than the compulsive competitors you have described as the new Black filmmakers in the USA?

JD: I think they do. These Black British filmmakers are almost ten years behind what's been happening here, for, say, seven years. Ten years ago we were very much into what is now called "critical studies" in relation to film, with Teshome Gabriel, Jim Pines, Clyde Taylor. Back then, we were having all these discussions about film and what is film and what are we going to do. Now everyone is just kind of pursuing what we talked about years ago. I think in the UK they are still just talking a lot. And I don't know, it might make some people angry for me to say that. They're talking a lot, but they have a lot more work to do, to flesh out, to experiment with.

HB: What place does Isaac Julien's *Looking for Langston* have?

JD: It's one of my favorite films. I think I like *Looking for Langston* a lot more than *Young Soul Rebels*. *Looking for Langston* is, for me, pure sensuality. It goes beyond the essentiality in content as well as in visual form. I think it goes beyond being a film reflecting a homosexual relationship. There's so much love in it for Langston Hughes and for his poetry. And there's so much love and sensuality depicted in so many different ways, in sound, content, form, color, and design . . . that it's just a very pleasurable experience to be a part of, to watch. *Young Soul Rebels* to me is more commercial, more like "Let's go to this more hip movie."

HB: More formula?

JD: Yes.

HB: Would you feel comfortable as a filmmaker—and I suggest that you wouldn't on the basis of seeing *Daughters of the Dust*—taking up the kind of relationship to history that the filmmaker takes up in *Looking for Langston*? I mean, it's been a controversial film. Hughes's best biographer (one could say his only "real" biographer) says that there's not a shred of evidence that Hughes ever had a homosexual encounter in his life. But where does a filmmaker stand in relationship to history, or something called history? We need to have the freedom to romanticize history, to say "what if. . . ."

JD: I think we need to do more than try to document history. I think we need to probe. We need to have the freedom to romanticize history, to say "what if," to use history in a speculative way and create speculative fiction. I think we need to feel free to do that. We need to expand upon an idea, upon our thoughts on fact. Whether Langston Hughes was a homosexual or not, *Looking for Langston* is one of the greatest love stories that I ever saw, and it made me appreciate Langston Hughes more, because it's looking at Langston through another window.

HB: So what kind of things do you put in your bag as a handywoman or bricoleur when you say, "Here's history"? I want to talk now about *Daughters of the Dust*, which is one of the most brilliant films I've seen. What kind of things, as a Black filmmaker, did you feel you had to bring to the "historical site" of the film? For your film is filled with the place of the Sea Islands, a region that you make seem storied since the beginning of time. What did you feel you had to bring to that project?

JD: I think I felt I had to bring a basic integrity of the historical events and issues, but I had to be free to be able to create some drama, to create some symbolism, to do whatever I wanted, basically. Because my point is, you can always do an ethnographic documentary and get the basic process, the day-to-day events down in a documentary type of way, and you could study that. But I needed to bring other elements to bear. For instance, a historian, or even a medical person, would point out that if you used indigo dye fifty years ago, it wouldn't still be on your hands. But it was important for me to show these indigo-handed people as a reminder, that these were the scars of slavery, this blueness. I needed physically to show the scars in a different way, because film is like poetry. You want to say something that's been said before, but in a different way. To show someone with scars on their backs from a whipping, I think, will have absolutely no effect on anyone anymore, because we've seen it so many times. And that's another reason why I didn't show the rape, the physical rape, in *Daughters of the Dust*, because we've seen it on television so many times that you just say, "Mmm, that's a good rape or bad rape." I wanted to visualize things that we already knew that we have known for years, but I wanted to show it in a different way. And so the scars of slavery were depicted by the blue hands.

HB: What did you feel as you came to your project and said, "I don't want to tell the same old story again"? When you decided to "get busy" and find other modes of doing your work, did you find precedents other than Paule Marshall? You use a really resonant passage from her *Praisesong for the Widow* in your film.

JD: That came late. I had written something already for my character to say while she was standing at the banks of Ibo Landing, and then I came upon Paule Marshall. I read it and said, "This is Ibo Landing; this is glorious the way she's written it." So we got in touch with her. I don't feel that I'm the greatest writer in the world, so why try to write something, when she sat down and wrote this beautiful thing?

HB: But almost everything in *Daughters of the Dust* that you needed in order to break, and to achieve an alternative mode of representation and to keep us away from cliché, formula, and stereotype, came out of ten years of hard work, right? What is your favorite invention for the film?

JD: One of my favorites is barely in there now because we had to cut so much. But one of my favorites came from having to show these phrases I had in my head: "the sons of drums," "the loss of warrior status," "the loss of manhood for African captives." How to show that without showing someone with tears in the eyes or whips on the back? So I decided to have a figurehead floating in the swamps. I was at a gallery in New York, and I saw a figurehead that was actually on the prow of a slave ship. It was huge, monstrous. It struck me as an awful joke, the idea that the people who built the slave ship decided to make the figurehead into an African warrior. And the vibes coming off of this thing were incredible, full of death. I just could not believe it. And if I had seen a photograph or a drawing, I would have just said, "Oh." But when you see the thing carved out and you know that the slaves boarding the ship saw their own representation of themselves, tied up on the thing, it was just awful. So I was going to have a figurehead, broken off of a slave ship, floating throughout the swamps, rotting—symbolic of the African warrior in the New World. This thing is forever floating and just rotting. I didn't want to say anything about it. I didn't want to have any dialogue going on about it, because sometimes dialogue actually diminishes things. Sometimes you will receive information and process it subliminally without someone standing on the edge of the swamp saying, "There goes that figurehead again." I remember my daddy used to tell me that time would float in and out with the tide. So I just had this figurehead floating, and that disturbed a lot of people. The way I see it is that those who know, know. For those who don't know, the story will still go on. And those who want to know, will find out.

HB: What other things in the film have the resonance of the figurehead for you?

JD: The drawings on the wall in the children's room of the shanty. Carrie Marshall, production designer, and Michael Kelly Williams and Martha Jackson Jarvis worked on those, and it was representative of the years of family children's drawings on the walls. Because you also see, within the drawings, ancient markings. Also, the graveyard—the plates and clocks and things left on the graves are reminiscent of what is done in Angola.

HB: Are you satisfied that this ten-year project has come off in a way that you can endorse, support, and recommend to others?

JD: I think I got 95 percent. There was so much that we had to lose because of time and lack of money and resources. A lot of the rituals and ceremonies had to be cut or eliminated.

HB: What, finally, would you say is the most significant lesson you have learned as a filmmaker?

JD: I guess the most important thing that I have learned is that you have to be true to yourself. You have to be true to your history and your culture. And just because someone else does not see or feel what you feel, you still have to give voice to what you feel, and you have to create what you know to be true even if there's nothing to reference it. People were saying, "Well, what is *Daughters of the Dust* like?" I can't really say it's like any other film that I've ever seen, but I knew that it had to exist. So you just have to go ahead and do it. And that's important. Things are changing now, with rap music, new images and so on; people process sound and image very quickly. I think the formulas are not going to be acceptable to the younger generation. It's a time of exploration.

"I Do Exist": From "Black Insurgent" to Negotiating the Hollywood Divide— A Conversation with Julie Dash

Michael T. Martin / 2010

From *Cinema Journal* 49, no. 2 (Winter 2010): 1–16. Reprinted by permission.

[Julie Dash] consistently intervenes in and redirects Hollywood images of African American women, offering aesthetically complex and compelling characters and returning to specific historical moments to recover and revalue the nuances of black women's lives and professional contributions.

—Joanna Hearne, 2007[1]

A raconteur of extraordinary discernment and vision, Julie Dash was born and reared in the Queensbridge Projects of Long Island City, New York, although her parents came from South Carolina, where on her father's side of the family the Gullah culture was practiced. In 1968, during her senior year in high school, she attended a film workshop at the Studio Museum in Harlem, which aroused her interest in filmmaking. In 1974, she earned a BA in film production at the City College of New York, then moved to Los Angeles to find work and learn to write screenplays. There she met and worked with Charles Burnett, Billy Woodberry, and Haile Gerima. In 1975, she became a producing and writing fellow at the American Film Institute, and in 1986, she completed an MFA in motion picture and television production at the University of California Los Angeles (UCLA).

It was during the UCLA period that Dash's filmmaking and political concerns coalesced to contest Hollywood's conventions of storytelling, as well as its complicity in American racism. Dash became part of a "study" group of Black student filmmakers at UCLA, dubbed the "Black insurgents" by Toni Cade Bambara (a.k.a. the "Los Angeles School" or "LA Rebellion"). The group, asserts Bambara, "engaged in interrogating conventions of dominant cinema, screening films of socially conscious cinema, and discussing ways to alter previous significations as they relate to Black people."[2]

The intellectual and cultural commitments of the first wave of this group were "inseparable from the political and social struggles and convulsions of the 1960s," contends Ntongela Masilela.[3] In contrast to Hollywood, members of the group engaged and were inspired by the writings of Third World theorists, the cultural texts and practices of the Black Arts Movement, and the anticolonial and postrevolutionary films and political tracts of the New Latin American Cinema movement. The group's project was to conceive and practice a film form appropriate to and in correspondence with the historical moment and their cultural and aesthetic concerns. For Masilela, a central preoccupation and organizing theme of the first cohort of what arguably constituted a movement—comprising Charles Burnett, Haile Gerima, and Larry Clark among others—was the "relationship of history to the structure of the family."[4] This theme is perhaps best epitomized by Burnett's neorealist take on urban ghetto Black working-class life in *Killer of Sheep* (1977) and, I would argue, by Michael Roemer's *Nothing but a Man* (1964), a seminal study of Black family life and race relations in the rural South in the late 1950s to mid-1960s. Dash, a member of the group's second wave, along with Billy Woodberry (*Bless Their Little Hearts*, 1984), would address this familial theme, as well as the Southern rural Black encounter with modernity, in her most original, experimental, and complex film, *Daughters of the Dust* (1992).

Dash's early films reveal the originality of her artistry and the themes that would inform her more mature work. For *Diary of an African Nun* (1977), adapted from a short story by Alice Walker and shot on Super 8mm, Dash received a Director's Guild of America Award. In 1982, she made *Illusions*, the story of two African American women—one passing for white—in the Hollywood film industry during World War II, for which she later received a Black Filmmakers Hall of Fame Award. With her critically acclaimed grand opus, *Daughters of the Dust*—selected by the Library of Congress for the National Film Registry in 2004, and the first feature film by an African American woman to have a national theatrical release—Dash is assured membership in the pantheon of African American filmmakers.

Despite the critical success of *Daughters of the Dust*, Dash continues to experience resistance in Hollywood to financing her projects. In the mid-1990s, she migrated to television, directing projects for CBS (*The Rosa Parks Story*, starring Angela Bassett, 2002), MTV (*Love Song*, 2001), BET Movies/Encore/Starz3 (*Funny Valentines*, 1998), and HBO (*Subway Stories*, 1996). She also produced shorts about health issues and music videos, including Tracy Chapman's "Give Me One Reason," which was nominated for an MTV Music Video Award in 1996. In 2004, she completed *Brothers of the Borderland*, a short film scheduled to run for four years at the National Underground Railroad Freedom Center Museum in Ohio.

This extended interview with Dash occurred on two occasions: during her visit to the Indianapolis Museum of Art on October 29, 2006, where *Daughters of the Dust* was screened as part of the museum's "Film with Artist Talk Program," and at Indiana University–Bloomington on October 3–4, 2007, when Dash gave the keynote address, "My Narrative: Experiences of a Filmmaker," and screened her film *The Rosa Parks Story* as part of a month-long celebration of the university's archives and special collections. The interview is organized in two parts. The first concerns Dash's work since *Daughters of the Dust*, including her current projects in development; the second, her film practice, the prohibitions of Hollywood and attitudes of executives that constrain Black filmmakers' creative impulse and "magic," and her views about Spike Lee and Black independent filmmaking from the 1960s to the present.

On the Margins of Hollywood

Michael T. Martin: Reviewing your website, I took note that you've worked on productions for CBS, MTV, BET Movies/Encore/Starz3, and HBO. Together, they substantiate your increasing presence and prominence in Hollywood. Apart from exceptional artistry and professionalism, how do you account for your success?

Julie Dash: I see myself working in and outside of Hollywood. Hollywood is still not quite open to what I have to offer. Angela Bassett was one of the executive producers of *The Rosa Parks Story*. She said, "I want Julie Dash to direct this film and to do some rewriting of the script." So it happened. The same thing occurred with *Funny Valentines*. I directed it because Alfre Woodard was one of the executive producers. She said, "I want Julie Dash on this." It's people like Bassett and Woodard who have helped me because Hollywood is still slow about hiring me to direct and write. They're curious, however, and like to keep up with me. I can have lunch with anyone and visit with executives, but they have not hired me. Some were put off by *Daughters of the Dust* because they did not understand it, although people in the African American community seem to have an affinity for it. In fact, they [executives] rarely want to talk about *Daughters*. Once I was at Universal Studios preparing to do *Funny Valentines* and a producer said, "Just don't do *Daughters of the Dust*." He actually said that. Another Hollywood executive said, "I've seen your movie—*Daughters of the Dust*. Let's not even talk about it, let's move on from here." You know, it's like having a skeleton in your closet; it's like we won't talk about that. It's interesting, and I would like someone to tell me what it means.

MTM: Given the demands of executives and the formulaic conventions of Hollywood fare, have you had to compromise your vision and artistry?

JD: I love making movies. I'm a filmmaker. I've been a filmmaker for a very long time. I know how to come at it from different angles. I will always maintain the integrity of the subject matter whatever I'm doing. I could do a music video, a very intellectual or highbrow porno film if I chose to. In production, I fight very hard to keep historical events and issues accurate. It's important to me because I don't really enjoy films that aren't multilayered, that don't resonate or are inaccurate. Of course, you can take dramatic license and stretch things to make them more interesting. All filmmakers do that. But I will not manipulate certain things that have to do with my culture to please someone else. I've been asked to do that and I have refused. Perhaps I'm seen as difficult. I see it as being true to myself. What's needed is financing from outside sources. From venture capitalists and private funds. As a people, we must finance the films we want to see. These kinds of changes have already begun with Tyler Perry, from people in the music industry, and with actors like Will Smith producing the successful film *The Pursuit of Happyness* [Gabriele Muccino, 2006], and now with Danny Glover—cofounder of Louverture Films—who is producing and directing the film *Toussaint* [2009].

New and Unrealized Scripts

MTM: Let's talk about your projects in development. *Digital Diva* was originally intended for CD-ROM. What's it about and when do you expect to complete it?

JD: I've worked so long on *Digital Diva* that it would now have to be a DVD. I went from a screenplay to graphic novel and to pitching the screenplay to every major studio, mini-studio, independent, Black-owned, what have you. They declined it. *Digital Diva* is about a young Black woman who is a third-generation computer encryption specialist. She's the digital diva. Her grandfather was a mathematical genius who worked for the Allies during World War II. And her father, a Carnegie Mellon fellow, was a Black Panther. I heard that during World War II they had Nigerians working in the Black Tower, which was a secret code-breaking site in Washington, DC. Why would they have Nigerians? Perhaps because the Igbo language is very difficult? I researched and found out that, while they acknowledged having employed chess masters, [Romani], and gamblers to break the codes, they omitted the Nigerians [from the official record]. So, I mixed this all together in the narrative. I put some Nigerians at Oxford—one of whom is the grandfather in the story—and had them go through the Alan Turing thing at Bletchley Park and then with the Allies in Washington, DC. Twenty years later, his son, a Black Panther allied with SDS [Students for a Democratic Society] and the Weathermen, is killed because he has become a very dangerous person. His daughter, the digital diva, is opposed to Black militancy because she lost the father she never knew.

MTM: There are aspects of *Digital Diva* that resonate with *The Spook Who Sat by the Door* [Ivan Dixon, 1973], which was adapted to film from the novel by Sam Greenlee.

JD: Absolutely. And the novel *The Man Who Cried I Am* [1967] by John A. Williams. I read it in high school and thought it was really good. Why hasn't the novel been made into a film? Time is running out to make *Digital Diva* because I have to tell the story within these time locks. I have not been able to get it financed.

In 1994, I was asked, "Don't you think it's a little confusing?" It's been picked up several times as an option by several sources who always want to make it something other than what it is. You know, there was one Black company that said, "Why don't you make it an AIDS film?" Then there was another that said, "Well, why don't you make it a white film?"

MTM: It's not about that.

JD: Right! We already have that. What's new? It's not just Julie Dash who has trouble getting films financed. It's also Charles Burnett and Neema Barnette and many, many others—including white filmmakers with a different voice. Everyone who works in the industry is working on this narrow channel. *The Rosa Parks Story* was made after fifty years had passed, and then they didn't want to tell it correctly. They said, "Add this to make her more likable, do this, change that." No, while Black filmmakers have progressed, we have a long way to go. Films are being made, but they tend to be comedies.

MTM: Negroes in Hollywood?

JD: Negroes in Hollywood. They now want buddy films. I don't know how to say it nicely; it's not about us. It's a very difficult situation, but it appears not to be so because now we're seeing more Black romantic comedies, which is wonderful. They're very relaxing, but who's deciding on which films will be made and which will not? What kinds of films are being made and why? Who is the audience? Are we still just performing for white audiences? Are we being funny, are we dancing, are we singing, or are we now the love interest?

MTM: At what stage of development is *The Colored Conjurers*?

JD: Same situation.

MTM: It sounds like a story that revisits the theme of passing in your earlier film *Illusions*, which I recall is a semiautobiographical work based on your aunt Delphine?

JD: *The Colored Conjurers* is a period piece. For years, I've been told that period pieces don't sell, especially period pieces about African Americans.

Recently, there's been nothing but period pieces from Hollywood. It's like approaching the Wiz in *The Wizard of Oz* [Victor Fleming, 1939]. The wizard: "Oh, today we're not doing this, today we're doing the other. Today the color is green, tomorrow blue." The rules change by the day and sometimes by the hour. The same companies have told me that they cannot do a period film and, before I hit the door, there's a period film being made. These companies claim the demographics show that they cannot afford to do films with a female lead. They can't do films about magicians because they can't sell them, then *The Illusionist* [Neil Burger, 2006] is released. The problem is that African American films are only allowed to be "this" or "that," depending upon when they need "this" or "that." There's not much variety. What's on my mind is not what's being produced or financed at the moment. And that's been going on for fifteen years now.

MTM: *Enemy of the Sun*, another work in development, exemplifies the range of your interests and appears to have more general appeal and commercial ambitions than *The Colored Conjurers*. This is suggested in the description on your website: "A sophisticated and sexy suspense thriller reminiscent of *Entrapment* [1999], *Body Heat* [1981], and *The Thomas Crown Affair* [1968, 1999]."

JD: A very well-known producer flew me to New York to talk about doing *Enemy of the Sun*. His development person, who also had *The Colored Conjurers* screenplay and *Digital Diva* script, said she didn't know any African Americans like that. I replied, "Well, where are you from?" She said from the Midwest and that was not her experience with African Americans. I said, "You could go to Atlanta or DC, we come in all colors, all shades, and we do many different things." I hate to say this but "they"—the people in development—have a very myopic view of who we are and what we are and what we want to do. If we don't fall into place exactly where and how they imagine us, as in *Daughters of the Dust*, it's like "What do you mean Gullah, I never heard of Gullah!" I've had people ask me why I didn't do a documentary about the Gullah before doing *Daughters*. Why do I have to do a documentary first? Some people insisted that *Daughters* is a documentary. It's strange. Or they'll say things like, "Was there a script?" No, we just met every morning at sunrise, and everyone knew exactly what to wear and what we were going to be performing that day. [*Laughs*] It's unbelievable. They think it all fell together, but if it all falls together and works but is something they don't know about, then they want you to "put that away and let me focus on what I know about you." It's very patronizing, but very interesting. If I were to do a remake of another film, maybe they'd be more interested? You know, just take a white movie and remake it with Black characters.

MTM: What's *Enemy of the Sun* about?

JD: It's about two con artists who travel around the US getting very wealthy women to give them their money. And when they hit Atlanta, one of them decides that they could continue their scams legally by becoming entrepreneurs and working within the system. The other argues, "We've got to stay on the run." So the story addresses the pull and tension between them.

MTM: The other project in development, *The Reader* . . .

JD: That's a remake of *La Lectrice* [1988] by Michel Deville and based on the Raymond Jean novel of the same title.

MTM: *The Reader* seems more grounded in Black life and the challenges and compromises of being an artist. The protagonist, Denise LaMarge, has literary interests, along with extraordinary musical competence. She's juggling the everyday as well as the personal, while struggling to make career decisions that work for her. Between these demands and roles is a complex identity. The close of the film (Act 3) visualizes a montage of and homage to cultural hybridity. What is it you want to convey in Act 3?

JD: That you can be a commercial success and maintain the integrity of your art or, in her case, performance skill, because she is a singer. It's also delving into magical realism because we never hear LaMarge sing, when she does, because her voice is angelic. It's a remake of the French film but with a lot of my own issues because she has a boyfriend who is a filmmaker and who can't get his films made. He loves to watch Russian movies, but all he can do to earn money is make music videos with dancing girls. And then you have the foreign business people telling LaMarge and her group that they're not really singing like African Americans, that they need to sing like African Americans.

MTM: African Americans?

JD: I experienced this directly. It was a foreign distributor who said *Daughters of the Dust* wasn't an authentic African American film. It wasn't, like, from the hood, which is interesting to me, having grown up in the hood. Ironically, those filmmakers who make the "hood" films haven't necessarily grown up in the hood. It's exotica to them. I hope to be around when history takes a look back at all of this. I think it's time for some Black social scientist to step in and ask some pertinent questions.

MTM: Given these four distinct projects in development, who is your audience?

JD: Anyone looking to see a great story! Everyone looking to experience the talent of and new worlds by African American actors.

MTM: Has your audience changed as you've worked increasingly in Hollywood?

JD: I think my audience has increased.

MTM: But not changed?

JD: With all of the new films being written and directed by African American filmmakers, including dynamic documentaries like *Rize* [David LaChapelle, 2005], our audiences are growing, and the demographics are changing.

Practice and Thematic Concerns

MTM: I would like to focus now on your practice as a filmmaker. Which do you prefer, narrative fiction or documentary?

JD: I prefer narratives to documentaries because of my mother. She'd come home from work and I'd say, "Would you come downtown? There's going to be a film showing that we made." She'd reply, "Is it a documentary?" And I'd say, "Yeah." "Oh, I'll see it later," she'd reply. So, I never forgot that. She was tired and wanted to see a movie. [*Laughs*]

MTM: So the choice of fiction over documentary was to please your mother?

JD: Yes. You never forget something like that: "I'll see it later. Bring your tape home." It was just like, "I'll see it later because I'm not getting up out of this bed to go down the street to see a documentary." She wanted to see a story. She wanted a beginning, a middle, and an end.

MTM: What's your method of narrative filmmaking?

JD: I try different things. Each film has its own history and personality. The narrative depends on the story. The story tells me how I'm going to tell it, what it's going to be. When I wrote *Digital Diva*, I didn't set out to do a suspense thriller, but it became one. When you're writing you hone the script and then tweak it to fall within the genre because you know there are certain points—post points—that you want to hit once you find out it's a suspense thriller. Maybe I shouldn't be saying this. Maybe I should say, "I set out to write. . . ." No, for *Digital Diva*, I just wanted to write a story about codes and ciphers, evoking W. E. B. Du Bois's "double consciousness" and Black people speaking and moving in coded ways. Transfer that, the same aesthetic and sensibility, to mathematics, and you have something really marvelous going on.

MTM: Do your films reflect a particular aesthetic style or sensibility that distinguishes them from other Black filmmakers, particularly other Black women filmmakers?

JD: I think so. I think that it's closer to Euzhan Palcy's work than anyone else's.

MTM: Palcy's early and most original work—*Sugar Cane Alley* [*Rue cases nègres*, 1983]?

JD: Yeah, that one. When you're directing, it's all about choices—a thousand choices. Every day you have what directors call the "four hundred questions" posed to you by different departments that you have to answer. You also have to plan ahead how you're going to address those questions when they come up.

Otherwise, you just go, "Hmmm" and easily acquiesce to a Eurocentric point of view. You have what we call the "locus of creativity" people around, questioning you: "Why did you put the camera here?" or "Well, the camera's sitting right over there, so why don't you move it over there?" And you say, "No, I'm not going to move the camera over there." [*Laughs*]

The thing to do is be prepared for it. I always return to the Black aesthetic. That's how I sort out and resolve my problems—from a Black aesthetic and from a woman's aesthetic point of view.

MTM: You're not making decisions by committee.

JD: Exactly, although it can easily become that. A lot of directors work with the actors and not the technicians. My fault is that I work more with the technicians than the actors, although I give the actors history sheets, summations of their character, etc. But there is so much to be done with the technicians, especially if you haven't made the decisions in preproduction, for example, of what color the cup is going to be. Otherwise, it becomes everyone else's decision—a mishmash of whatever that could be wrong or inappropriate. The director has to make these decisions.

MTM: Among the writers who discuss your work, several register but few remark upon the people who have influenced your mode of storytelling. I'm going to invoke their names and ask you—in a sentence or two—to explain why or how they influenced you. First, Randy Abbott (a.k.a. Omar Mubarak)?

JD: My first film teacher. Through him my first questions about filmmaking were uttered.

MTM: Larry Clark?

JD: There are two Larry Clarks. There's the white filmmaker Larry Clark and the Black one from UCLA.

MTM: The latter.

JD: Among the reasons I went to UCLA was to work with Larry Clark, Haile Gerima, and Charles Burnett. I did my first film test with Larry Clark in the 1970s.

MTM: Haile Gerima?

JD: I met him at the LA Film School. I never worked on any of his films, but I went to a lot of his screenings during the early UCLA days.

MTM: Akira Kurosawa?

JD: That's when I realized that you make films from within you.

MTM: Vittorio De Sica and the Italian neorealists?

JD: Their films reminded me of Harlem.

MTM: Charles Burnett?

JD: He reminds me of the neorealists.

MTM: St. Clair Bourne, whom you have acknowledged "became a model" for you?

JD: I worked for him through work study when I was at Chamba Productions in New York. It was the first summer of my first year in college. I became his slave. He only once took me out on the set. I had to stay in the office and go to the store. [*Laughs*]

MTM: Paid your dues.

JD: Yes, I did. But I also was able to meet the "Chamba Brothers": Charles Hopson, Stan Wakeman, and Stan Lathan, whom Kathleen Collins was editing for. And, earlier at the Studio Museum of Harlem, I met African American female filmmakers who had come before me. I saw Madeline Anderson's documentaries and Jessie Maple's first feature film [*Will*, 1981].[5] They were unable to distribute them broadly.

MTM: Wasn't Stan Lathan with *Black Journal* at the time?

JD: Yes, and he was one of the "Chamba Brothers." They were working directors.

MTM: Making documentaries?

JD: Yes.

MTM: Has Kathleen Collins influenced your filmmaking?

JD: Kathleen Collins had her editing suite and was editing something for St. Clair Bourne. She would let me come in and watch her edit. She was so efficient and with a baby in one hand. We became friends, and she taught me about editing.

MTM: What about the Black women writers that influenced you? You said, fifteen years ago in an interview with Houston Baker, that Toni Cade Bambara influenced your approach to narrative.[6] Has Toni Morrison influenced your approach to storytelling?

JD: Her writing, whether in *Song of Solomon* [1977], *Tar Baby* [1981], *The Bluest Eye* [1970], or even *Beloved* [1987], is so visual that I would talk back to the pages and visualize the movie. You sit there crying, pat your eyes with the towel, and pick up the book again. I mean, it's very interactive when reading Toni Morrison because you're engaged.[7] I sometimes reread her novels, especially the *Song of Solomon*, through the audiobook. Someone said to me, "Oh, that could never be made into a film because it's so complex." So I listened to her voice as she read it and was able to visualize the story.

MTM: In an interview with Felicia R. Lee in *The New York Times* nearly a decade ago, you said that "I'm tired of seeing films about ourselves as victims ... reacting to external forces. . . . I hate the urban testosterone films."[8] Would you elaborate on this genre?

JD: I'm getting myself into trouble here. Actually, I suggested that in *Illusions* [1982]—how we're portrayed in films to entertain other people. Less so now because of Spike Lee. But Spike is one person. You want me to elaborate on the testosterone films? Because they've changed; it's romantic comedies now.

MTM: What's a testosterone movie?

JD: The young "urban male" films made in the 1990s. I can look at these films and say, "Well done, bravo," but I'm not a guy. I grew up in the Queensbridge Projects and could watch the same thing by looking out the window. I did not grow up in a middle-class environment, so I don't see poverty, drug abuse, violence, and ignorance as being exotic or something worth imitating. I did not sit up at night worrying about Dracula either, because growing up I knew vampires would not pass 12th Street in Queensbridge. To me, a horror movie is watching a story about families suffering from drugs, poverty, etc. Perhaps that's why I want to see a lot more when I attend a movie theater or purchase a DVD.

MTM: What kind of films do you want to see about African Americans?

JD: I want there to be more of every type of film you can imagine. I want to be able to see us in Middle Earth. We don't get to go beyond certain boundaries. We have to stay in this country and do this, that, and the other. Maybe we can run around in war a bit, but we're largely portrayed working that plow, walking the streets selling drugs, or being victims of drugs. I want to fly to the moon. Where's our *Lord of the Rings* [Peter Jackson, 2001–2003] trilogy? Where's our *Narnia* [Andrew Adamson, 2005, 2008]? As a child, we grow up knowing that we can't go there, and if we do, we'll get shot. We can't imagine ourselves running with antelope. We have to be practical. We only get to be young until we're old, and often we're old as very young people. Where's our magic? We're not allowed this magic, this space to explore. How do you grow up to be a full human being? I didn't have that space when I was growing up. I knew that you couldn't be this, you couldn't be that, so many of us don't even try. And the result can be disastrous. Today there's more of us to see in movies, but it's largely the girlfriend with the turkey neck.

MTM: Have your views about Hollywood changed since the interview with Lee?

JD: What did I say then? [*Laughs*]

MTM: You said it was a bad scene.

JD: Let me say this: It's now an even more complex scene than ever before. With the success of Tyler Perry, F. Gary Gray, Gina Prince-Bythewood, Will Smith, Tim Story, Mara Brock Akil, and Shonda Rhimes, one wonders why it is still so difficult to convince the powers that be that we do, in fact, have an audience. It's a constant fight. You will have to fight for your ground and how you see the world, for not only your own mind's eye, but also for your children and their children. We need to be dedicated, with a concerted and focused effort to demand more balanced images of ourselves out there. People say things have changed. They have changed, but in many ways they have not.

MTM: What was your experience transitioning from filmmaker to novelist to producer and now to all of the above? Are there differences and similarities between literary and visual modes of narration?

JD: I think it's easier to be a filmmaker than a novelist. I've been a filmmaker longer than a novelist. Last summer, I was working on a novel, and I can't express myself through words like I can through images, through pictures. I'm not as fluid.

MTM: In *Why We Make Movies*, you were queried about Forest Whitaker's direction of *Waiting to Exhale* [1995]. You replied, "I think he did a fine job, but it would have made a big difference had a woman directed it. . . ."[9] Is there a woman's sensibility to filmmaking that is different from a man's?

JD: I think it would have made a difference in the directing, and there is a difference of sensibilities between men and women. It's in the tiny specifics. I know it sort of flows from the top down. You need a strong woman in the producing, writing, directing, as well as editing areas to retain the tiny specifics and integrity of the film. The director now supervises the editing because it's easy to cut something out. A director can shoot something, and it'll never make it into the finished film because someone else says, "What is that? We don't need that." It's always "we," or my favorite line . . . , "It goes off story, it's off story." But men and women think differently. They want to see different things. If you have an all-male team working on a woman's film, it will be missing some things. Like music, if it's the beat, the beat is just off, but that doesn't mean that men cannot direct women's movies and that women cannot direct men's movies. I'm saying, if it's going to be an all-male team—producer, director, writer, and editor—you better bring in some women to say, "Hey! You missed a beat here."

MTM: What would you have changed had you directed *Waiting to Exhale*?

JD: I'm gonna stay out of it.

MTM: Regarding *The Rosa Parks Story*, you said that you were "determined to get a more womanist vision, a female version of what was going on because it was a very male-centered script."[10] What's a "womanist vision"?

JD: The script I was handed was more about Raymond Parks and his point of view than Rosa Parks. It was not about her. And I think that's why Angela [Bassett] wanted me to massage the script by Paris Qualles—the writer of record. Together, we made the appropriate changes.

MTM: You were also especially critical of how the meaning of independent film has been appropriated and co-opted by Hollywood. Regarding companies like Miramax, you said that it's "not independent. It's not a filmmaker's vision. They're not signature films."[11] What do you mean by "signature films," and are they different from auteur films?

JD: A signature film is like an auteur film. It implies the director has control over everything. However, filmmaking is a collaboration, unless the film is some kind of surveillance with one camera.

MTM: Is there a Julie Dash signature?

JD: I hope so. I'm working toward one. I think each project develops organically, even if you're handed a script as with *The Rosa Parks Story*. You sit with it and walk the site. You do your own research, which I did and discovered wonderful things like putting additional period buses in the film, changing locations to enhance the drama, and sometimes narrowing the focus of the story beats.

MTM: If I saw any one of your films, is there something about it that would identify you as the author? For example, I think Euzhan Palcy's *Sugar Cane Alley* is her most original film. Once she migrated to Hollywood, her unique style was less discernible and apparent, in my view.

JD: She has made other films that they have not distributed in the US, including a musical. There's a film about a little girl who sees a ghost or is a ghost of a little girl. They did not release it here because they said, "It'll confuse people with subtitles." Another factor is when you have four hundred questions and 101 people with the legal right to tweak a film after you have completed it. They own the film and have a right to tweak it, so they say.

MTM: You have asserted on several occasions that you "want to see authenticity."[12] What do you mean by "authenticity"?

JD: By that, I mean you can feel that it comes out of the filmmaker, out of the community, out of the issues, out of the events, out of history. You don't want something just grafted onto a film. You don't put a hat on a person without feeling a natural sense that it's right. It means that you know that something is flowing and moving right and that the history is there and recognizable to you. When you know that the parallel streams of information, symbolism, and metaphor coming together are not silly or stupid. We know, we feel the natural rhythm of the story, situation, or event. It's a glorious feeling. Unfortunately, I feel it more with foreign films than I do with those made in the US.

MTM: Can a filmmaker retain a critical and independent stance in Hollywood given the pressures we've talked about?

JD: Beyond the overused argument about "commerce versus art," I think the main goal we have to keep in focus is that we can have both. Everyone else does. Why do we have to remain especially limited in our thinking and doing? It's not just about putting Black folks in front and behind of the camera. If you hire people who tell the same stories the same ways that other folks do, then what's the point? I see that happening a lot. They are fulfilling quotas. And it's like, "Well we have to do it this way because this is the way we've always done it."

MTM: Let's revisit the interview you had with Houston Baker in 1992. I want to read a statement that you made because I think that it is as relevant today as it was fifteen years ago. Regarding your narrative approach to *Daughters of the Dust*, you rejected "the male Western narrative" for the narrative mode based on oral tradition as exemplified by the African credo."[13] Since *Daughters*, have you changed your view about this mode of narration?

JD: I think there was some confusion there, and my statement was misrepresented. I was saying then, that before *Daughters of the Dust*, I was not using the Western male narrative based upon the "tall tale of the once upon a time" and the linearity of Act 1, Act 2, and Act 3. Now, in some of my other films, I'm working within the Western narrative because it is easily grasped by audiences. But you can insert other things in there to make the audience consider and feel that there's something more that you're trying to tell.

Black Filmmaking: Making Progress?

MTM: You have noted that during the 1960s and '70s, Black filmmaking on the East Coast was largely devoted to documentary, while on the West Coast, to narrative film. Apart from the dominance of Hollywood, its commercial concerns, production practices, and narrative conventions, were there other factors that account for this difference?

JD: I think the West Coast got lucky, first with *Sweet Sweetback's Baadasssss Song* [Melvin Van Peebles, 1971] and then with *Shaft* [Gordon Parks, 1971]. "Hey, we've got a good thing going, let's make some Blaxploitation films." They really took off.

MTM: And why the documentary on the East Coast?

JD: Because East Coast filmmakers were more interested in authenticity, the truth, answering questions, and exposing situations. Of course, the budgets for documentaries were smaller than for narrative features. You don't need a large crew; you can do it faster and more efficiently. I came out of that East Coast filmmaking tradition and wound up on the West Coast trying to apply that same aesthetic to narrative films.

MTM: Have the dynamics and practices of filmmaking now changed the trajectory of the West Coast narrative, East Coast documentary?

JD: Yes, there are many narrative films being made on the East Coast, even in the Midwest, including here in Indiana. The playing field is now leveled by digital technology.

MTM: You have asserted that during the 1990s the climate for Black filmmakers was more difficult and competitive. You said, "We don't even see ourselves right now as a movement. I don't think these filmmakers are thinking in terms of history and progression."[14] Is the climate for Black filmmaking any better today?

JD: During the 1990s it was very competitive. I now realize that the competitive climate for Black filmmaking was created by Hollywood, [which was] determined to make "testosterone films." Hollywood made sure that when they took pictures of these homeboy films from the hood that they didn't include women. I remember someone said, "Well, they didn't know where you were." I was with Mario Van Peebles in Germany attending a film festival. My entertainment lawyer also represented the Hudlin brothers and Mario, so how could he say they couldn't find me? I'll never forget that they got a Black woman and cultural critic—Karin Grisby-Bates—to say that these were the [male] filmmakers making it and that my movie [*Daughters*] was a television movie. She wrote that in *The New York Times*, and people repeated that it wasn't theatrical. I said, "No, it's not a television movie." It was American Playhouse that coproduced my film, along with *Straight Out of Brooklyn* [Matty Rich, 1991] and *Stand and Deliver* [Ramón Menéndez, 1988]. But *Daughters* became a "television movie" because it suited their purposes. At Sundance, we were all interviewed, but all the interviews were skewed toward the Black male filmmakers while the female filmmakers were tossed aside. I now understand that it was a concerted effort to promote Black male filmmakers while they ignored everyone else, as if we didn't exist. We do, and I am still around.

MTM: Are Black filmmakers as self-serving and opportunistic today as you, seemingly, have suggested that many were in the 1990s?

JD: What was going on back then was frightening. I recall an incident at the Sundance Film Festival when the director Matty Rich said, "Hey, Julie, I was wanting to meet you." I replied, "Hey, Matty, how you doing?" A publicist immediately cut in and said, "You two don't talk." I was, like, when did this happen?

MTM: And now?

JD: It's not like that now, but it's certainly not like the way it was in the 1980s when everyone would meet at the film festivals. It was the only time we got to see everyone, and it was great. I think we've learned that the competitiveness of the 1990s didn't help anyone; no one got to make any more movies. Since the 1980s, the only one who's been consistent is Spike Lee.

MTM: You said to Houston Baker that in *She's Gotta Have It* [1986], Spike Lee "brought life back into the Black independent film movement."[15] Now, with Spike Lee ensconced in Hollywood—except for occasional departures, like his recent take on the Katrina debacle—is the US Black independent film movement overshadowed by his prominence in Hollywood?

JD: No. And we need more filmmakers like Spike Lee. He just keeps exploring and stretching the envelope. People don't understand how much battering he took. He just keeps coming back, putting blinders on, and doing what he's going to do. I love that he takes chances. If we had ten more Spikes, we'd be in good shape. And some female Spikes, too. The documentary on Katrina [*When the Levees Broke: A Requiem in Four Acts*, 2006] had you weeping. I understand that he's going to do a dramatic film on Katrina. Then he had the thriller bank robbery movie [*Inside Man*, 2006], although it didn't feel at all like Spike. I won't let anybody talk badly about him. He took a chance with *She Hate Me* [2004]. It was five different movies in one and had a little Spikeness in it. Okay, it was French.

MTM: Is there another Spike Lee out there to revitalize the Black independent film movement?

JD: I know there are many Spikes who have that drive and sense of wit.

MTM: Do you have anyone in mind?

JD: Shola Lynch, Sylvain White, Darnell Martin, and Antoine Fuqua.

MTM: Let's conclude here with your current project. What's it about?

JD: There's a Nancy Wilson song, "Now I'm a Woman." Everything is music. You carry that around and one day you say, "Hey, I'm going to do a film about 'first I was a child, now I'm a lady.'" [*Laughs*] It's a romantic trilogy. The main character—a woman—is a perfumer, and her life has been influenced and informed by three distinct fragrances.

MTM: Thank you, Julie Dash.

JD: And thank you too.

Notes

1. Joanna Hearne, "Julie Dash," in *Schirmer Encyclopedia of Film*, ed. Barry Keith Grant (Thompson Gale, 2007), 376.
2. Toni Cade Bambara, "Reading the Signs, Empowering the Eye: *Daughters of the Dust* and the Black Cinematic Movement," in *Black American Cinema*, ed. Manthia Diawara (Routledge, 1993), 119. According to Ntongela Masilela, Dash was among the "second wave" in this movement, which included Alile Sharon Larkin, Bernard Nichols, and Billy Woodberry. See Ntongela Masilela, "The Los Angeles School of Black Filmmakers," in *Black American Cinema*, ed. Diawara, 107.
3. Bambara, "Reading the Signs," 119.
4. Bambara, "Reading the Signs," 111. Note that Charles Burnett's films *Killer of Sheep* (1977), *My Brother's Wedding* (1983), *The Horse* (1973), *Several Friends* (1969), and *When It Rains* (1995) were released in a box set by Milestone Films (2007).
5. See the Jessie Maple Collection at the Black Film Center and Archive, Indiana University–Bloomington.
6. Houston Baker Jr., "Not Without My *Daughters*," *Transition* 57 (1992): 151.

7. For more on Dash's thoughts about Morrison, see Baker, "Not Without My *Daughters*," 151–52.
8. Felicia R. Lee, "Where a Filmmaker's Imagination Took Root," *The New York Times*, December 3, 1997.
9. George Alexander, *Why We Make Movies* (Harlem Moon/Broadway Books, 2003), 236.
10. Alexander, *Why We Make Movies*, 241.
11. Alexander, *Why We Make Movies*, 236.
12. Alexander, *Why We Make Movies*, 242.
13. Baker, "Not Without My *Daughters*," 151.
14. Baker, "Not Without My *Daughers*,"159.
15. Baker, "Not Without My *Daughters*," 161.

6° of Geechee

Stephanie Hunt / 2015

From *Charleston Magazine* 29, no. 5 (May 2015): 128–33. Reprinted by permission of Stephanie Hunt, freelance writer, editor at large, *Charleston Magazine*.

Filmmaker Julie Dash, celebrated for elevating African American heritage on the silver screen, is chronicling the worldly vibrations of culinary griot and beatnik Geechee girl Vertamae Smart-Grosvenor. Her New York accent is all Queens, her hair a commotion of curls, her eyes strong and bright. Julie Dash gets your attention, if not with her striking presence and persuasive smile, then with her impressive body of work. Mention her name around film aficionados and you get knowing nods: "Oh yes, Julie Dash." In academic circles related to film studies, African American history and culture, and women's studies, her name is even more recognizable, almost approaching cult status.

With fourteen directorial film credits, a Director's Guild Award, and the distinction of being the first African American woman to direct a wide-release motion picture—*Daughters of the Dust* (1991)—Dash is more or less a female Spike Lee. She's worked with actors Angela Bassett and Cicely Tyson and singers Tracy Chapman and Sweet Honey in the Rock, as well as scores of others, including filming actor Danny Glover and musician Hugh Masekela for her current project, a documentary on Vertamae Smart-Grosvenor. But to students at the College of Charleston, where she's been a visiting artist and scholar at the Avery Research Center, a division of the College of Charleston libraries, since 2011, she's simply "professor," the one who's teaching them the finer points of cinematography—even how to make a film using the smartphone iOS platform. The best camera these days? "The one that's in your pocket, because it's accessible, it's right there when you need it," Dash says, paraphrasing photographer Chase Jarvis.

She's no nonsense—it's all about the work. Dash doesn't dither with showbiz pretense or Hollywood aura, even though she's "officially bicoastal," with her home in LA when she's not in Charleston, and hails from a glam pedigree: her older sister, Charlene, was one of the first Black supermodels with the Ford Agency in the 1970s, gracing international runways and fashion spreads in magazines from *Vogue* to *Ebony* to *LOOK*. And her uncle Julian Dash, one of her father's six brothers who were born and raised in Charleston then moved north, was a noted jazz saxophonist and cowriter of the iconic tune "Tuxedo Junction."

Dash simply does what it takes to get the job done—just ask the crew members who worked on the filming of her breakout *Daughters of the Dust* and joined her in traipsing around Hunting and St. Helena Islands' beaches, swamps, and maritime forests wearing Dracula capes as rain gear. "It was after Halloween, and they were on sale. That's low-budget Hollywood for you," says Dash, who shot the film for $800,000—and that's including a hefty line item for DEET and Skin-So-Soft, thanks to ravenous post-Hurricane Hugo mosquitoes and gnats.

On the Map

Daughters of the Dust, which Dash began researching in the late 1970s while she was a fellow at the American Film Institute in Los Angeles, is a dreamy, ethereal, winding tale of an extended Gullah family at the turn of the century as they prepare to leave their matriarch, Nana Peazant, and their moss-draped, memory-drenched Sea Island homestead for "progress" and migration to mainland culture. Released in 1992, the film received critical acclaim—"mesmerizing," according to *The Boston Globe*; "poetry in motion," said *The Atlanta Journal-Constitution*; "an unprecedented achievement," heralded *The Village Voice*—and won the 1991 Sundance Film Festival Best Cinematography Award. *Daughters* not only put Dash on the map, it introduced the Gullah Geechee culture, language, and food to a much broader audience than ever before. Though now more than twenty years old, the film is still screened nationally and internationally and was inducted in 2004 into the Library of Congress's American Film Registry as one of 400 national film treasures.

"This movie really changed my life," says cultural anthropologist Dr. Patricia Williams Lessane, executive director of the Avery Research Center, who remembers attending a screening in Atlanta ("the Mecca of all things Black") the summer before she went to graduate school at Dartmouth. "It was the first time I'd seen a film that situated Black life and Black women's lives so straight in the middle. It was so magical, so beautiful; historically correct and yet ethereal. I was obsessed." Lessane went on to incorporate aspects of *Daughters* as a post-slavery slave narrative into her doctoral research, and today she frequently uses the film in her classes when discussing Africanisms in the American and the African American experiences.

Many viewers with no previous exposure to Sea Island history and Gullah culture compared watching *Daughters of the Dust*—with its impressionistic cinematography, moody and wild landscapes, and mythic narrative delivered in mysterious, lyrical dialect (with no subtitles)—to watching a foreign film. Perhaps that's not surprising, given that going to esoteric foreign flicks in Manhattan with her older sister was how Dash first became entranced by the silver screen as a young teen. "My sister had traveled to France (she modeled in the infamous Versailles Battle of 1973), and she took me one afternoon to a French film, and then to a French restaurant, and I was hooked," Dash says. "It roused my fascination with films of unknown cultures."

This early intrigue led Dash, then in high school, to enroll in an after-school workshop in filmmaking at the Studio Museum of Harlem, and from there to the City College of New York for her bachelor's of art in film production, followed by a fellowship at the American Film Institute's Center for Advanced Studies in LA. She then earned her MFA in film and television production at UCLA. "I was lucky to have teachers who were hippies, who encouraged experimentation," says Dash, who initially wanted to be a cinematographer, "until I discovered I wasn't very good at it," and then gravitated toward producing and directing. In addition to her long list of credits . . . Dash has been a frequent lecturer at universities, including Harvard, Stanford, Yale, and of course, the College of Charleston, where Lessane, a die-hard Dash fan, was thrilled to lure her mentor and idol.

Geechee Vibrations

Teaching at the Avery Research Center, her father's and uncles' alma mater (then the Avery Normal Institute), has been an ironic homecoming for Dash, who spent summers traveling from Queens to visit her extended Charleston-based family; her mother was from Union, South Carolina. "When my father was growing up and in school, being 'Geechee' was frowned upon. Their teachers insisted they speak properly; they had it [Gullah accents] worked right out of them, here at Avery," says Dash, whose film showcased the endangered dialect, in essence reversing her Avery predecessors' efforts. Dash hired Gullah language experts to consult on both *Daughters* the film and her subsequent novel of the same title (a sequel to the film). "I wanted the dialogue to be authentic," she says. Enter Vertamae Smart-Grosvenor, a proud "Geechee girl" and Gullah language and food consultant extraordinaire, a force to be reckoned with, and now the subject of Dash's current film project.

Dash vividly remembers her first encounter with Smart-Grosvenor in the mid-1980s. "I saw this title at a bookstore in New York, *Vibration Cooking: Or, The Travel Notes of a Geechee Girl*. I was stunned that she had used the word 'Geechee.' People just didn't use that term—it was like the N-word," says Dash, whose family was proud of being from Charleston, but "Geechee" references were only whispered privately. "If you were African American and you wanted to call someone out, you called them a 'Geechee,'" she recalls.

Smart-Grosvenor—a native of Fairfax, South Carolina, who eventually lived in Philadelphia, Paris, and New York—however, embraced the moniker and celebrated Gullah traditions and gumbos in her 1970 culinary memoir, with its folksy, straight-shooting, blog-like tone that was fresh, funny, and thoroughly '70s-ish ("I dig it"). Readers "dug" it, as did the media—Smart-Grosvenor's *Vibration* ("I never measure anything . . . I cook by vibration," she wrote) became a best seller and has had a four-decade-long ripple effect. She's appeared on *The Today Show* and *Nightline*, was an NPR commentator and host of the series *Horizons*, served as editor of *Élan Magazine*, worked on the film *Beloved*, and was close friends with Maya Angelou and Nina Simone. Tall and cosmopolitan, a woman of pageantry and style (elegant hats and African-inspired garb), Smart-Grosvenor became a high, cool priestess of Black pride, brilliantly commandeering rice, pork, gizzards, and greens as her cultural bridge. She served up the history of race in America with sass and a frying pan.

Dash worked closely with Smart-Grosvenor on *Daughters* (she plays the part of Hair Braider), and in 2012, Dash and Lessane began interviewing Smart-Grosvenor, who was then seventy-five and living back in her native Hampton County, as part of the Avery's oral history project. "She'd talk about her first dinner party back in New York on the Lower East Side with Yoko Ono as a guest. There were tales of her living in Paris at the Beat Hotel with Alan Ginsberg and William Burroughs, pictures of her with Muhammad Ali. She once suggested I take a photo of the two of us, and she'd send it to her friend, Jackie Onassis. Patricia and I realized, whoa, there is just so much here that hasn't been told," says Dash. "It's like that Kevin Bacon thing—six degrees of Vertamae. She showed up everywhere, had all these madcap adventures, and was connected to so many significant historical movements and people."

Last year, Lessane secured the Avery Research Center's largest National Endowment of the Arts grant to date, $75,000, for Dash. With the support of Avery researchers, the filmmaker began work on a new film, *Travel Notes of a Geechee Girl*. An Indiegogo campaign to crowd-fund additional financing for the project is underway. Numerous interviews for the biopic have already been shot, including those with Danny Glover and South African jazz trumpeter Hugh Masekela; Fabio Parasecoli, a culinary scholar at The New School; Nancy Grace, author of *Girls Who Wore Black: Women Writing the Beat Generation*; and Sue Goodwin, former producer of NPR's *Talk of the Nation*; and many more are in the works.

"As a filmmaker, this project is challenging and exciting, and a little hard to contain," says Dash. "Every time I interview someone, I learn something new, some fascinating side road of Vertamae's life. We're bringing in scholars and artists who can lay a foundation for what the world was like as this six-foot-tall Black woman from rural South Carolina was passing through it." Indeed, Smart-Grosvenor was like a Gullah Zelig, playing a part in five different cultural movements: the Beat Movement, Black Power, Black Arts, New Black Cinema, and the culinary revolution. She was bold, brave, and determined to pursue excellence, notes Dash. "If this Black woman in the 1950s could get on a boat and find her way to Paris, become a Black beatnik and bestselling author, then maybe it will inspire women today."

Which, of course, is not unlike Julie Dash herself, who has become a role model for many, including the Oscar Award–winning director Ava DuVernay, of *Selma* fame. "Julie's work leaps off the screen and into my bloodstream like a drug," says DuVernay, who, when honored by the African American Film Critics Association in February, asked Dash to present her award. "I'm in awe of her commitment and courage to intentionally and wholeheartedly show the imagery of Black women. This inspires me. This shows me all is possible."

And here in Charleston, Dash brings definite cachet to the African American studies program, says Lessane. "Julie is a great mentor to students. She's not only a cinematic genius, she's giving of her craft and ideas, and so supportive of others. She's the yin to Vertamae's yang. Vertamae is wily; she takes control of a room and wants to be the center of attention. Julie is unassuming and is more interested in shining the light on others. She is that kind of person."

Interview: Julie Dash

Cassie da Costa / 2016

From *FilmComment.com*, February 29, 2016. Reprinted by permission of Film at Lincoln Center.

It's been twenty-five years since the theatrical release of Julie Dash's *Daughters of the Dust*, which had a week-long run at Film Forum in 1991. Dash's groundbreaking film follows the Peazant family in the early twentieth century, as the younger generation is about to leave their Gullah Geechee community off the coast of South Carolina and head up north and onto the mainland. Seeking to take advantage of "civilized" society and opportunity, they prepare to leave behind their matriarch, Nana Peazant, who holds fiercely onto her roots and insists that her children and grandchildren do the same.

Daughters of the Dust was originally met with confusion about its portrayal of a part of African American history that was, up to that point, unrecognized in the mainstream. The film's focus lies firmly on the lives of the Peazant women, interweaving narratives of the past, present, and future and using two narrators (Nana and "the Unborn Child"). Its images are as immersive as they are elusive, with bodies always carefully situated in relation to each other as generations intermingle, conflict, and ultimately make their peace. Tableaux of the Peazant women show them as they dance, eat, argue, dream, grieve, and reminisce.

The entire film takes place outdoors, in the woods and on the beach, as Black history from West Africa to South Carolina is relived through its physical marks on the present. Cinematographer Arthur Jafa brings out both the boldness and softness of blues and browns, and the dulled whites of turn-of-the-century Victorian dress, worn down by their constant exposure to nature. In this way, the keen attention given to composition, framing, texture, and hue is crucial as *Daughters* conceives of new symbols for Black American struggle and resilience. For example, rather than whip marks, indigo-stained hands are the scars of slavery. Indelibility—physical, filial, and historical—rings throughout an unforgettable film that imagines Blackness in America as legacy rather than as a story of destruction.

Daughters of the Dust was the first feature film by an African American woman to have a theatrical release and has since been widely written about by academics, critics, and filmmakers. *Film Comment* spoke with Dash, who teaches at Morehouse College, about making the film, its legacy, and what the past twenty-five years have been like for her as a working director. Cohen Media Group and UCLA have been restoring *Daughters of the Dust* under the supervision of Dash and Jafa, with a rerelease slated for the Wexner Center for the Arts at the Ohio State University in May and a home video release by Cohen.

Cassie da Costa: I spoke to Chris Horak [director of the UCLA Film and Television Archive] about how the new restoration is going to change how we see the film and bring all these new layers of the images to light.

Julie Dash: They did a *terrific* job. I was stunned. I hadn't seen the film look like that since we edited it on film. And I remember, you just get used to what it is—it wasn't fully color-corrected because at the time it was very expensive to go to the studio and get a better print. After that, we were out of money, so we just had to go ahead and release it, but it wasn't there yet. But now it is. And it's like, "Whoa, you can see the people's faces!"

CdC: I was reading the book you wrote about the making of *Daughters*, and in the interview with bell hooks, you talked about how men would "fly out of the theater" seeing the lives of Black women portrayed.

JD: [*Laughs*] They'd be in the back of the theater and come rushing up the aisles! They either needed to go to the bathroom really badly or they were just like "I'm getting out of here because where's the men?"

CdC: And now you're teaching cinema at Morehouse, an all-men's college!

JD: Well, this is two generations later—they weren't even born yet. Plus, I don't know how many of them have seen *Daughters*. They've seen some of my other work like *Love Song* [2000] or *The Rosa Parks Story* [2002]. But one of the classes I'm teaching is called "Black Women Filmmakers." And we say "Black women" rather than "African American women" because I'm including filmmakers from all over the African diaspora like Euzhan Palcy and Sarah Maldoror, all of our great filmmakers. And they're all in the class saying, "I've never heard of her, I've never heard of her." Of course you haven't, but now you have—enjoy! Yvonne Welbon, all these people.

I'm just contracted for this year, 2015–2016. It's a good thing because it puts me on the East Coast—I'm working on *Travel Notes of a Geechee Girl*, and everyone I'm working with is on the East Coast.

CdC: It's been twenty-five years since *Daughters* came out, but press reports usually make it sound as if you haven't been doing anything in all that time when you really have been.

JD: They don't mention anything but *Daughters of the Dust*. And the public tends to believe I haven't done anything, and then they start making these lists, and they say, "Well, list the Black filmmakers," and I never make that list because it always has that little caveat "working within the last ten years." And it's like, "Oh really? That's the way you're going to list things?" But do they know about the commercials I do? I did a couple of Coca-Cola commercials last summer. I do car commercials. I do TV. I have never stopped working. It's just that I'm not in the public eye that way. I had a good run with being highly visible, and now it's time for other people to be highly visible—I have no problem with that. Let me just support them, and let me just keep doing what I'm doing, because at the end of the day it's about the work.

CdC: I wanted to talk to you about *Daughters* both in terms of the film itself, but also in terms of what it's generated over the past several years since its release. You were inspired by novels by Toni Morrison, for example, and also by foreign films in creating a narrative structure that actually speaks to the ways that stories are told within the diaspora and not adhering to A-to-B-to-C narrative.

JD: Right! Binary narrative. In the culture we're not binary, we speak in rhythms and sensibilities, we're circular. We're agrarian, we do improvisation, and movement and dance and speech and art and design, and it's possible to communicate in these ways through cinema too.

CdC: And you brought together so many artists to do this. In reading the book you wrote about *Daughters* [*Daughters of the Dust: The Making of an African American Woman's Film*], the entire production sounded like a truly collaborative experience, people pitching in in all these different ways. I know people talk a lot about film being a collaborative experience, but the idea seemed to be taken to heart.

JD: It *was* collaborative. And back then, Arthur Jafa talked about it as a jazz band, like a jazz orchestra out there. Working with [production designer] Kerry James Marshall and [art director] Michael Kelly Williams and the costume designers—it just started flowing. It was a huge production for an independent film. We had these big warehouses where we had the costumes stored, where they were being dyed. The art department had their warehouse where Michael Kelly Williams was making the chair and he and Kerry were making the tombstones and the figureheads. It was a museum, if you will, walking through the art department.

And it started even before we got down there. With Kerry, we were pulling images as references for the indigo plantation flashback scene, and Kerry actually built those indigo dyeing mounds, all based upon what we could find or pull together or read about how they did it in West Africa as the foundation for what was done here. I believe we were the very first ever to have indigo as a visual theme or motif that went throughout the story. I decided, instead of showing the form of enslaved people with whip marks or scars of slavery, their scars would be the permanent blue hands from working the indigo fields, and that's how you could tell who was a former enslaved person of the elders.

CdC: Some responses to the film were incredulous that you would dare to imagine anything through a fiction narrative rather than construct a biographical or documentary-style feature.

JD: Yeah, and I thought about [doing] that at first and then was like, well, why do I have to? It's cheeky to say that—that of course I have to tell you what you don't know first and *then* I can do it as a drama? Come on.

CdC: That's why I think the film was so ahead of its time and continues to resonate. It imagines so many things instead of just trying to tell people who they were, and it was as much about the people who made it as it was about the history, which is such a difficult thing to do in your first feature—to put so much of your imagination in a history-referencing narrative without adhering to any sort of template.

JD: It was my first feature, but I had done quite a few shorts. I had pretty much done the same thing in—well, I got hit in the head for doing *Illusions* [1982]. At the time, people were saying, "How dare you? Isn't that just like *Imitation of Life* or *Pinky*?" and I was like, "No, it's totally different." Like, how dare I deal with the color caste when Black filmmakers weren't doing that then. Because I made that in '82. And with *Illusions*, I remember being in Rennes, France, at a Black film festival, and some people, Black French people, got up and walked out of the screening because they weren't getting the full translation and simply thought I was doing *Pinky* or *Imitation of Life*, a Black woman ashamed of passing for white. But I was using passing for white as in, she was like a guerrilla fighter. But they couldn't grasp that because all they could think of was the 1930s or 1950s Douglas Sirk. So I've been creating new realities for a long, long time.

CdC: *Daughters* had a theatrical release, so you see so many more people coming into contact with it, and it had the ability to surprise them. But that was the way your career was setting up to go, because you had been making that kind of work already, pushing boundaries.

JD: I also think independent filmmakers, Black or white, at that time we were exploring new ways of telling the stories that we already knew. We were reframing it. Hollywood had framed things a certain way—the baseline Southern historical film was *Gone with the Wind*. So everyone wanted to do something that was not that. It's amazing because now I still get screenplays sent to me with that same *Gone with the Wind* aesthetic. And I see it on TV all the time. That's a false notion of the antebellum South and the postwar South. It's still false, but people are still going with it. It's all cotton picking when cotton wasn't the only thing—it's indigo, it's tobacco, it's all kinds of things. And then there were the enslaved people who lived, for instance, in Charleston. In the city, where my people are from, they didn't work plantations; they were craftspeople. No one really showed that type of slavery because it doesn't depict the aesthetic frame that's been established with *Gone with the Wind* with picking cotton. They'd put on their metal badge and get up in the morning and go to work making shoes in a factory, but we're not allowed to see that. In Philadelphia they worked in mines—in the coal mines. You never see that.

Can we change up now? It's been sixty, seventy-five years of the same thing over and over again. And I just turn on television now, and it's that same old antebellum farce that we're seeing with Mammy in the kitchen who's overweight. And scholars have already come up and said that that's not true at all. She wasn't fat; she was the sexual toy of the master of the house—but they create that Mammy because that image becomes the beard, it's the cover story because no one would think that the master of the house is going down every night to sleep with Mammy because she's big and fat. That's been disproven. But every film you see comes up with that one. I don't want to operate within the same frames of what's been said.

CdC: It's this idea that white imagination is more honest or truthful or valuable than how Black people imagine their own lives. And that's why your bringing so much of the complexity of diaspora into *Daughters* was so important, because even now Black people working in film can still feel constrained in their efforts to portray unexpected elements of Black life.

JD: But those unexpected things have resonance, and they are actually a visible delight, metaphorically, emotionally. It's just like an awakening when you're watching a film and you go, "Oh, okay, wow!" And I think that's why I like foreign films so much: I'm learning, I'm seeing something new. It's the same genres and dramas that we're familiar with, but you see them through fresh eyes, through new voices. It's an experience. It's the way cinema is supposed to be.

CdC: But what can also happen is that when you are that new voice and you're telling a new story, on the flip side, you're asked to become a spokesperson for that perspective, a token, and you're expected to do the same kind of work over and over again. Did you feel that pressure after *Daughters*?

JD: Yes. That's why I think people can't really understand how I did *Love Song, Funny Valentines* [1999], *Incognito* [1999], *The Rosa Parks Story*. They're all very different types of films, different genres. But they just don't mention it because they think, "She does historical dramas, she can't do something like a *Love Song*, a romantic comedy, so we won't even mention it."

CdC: It seems as if this idea of a Black filmmaker having to "break out" is less about their finally making a strong film and more about being able to push past (or even align with) the "expectations" of their audiences.

JD: And things have not really changed that much. I saw this film on TV—you know, because it's Black History Month, and there are all these Black films on TV—and it's got the same *Jane Pittman* ending! That movie must have come out forty years ago, when I was in the eighth grade, *The Autobiography of Miss Jane Pittman*. It's the same old thing, but you're supposed to be happy because now it's a digital production.

CdC: *Love Song* to me feels like a precursor to a wave of Black romantic comedies that I think now have been getting theatrical screen time. It's one of the films that pushed toward this idea of showing the modern lives of young Black people.

JD: A film about a group of Black women who are not talking about race. Trying to get through their daily lives without trying to be Atlanta housewives.

CdC: I haven't seen *Daughters* be put into conversation much with other films. It definitely stands on its own as a piece of work that's incredibly unique, but at the same time, this idea that people hadn't seen this type of story before or were surprised by it really prevented people outside of academia from engaging with it as a film that's in conversation with other films.

JD: It's funny how it plays outside of the country without people saying it's complex or anything. There was a retrospective of it in Taiwan in 2009. It's played in India, all across Asia, Poland, Germany, and no one ever says anything about it being slow or difficult to follow. Nothing like that. And I think, "I have to return to those places with the film." It's always been received differently outside the country because they don't have the same expectations of, when you say "a Black historical film" and people think, "Oh, I know the story, roll the film." And when they're not seeing what they expect to see, then there's some kind of resistance.

CdC: That's also one thing bell hooks really hit on in that conversation [in *Daughters of the Dust: The Making of an African American Woman's Film*]. You say earlier in the book, "I realized early on that even a lot of my own people sometimes would be against me"—this idea that it was white men, then white women, then Black men, and after all of that . . .

JD: I even spoke to a lot of Black women film executives, and they had a lot of the same reactions as white men because their jobs were to be white men. So that's why I realized it's not just race, it's bigger than that—it's race *and* gender. And the systemic racism—those Black women executives have to hold a line so that they can keep their positions. It was interesting to learn and I'm glad that there's now movement forward with Ava [DuVernay], with Dee [Rees], and with Gina Prince-Bythewood—that they're able to make films and have more traction.

CdC: So how did you move forward from that?

JD: It hasn't stopped me from working in the independent sector. I was working for Disney, Imagineering, designing multimedia pavilions. I worked for the National Underground Railroad Freedom Center museum making a $1.5 million film that plays there continually. I'm still writing and I'm still making films. I've never stopped. That's the thing that some people don't understand. They think that if you don't get a Hollywood film, you just stop in your tracks and become a nurse. I'm a filmmaker, I was a filmmaker long before those people were in the studios, probably, and I think it's a little bit too late to turn and run now. This is what I do: I make a film, and if I can't make a film, I teach, or I teach while I make it. I will always be a writer. Filmmaking is filmmaking. I tell stories, I like to take an idea and turn it into something visual that's compelling, exciting, meaningful. And that's the task at hand no matter whether it's a five-minute-thirty-second commercial spot or a feature film. That's what I enjoy doing, and that's what I have been doing.

Audio Story: *Daughters of the Dust*— Julie Dash Interview

Andrea Chase / 2016

From "Audio Story" on PRX.org, October 14, 2016. Transcribed by Jaiden Canteen. Printed by permission. Interview has been edited for style.

Andrea Chase: I know there were a lot of struggles to get this film made, but talk a little about the exhilaration of making this film while you were making it.

Julie Dash: Well, I think the exhilaration may have come from more so the location than anything else, because wonderful, seismic, organic things were happening with the weather.... Before we began shooting, we had to evacuate because of Hurricane Hugo. We returned, the terrain was a little bit different, but that tree that I use at the very end—one of the last scenes—that was knocked down by Hugo, and I was able to use that; that wasn't in the original plans. The sand dunes were not as high as they were pre-Hugo. I was able to cast better and able to get crew from Charleston because they were a part of the clean-up crew from Hugo. So I was able to get some of the carpenters from Charleston to come and not only work on the preproduction and building of the shack, but also, like Umar Abdurrahamn, we got him to be the Bilal Muhammad because he had the right look. So the cast and crew was upgraded due to Hugo and that was—sheer delight. It was an exhausting, deep woods, mosquito- and no-see-um insect-infested environment even on the sand dunes.... Blood-sucking gnats were biting everyone. So it was not an easy shoot. We were twenty-three days out there, but something about it was just so awe-inspiring by being there before sunrise and working until sundown because, you know, we were shooting without artificial lights and using only daylight, sunlight. Something about it each day was exhausting, but complete and refreshing and awe-inspiring.

Chase: Do you feel like the old ones, the old gods, were sort of watching out for you—I mean, knocking down a tree so that it would be perfect?

Dash: The gods were certainly with us. There were things that happened—we would have to stop shooting one scene because a wind storm would pick up and it would be pretty dangerous—and I would start shooting another scene that I had prepared for such an event, because I once read in a book written by John Sayles to always have these special scenes in your pocket that you could just pull up and continue shooting. And that was a director's trick that I continue to use to this day, to always have scenes in your pocket that you could substitute for the major scene that you're shooting when you could no longer continue shooting that.

Chase: I'd also love for you to talk about the incubation process for this film. When did you first want to tell this story cinematically, and what compelled you? I mean, this is like a film that had never been seen before. You were changing a lot of the languages of cinema, a lot of semiotics we were used to.

Dash: Yeah, there was a long incubation period. I began writing this when I was a student at the American Film Institute. I was a producing-writing fellow there '74 through '76—and I continued writing after I had completed AFI and went into, you know, graduate school at UCLA. And I continued to write that along with other things, but I always came back to this story that I wanted to tell—because I wanted to challenge myself to create an African American historical drama that was authentic to my culture and to things I had been learning in graduate school and all along the way and after having my daughter. When my daughter was born in '84, then I knew I had to add the Unborn Child to the story. As I grew and as I developed and as I learned more about life—the poetics and the metaphors of life—I included those events and issues and historical moments inside of *Daughters of the Dust*.

Chase: And I love the way you always challenge yourself. You're someone who will drag a wind machine into a subway to get just the right effect. [*Laughing*]

Dash: You remembered that!

Chase: Oh God, yes!

Dash: Oh gosh, I got teased about that for days! [*Laughing*]

Chase: But it was the effect. This was for a short film you did as part of—

Dash: Right, "Sax, Cantor, Riff" . . . from *Subway Stories: Tales of the Underground*. And when the [protagonist's scarf] wasn't blowing enough, we attached it to microfilament and, like, a fishing rod and put it out there and turned the wind on it so it could stay in the air longer and float and not go into the track because no one was gonna go after it.

Chase: No, there were runaway trains you were dealing with down there too.

Dash: There was a runaway train, and that changed everything because we were supposed to get into the track and shoot something prior to the runaway train, and it was like, "Oh my God." [*Laughing*]

Chase: Yeah, no. . . . Have the other scene or the other idea in your pocket, as John Sayles taught.

Dash: Right, exactly, and moving on very quickly—we will not do that.

Chase: Talk too a little about once you've gotten the film made, of course then it has to be seen, and no one really knew what to do with this, but it ended up playing for ages everywhere. What was that like for you? Talk about that—that validation, the vindication.

Dash: Well, by the time it was playing at the New York Village East for thirty-six consecutive weeks—wow. It was amazing and we were all very happy and we were all moving on. I was already writing the novel, the continuing story, and working on other projects, so we were happy about it, but we had moved on a bit, and we thought things were gonna go along a lot faster—because it took a year from the Sundance award—the award we got from Sundance for best cinematography—to get distribution.

Chase: Wow.

Dash: Yeah, when everything else was being picked up at Sundance.

Chase: Yeah.

Dash: So I still had a lot to learn—I had a lot to learn from the distribution companies and about gender issues and about films that were labeled nonaccessible—which *Daughters of the Dust* was labeled as too culturally specific and nonaccessible. And I was like, "Ooh—no, no, no, no."

Chase: When you get a note like that, what is your reaction?

Dash: I understood it! [*Laughing*] But I understood it, so I thought everyone else understood it too.

Chase: Of course.

Dash: But really the note was saying, "That's not for us, and we really don't think it's for anyone else, and bye-bye." However, here we are.

Chase: Yes.

Dash: Twenty-six years later, and it has been playing in theaters and universities and everywhere for the last twenty-six years—and now it's going to be rereleased theatrically.

Chase: Talk about being able to do this restoration.

Dash: The restoration. Well, it was Tim Lanza at the Cohen Media Group who gave us a call and said, you know, "We're going to be distributing it. How about taking a look at ideas of restoring the color?" And I was saying, "Yay! Absolutely! Yes, yes, yes!" So he supervised that, and we brought in the cinematographer, AJ [Arthur Jafa], who sat with the people in the lab and worked on the digital restoration to bring the colors back to where they once were and to move from analog, from celluloid, to the digital space to do the scans. It took a while and it wasn't easy—it took a couple times. We tried it a couple times before we finally got to where we needed to be. And then it was converted into 35mm film again for certain prints. I saw a digital version of it and I was just very happy. It was just beautiful.

Chase: Was it hard, getting the color back to where you wanted to? Did you have reference things?

Dash: We had memory.

Chase: Ah, okay.

Dash: Our reference was our memory, what it looked like on the set and what it looked like on what's called the work print. We had a physical film work print. Because we shot in 1989, and so we were editing in 1990 and preparing for Sundance, which was 1991, I knew what the work print looked like. AJ knew what the work print looked like. We just were not able to achieve that as an answer print back then because answer prints were just so expensive each time you go to another answer print. So finally we have our release print in the digital space.

Chase: Are you able to watch the film and just enjoy it as a film? Or are you just sitting there going, "Oh, that was the day the mosquito got into . . ." or "That was the day that . . ."?

Dash: All of that—all of that.

Chase: Yeah—aw.

Dash: I sometimes watch the opening and the closing, but I just let it be now for what it is. I've seen it so many times, you know, with the editing and with the screenings—all the time, you know, around the world—that I just let it be now, and I think about—well, about what I'm working on now.

Chase: Vertamae Grosvenor.

Dash: Yes.

Chase: [She] was a commentator for many years on NPR, culinary anthropologist, and I was just so delighted to read that you were going to be doing this. Talk a little about Vertamae and, of course, the film you're going to be making.

Dash: In 1970 Vertamae Smart-Grosvenor published a book called *Vibration Cooking: Or, The Travel Notes of a Geechee Girl*—wow. Last month, she passed away. In between, she was not only a famous chef and personality and an actor and performer and all that, she became a culinary anthropologist and a broadcaster on NPR, a roving reporter, an actor in *Daughters of the Dust*, a consultant on *Daughters of the Dust*, and also an actor and consultant in *Beloved*. She was a remarkable woman who crossed so many borders and boundaries that several years ago I, you know, sat down with her and told her that I wanted to do a film about her life because I never met anyone quite like her before. And the more we interviewed her and the more we spoke to people who knew her, it became even more so. And I found out that in the 1950s she became a beatnik—and here she was this tall skinny girl from South Carolina, a Black girl who traveled alone to Paris and set up shop in what became known as the Beat Hotel and was living there, working and writing and interacting with the other artists—and the other artists included Allen Ginsberg, William Burroughs, Johnathan Kozol, Robert Cole, and a young artist who would become her husband at the time, Robert Rovner. She returned to the United States and became involved with the Black Arts Movement, the Black Cinema Movement, of course, you know, broadcasting, and acting—and at one point she was even a moon goddess with Sun Ra. [*Laughing*]

Chase: I'm not surprised somehow.

Dash: Yes—and I love that part. A moon goddess. Not a sun goddess—a moon goddess, you know. And she was also making costumes for us. So Ms. Vertamae Smart-Grosvenor was quite an individual. And she has quite a legacy that she has left behind for everyone to enjoy and to learn from her—her movement, her travels, and her life, which represents what we now talk about intersections of race, gender, and boundaries—crossing boundaries.

Chase: I think uh she didn't accept boundaries. She just went forth.

Dash: Borders and boundaries did not stop her—no. [*Laughing*]

Chase: Tell me about her cooking for you.

Dash: Oh, my goodness.

Chase: 'Cause I'm, like, so jealous. [*Laughing*] I'll be honest.

Dash: The first time I read her cookbook, I just laughed and laughed and laughed. I mean, she had recipes for possum, she had something called Harriet Tubman ragu, she had Larry Neil fried chicken. I mean, it was some hilarious stuff, and then a little aside story she told, the memoirish type story she told in between the recipes—it was just, like, a hoot. She gave me confidence to call myself a Geechee because prior to that, you know, it was a secret. You know, no one wanted to be known as coming from Gullah Geechee culture because it was considered lowest of the low—and so her book alone, just on the cover saying *Travel Notes of a Geechee Girl* was pretty radical at the time—pretty radical.

Chase: Now, after *Daughters of the Dust* you were offered a lot of scripts that weren't yours, that you weren't particularly interested in doing.

Dash: I did several television movies.... *The Rosa Parks Story, Funny Valentines, Love Song, Incognito*—things like that. But I was never able to get a story that I had written funded or to do a movie that I wanted to do. I'm still writing, and I have a miniseries that I have written and several feature films that I've written—and I'm talking to people still. But I'm still optimistic. [*Laughing*] But I think in many ways *Daughters of the Dust* just frightens people, certain people who do green light films, who felt that they certainly could embrace an African American woman as a film director, but it was not going to be me.

Chase: Oh! But it ran for thirty-some-odd weeks and ...

Dash: Well—yeah, and in many ways, it was not going to be me because I proved them wrong.

Chase: Julie Dash, thank you so much for talking with us today.

Dash: Thank you.

Chase: The film is *Daughters of the Dust* and I am Andrea Chase.

Interview: Julie Dash

So Mayer / 2016

From *Raisingfilms.com*, October 12, 2016. Reprinted by permission.

Julie Dash has been making films and television for four decades and is part of the LA Rebellion generation of filmmakers. Her feature *Daughters of the Dust* (1991) was the first full-length film by an African American woman with general theatrical release in the United States. Dash is the film's producer, screenwriter, and director. In 2004, *Daughters of the Dust* was included in the National Film Registry of the Library of Congress. Dash has also made numerous music videos, commercials, and television movies, the latter including *Funny Valentines, Incognito, Love Song,* and *The Rosa Parks Story*. Her *Brothers of the Borderland* was commissioned by the National Underground Railroad Freedom Center. She is also a screenwriter and novelist and is currently working on a feature-length documentary about Vertamae Smart-Grosvenor. *Daughters of the Dust* is currently touring the world in a restored 35mm print. It screens at the London Film Festival 2016, on Saturday October 15.

So Mayer: Your daughter N'Zinga grew up with the making of *Daughters of the Dust*. . . . How was that?

Julie Dash: We started making the film prior to her arrival, and I'd already been making films for a decade. I never brought her on set when we were shooting, but I took her to the edit suite all the time. It was definitely much easier to work when she was small, because she was in a child seat that I could put under the edit table, and she'd sleep. When she was older, she was more impatient, asking, "Are you done yet?" But children are useful to filmmakers, too. They're a great source for dialogue. They say things like, "Why are we here on earth?" and you say back, "Well, because here is where we are." I remember when my daughter was little, I told her that when I was her age, I'd had a bird, and that it had died. She asked why, and I said I didn't know. She looked at me and said, "I know. [*Emphatically*] Drugs." And I thought, "What?" But I realized later that it was because they begin telling them in kindergarten that drugs are bad, drugs kill you. But you don't get dialogue like that without kids, and they don't realize what they're saying. It's great.

Mayer: Was it a particular challenge to be a two-filmmaker-parent household?

Dash: AJ [Arthur Jafa] and I worked together on several films, but then we divorced, and it was me and my daughter. I was shooting music videos and commercials, working a lot, and the one repercussion I remember is [that] she got thrown out of Brownies because I couldn't go to the zoo. So she never made it to Girl Guides because her mom was too busy to go on all these trips!

On the other hand, there was some sense of a film family that she was part of. Once when I was editing on a later project, the assistant editor picked her up from school. She was really happy about it. He's gay, and she said to me, "Oh, Mom, he's so much more fun than you are." And once she got her eyebrows arched on set: there was some downtime, and she was hanging with hair and makeup.

Mayer: What did she think of your work?

Dash: She always knew what my job was, but no one else's mother was a filmmaker. I was always shocked when people said that *Daughters* was the first feature film by an African American woman to get distribution, because I was part of a group of Black women filmmakers in the 1970s and 1980s: I just happened to get distribution first. So one day, when the kids in my daughter's class had to say what their parents did, she told them I was a supermarket cashier! Because it didn't make sense to her to say I was a filmmaker. I'll never forget that.

She said we were crazy to be filmmakers—and now she's a postproduction supervisor at Mattel for Barbie commercials. She loves Barbie. I don't know how it happened. I was always such a tomboy and raised her the same. I put her in Osh Kosh dungarees and so on. But she was so super femme! I learned hair and makeup from my crew—from the glam squad, that's what I call them. And I'm wearing nail polish right now because she taught me how to.

Mayer: How did you get into filmmaking?

Dash: I always wanted a train set as a kid, and my parents were worried. So what drew me to filmmaking was working with film cameras, the lights, editing, to conquer all the technology. Now I want a drone for my birthday! I told my daughter that already. It can be a bedazzled one, like this phone case she gave me, I don't care. We had a helicopter on *Daughters of the Dust*, but a drone would have made things so much cheaper! I think about all the shots we could have gotten. You'd have a whole different lighting situation. We were shooting in natural light with reflectors, because it was filmed in a conservation area and we weren't allowed to use any four-wheeled vehicles: we had to carry in *everything*, lights, cameras, generators. That shoot felt like it would never end.

Mayer: *Daughters of the Dust* remains quite unique in American cinema, as the story of a matrifocal, multigenerational, complex African American family. What was your aim with the film?

Dash: I wanted to tell a story so authentic to African American culture, it would feel like a foreign film. Nothing I saw on TV growing up felt like my life. So it was a challenge and a mission to find a way to bring that story to the screen. I wanted to tell a story about the first generation of African Americans born free, migrating north: what's their future? And how is it connected to their past? This generation is moving into the effects of the Industrial Revolution, it's the first years of the twentieth century, but they have older relatives that were slaves. The film is about the tipping of the scales, about youth wanting to go forward but asking, "How can you balance moving toward progress and change, but hold on to your culture?"

Yellow Mary is an important character for that: she's lived on the mainland, and she's a woman of independent means, which at that time meant she had to be a prostitute. She is shunned by the family, but she holds power, she inspires fear and admiration, and the family comes to embrace her over the course of the film.

Mayer: Do you feel like there's a new generation of filmmakers, particularly women of color, who are daughters of *Daughters of the Dust*? What advice do you have for them?

Dash: Now there are more women making films, and they're getting them out there. It's wonderful. Just by being visible they are making it possible for other people to say, "I could do that—and I could do it better!" That's important too, that vision. What's needed is visibility, but then also recognition of good work being done, and the sharing and promotion of good work. We need to be celebrating and mentoring—I always have young filmmakers I'm mentoring, as well as in my teaching work.

Mayer: Are any of them parents? Do you have any particular advice for them?

Dash: I do have some young filmmakers around now who are parents—it's not easy, there are tough choices to be made. I've always been upfront about that. I had a child while *Daughters* was in development, and then right before the shoot I found out I was pregnant. I knew from the first time that I would be sick, and that it just wasn't going to work, so I had an abortion—and I wrote about it [in the book *Daughters of the Dust: An African American Women's Film*]. There was blowback—subtle blowback—from some filmmakers, but I knew that I wouldn't be able to do that, to make a film while pregnant.

Mayer: Given that kind of criticism, and other barriers, how have you kept going?

Dash: If you're going to be a filmmaker, you have to make films because you want to, because you have a voice and something to say. If you get criticism, read it and say, "That's your point of view." You're not making the film to please anyone other than yourself. There can always be growth from dealing with criticism, but you can't let anyone shut you down or insist you only do one thing—after *Daughters of the Dust*, everyone just wanted me to remake that film. But I did *Love Song* [an MTV original movie starring Monica], I made car commercials, I made industrial films: most people don't know that. And because of how filmographies are presented, people can't see it. I would love to have made another feature, but I also chose work because it was interesting, as well as because it paid. Movies for television are the same amount of work and storytelling as for cinema. The largest-budget film that I ever made—$1.5 million—was a twenty-five-minute film that's part of an immersive exhibit for the National Underground Railroad Freedom Center, *Brothers of the Borderland*. It's a historical drama, we had to stage river crossings, and it has narration by Oprah Winfrey. But no one knows. [Editor's note: It is listed on IMDb, but Dash's name is not on the exhibit's web page.]

I work to make myself happy: to challenge myself. You can't be swayed—or dissuaded—by critics. I think some people thought I would just go away—but here I am, I've survived them all. I'm not going away. I'm too old to retrain as a nurse. And I love it, too! It's so hard to be at this film festival as a guest, only for a short time: I want to be watching films! When I was a student, we would take a week off classes and go to film festivals, and go to films day and night.

Mayer: You are working on a feature film right now, *Travel Notes of a Geechee Girl*, a documentary that you've crowdfunded. How is that going?

Dash: We're still shooting on *Travel Notes*, but it's a little strange because Vertamae [Smart-Grosvenor, the film's subject and a long-term friend and colleague of Dash's] passed away September 2. What I've actually been doing for the last while is organizing her memorial, which happened two weeks ago. I'll be showing some footage from the film for the first time. She was so well known, and that's documented, yet she's gone unheralded. But she cooked for everyone and made over one hundred broadcasts about food and culture on NPR [which has a moving memorial essay by Jacki Lyden, with clips of Smart-Grosvenor's commentaries]. Her story should be told.

We raised $32,000 through the crowdfunder, which is very nice for a documentary. We shot twenty-two interviews, but now we're fundraising for the edit. I contribute to Kickstarters and Indiegogos all the time, even if it's only five bucks. I try to finance films where I don't know the director, and I do it anonymously. That way I'm contributing to the future of film.

The "Daughter" Returns: Julie Dash Speaks About Her Triumphant Revival—And Where She's Been

Bilge Ebiri / 2016

From *The Village Voice* (November 16–22, 2016): 37–38. Reprinted courtesy of *The Village Voice*.

One great shame of American cinema is that we didn't get theatrical releases of Julie Dash films in the twenty-five years since *Daughters of the Dust*. But that didn't stop Dash from making plenty of exceptional work over the years—sometimes under difficult circumstances. She even made a few superior TV movies along the way. We recently talked to her about both *Daughters of the Dust* and some of those lesser-known later films.

Ebiri Bilge: I always find it odd nowadays when people who are interested in film haven't heard of *Daughters of the Dust* or *Illusions*. I was in college when *Daughters* came out in 1991. And we had watched *Illusions*, your 1982 short, in my Introduction to Film class. *Daughters* played for months in New York—a real phenomenon.

Julie Dash: It did turn into quite a year for us. As an independent filmmaker, to tell you the truth, I was like, "Oh my god, I'm not ready for all of this. I just want to make movies!" A lot of filmmakers nowadays are actors or comedians or this and that, and I'm none of that. I'm just a filmmaker. And I was really not used to being in the public eye like that. But it was life changing, to say the least. What a time of discovery and wonder.

Bilge: Were you taking Hollywood meetings?

Dash: I was taking a lot of meetings, but nothing ever came of it. The way people used to look at me from across the desk—like, "So, you're the one who did *that*." I remember one young woman. We were shaking hands as I was leaving their office; she said, "Oh you're not so bad." It was almost like she had to take the meeting with me but was actually kind of frightened. A lot of industry people didn't know what to make of the film or of me.

Bilge: *Illusions* was set in the film industry. Years later, when you were having more industry interactions in the wake of *Daughters*, how did the reality of the industry match your earlier conception of it? Was it different?

Dash: No. In fact, it was even more so and still the same. Now that I know more, I could redo *Illusions* and put in even more things that I've learned. It was kind of shocking. Let's just leave it at that.

Bilge: *Daughters*, while it does have a story, is not so much a movie you follow as it is a movie you luxuriate in, just spending time with these people.

Dash: Many people say, "I kind of drifted off and thought about my family." This is part of the experience. It is not by accident or happenstance. I wanted the film to be like a widescreen tableau, to make you feel like you're looking at a scrapbook, a family album. And the music. We have talking drums throughout. Audio of a Nigerian master drummer playing, "Remember me, remember my name." Of course, an average person on the street cannot understand talking drums, but I do believe it has resonance. We take them on a journey where they don't really know what's going on, and it's not a Western plot—which is by design.

I was just up in Northern California. And there was a young girl in the audience who said, "Clearly, there was no script, and the film was improvised." And I just said, "No, dear, there was a full script. You can't have this many people out on a beach with no idea of what they're going to say and do." I think so many people have preconceived notions—well, I know they do—about African American culture, about who we are, or why we are. And another woman in that same audience—I think it was her professor—kept wanting me to explain why they were wearing white. Number one, it was post-slavery period. It was post–Gibson Girl, and they were wearing Gibson Girl–style dresses. Some of them were seamstresses. It was a family celebration, to say goodbye. Why would they be wearing work clothes? You usually had two outfits: Your Sunday clothes, which you're going to be buried in, and your work dress.

This came up in *Daily Variety* twenty-six years ago, too, where the reviewer said it looked like a Laura Ashley commercial, which was so snide. It was beyond their imagination to be able to see African American women in white dresses on a beach. She also mentioned the suits that the men were wearing. None of the suits were new. They were very old, and frayed, and all that, but that was not in the data box. For them, it was like, "Error, error. Why is she doing this?" It was not anything that they'd seen before pertaining to African Americans in the South. And no matter how many times I explained that we worked from photographs that were taken in 1902, they had a problem with it.

Bilge: In this and a number of your other films, movement feels very important. The shorts *Four Women* and *Praise House* are, in part, dance performances. In *Daughters*, too, it's in the way a character carries himself, or the way you use slow motion and step-framing. There's a lot of great dialogue, but there is also a silent movie-like quality.

Dash: Well, I'm a film school rat! We took on a lot of things with that little movie. We played with the motion, to create visceral responses. We'd start out at twenty-four frames a second, and then fugue into sixty frames a second—almost like the effect you'd have in dub music.

Bilge: Let's talk about film school. You went to AFI and then UCLA. You're identified with the "LA Rebellion" filmmaking movement, which was focused in and around UCLA. But the way people often refer to it nowadays, it makes it sound like this small group that emerged briefly. Reading more about it, I was really struck by the fact that this was a program stretching across many years, with lots of very different filmmakers coming through.

Dash: Yeah, absolutely. And of course at the time, we didn't call ourselves the LA Rebellion. We were named that post-graduation, which was interesting. But, yeah, my understanding is that it began in the late 1960s, early '70s, and went on into the '80s. I graduated in '85. And another thing that people don't understand about the LA Rebellion—they think that it was all Black. It was not, at least as far as I was concerned. Elliot Davis was a part of it. He just recently shot *Birth of a Nation*, with Nate Parker. There were so many other people: Monona Wali was Indian American, Amy Halpern was Jewish.

Bilge: You're originally from New York. I've read that it was at the Studio Museum of Harlem that you first discovered cinema.

Dash: That's where I fell in love with foreign film, specifically, sitting in the museum, which was in a different location at the time. Sitting in the middle of Harlem, watching Eisenstein's *Potemkin*, or *Jules and Jim*. I was a teenager. Everyone's always so surprised. Who would have thought it? But that's when it began—my love of films that went beyond anything in my known world. I think that's the age when you can imagine. You're taken on a journey, and when the lights come on, you look around and it's like, "Oh, I'm back home." It's a *Wizard of Oz*–type of feeling.

Bilge: There's very little discussion about the TV films you made after *Daughters of the Dust*. But they're all interesting, and a couple are great. I adore *Love Song*. It's not a startlingly original story, but we really get to know them and like those characters.

Dash: That was my foray into pop. It was just a great cast, written by Josslyn Luckett, who left the industry and went back to Harvard to study theology. I saw her at the Black Star Film Festival. I so wish she would come back.

The characters in that film are fun and cool, and they have their own voices. I also loved the idea of casting a darker-skinned mother and a light-skinned father. That was the situation in my family, where my mother was dark-skinned and my father was very light-skinned. It's the "brown paper bag" issue. Back then, if you were a woman and you were darker than a brown paper bag, in middle-class Black life . . . things were different, let's put it that way. I kind of eased that into the dialogue. It's fun being able to do that, because we need to hear more about that. We can't have that history lost.

Bilge: In a film like *Incognito*, which is a very standard-issue erotic thriller, the opening image is a woman in white running on a beach. I remember seeing that, and thinking, "Wait, we're right back where we left off with *Daughters of the Dust!*"

Dash: I know! I wanted more of that! And they kept cutting it down, and then they laid the titles over. Oh, I had so much on the beach. It was *fabulous*! I love it, with the wedding dress.

Bilge: And the film also has these real cinematic reveries. The character is having these flashbacks and dream visions. You really kind of went to town with those.

Dash: Let's just say *Incognito* is a film you need to have a beer before you watch. [*Laughs*] It was shot in sixteen days, like *bam bam bam*. It's based upon a romantic novel—part of the whole Arabesque series of romance novels. We had fun playing with the genre, playing with hyperreality. The scene with the guys painted in silver. Those weren't written into the script, but I was like, "Why not?"

Bilge: It's been a long time since I've seen *Funny Valentines*, your film about a woman going back to her hometown to reconnect with her mentally challenged cousin. But I remember being very moved by it.

Dash: Oh, yes. I got a call from Alfre Woodard. She wanted me to direct a movie that she was going to do in several months. They had a production, but the script was not there. It was based upon a short story by J. California Cooper. The film that we made had very little to do with that short story. We just had the characters. We got Amy Schor Ferris to do a rewrite, and she did a terrific job of making it meaningful. And that's always what I want to do. Whenever I do a film, it has to take us one step further to making the world safe for everyone, let's say. It can't just be a movie about race and someone being disabled. Why are they "slow"? Is it autism, is it Asperger's? Is it because you were born a breach baby? Okay, then, let's make it about that. I always want to find the back story, you know—what happened before the story began.

I had also been reading a lot of books about canned fruits and vegetables, just by happenstance. And I said, "You know, let's have this rape victim do something more than just hate her life. Let's have something more sustainable than just anger. So let's have her preserve fruits and vegetables from each year's crops." That became part of the story. For the costuming and for the props, that worked out. It just kept falling into place, once you came up with an overall visual metaphor and a theme.

Bilge: Elements like that also create a cinematic space where we can appreciate the actual work that these people do—which is something you don't see in movies very often.

Dash: Well, it's always a struggle, too, with producers who just want to hammer that out—"Just the story, just the story." But a movie has to be more than a story. It has to be multilayered. We had to go through a whole lot of machinations to get the fruit in. Oh, and to get the usher board in! A lot of people didn't get it. It's a very Black thing, you know—church ushers. If you don't know that, then you'd think that it's not very important, the thing about the competing ushers in church. That was big in my childhood. Every year they would have some kind of celebration where they would all march in uniform, and they'd get an award or something—the fittest and the finest ushers, the largest.

To me that was normal, but to get it into the film was difficult, because some people could not understand where I was going with it. But I still get letters. Even on this tour with *Daughters*, people are saying, "Well, where can we get a home version of *Funny Valentines*? That's my favorite film, my grandmother's favorite film. . . ." And I think it's because of these elements that are so familiar to Black culture. Everyone knows the ushers run the church. When you see a Black church in a movie, it's always about the power of the preachers. Yeah, well, look to the left and the right and the ushers standing there, like military generals. *They're the ones running things.*

Bilge: *The Rosa Parks Story* was a bigger TV movie and nominated for awards. But you haven't made more theatrical films since then.

Dash: Yeah. I think because of *The Rosa Parks Story*, maybe I was labeled as difficult because I wouldn't do certain things. Like one of the things I would not do was have Rosa Parks say, "Well, I didn't get up because my feet hurt." That became a big issue. I said it was not true that she said that—it's a myth. Some of the producers wanted me to have her say that. Right at the end, they wanted me to ADR [automated dialogue replacement] a line, but I absolutely refused to add that line, because it's not true.

There were so many no-no's that I did on *The Rosa Parks Story*. Those scenes of her hanging the sign saying, "A man was lynched today." Well, that was something the NAACP was doing in the 1950s during a period of violence. Every day they'd hang a sign up when there was a lynching, kind of like with Black Lives Matter now. That was not approved by the producers, so we snuck it in. I was lucky to have Angela Bassett and Cicely Tyson on my side, sneaking things in with me.

Or when she leaves the bus and crosses the street at the theater, and there's *A Man Alone*, a Ray Milland movie, playing. I studied the period. I knew there was a theater across the street when she was taken off the bus. And it was important to me to find out what was playing at that theater. I had the art department put that up. The theater was still there. And when I found out that it was days before Christmas, I said, "We have to put Santa Claus there." Little things like these tiny specifics will give a story resonance. But it became such a big deal because people thought I was messing with the myths of American history. And then I also added the bus driver going across the street to call his supervisor. Because that's what he always said he did. And his supervisor told him, "It's your job to call the police, and to get her off the bus." So I added that, too, rather than just the same old image of "Get off the bus, get off the bus, you can't stay." All of those things add tension, drama to the moment.

Bilge: The scene with the bus driver is fascinating because it also places the historical event in the context of a system. It's not just like one racist driver and brave Rosa Parks. There are all these other things happening around them, driving them towards their actions.

Dash: Yeah. And the fact that the colored section of the bus was fluid. If there were more colored people sitting than white people, you moved that sign back and gave the whites more space. I learned so much from making that movie. Like the fact that they literally had to get on the back of the bus—that you pay up front, and then get off, and then go around the back. But in almost every American film you see, they walk *through* the bus to the back. When I found out that you had to get on, get back out. . . . Little details like that were important. And I remember getting a fax from the network, saying, "It's too much!"

Bilge: What were some other projects along the way that came close to happening?

Dash: There was *Secret Agent Mom*. . . .

Bilge: I love it already.

Dash: Right? We were down in Albuquerque on location, on set, when the plug was pulled. And then there was another one, *Tupelo 77*, where the producers agreed to disagree among themselves, and after working on that for more than a year, it went away. There were many projects that just didn't happen. But that happens to everyone.

Bilge: Watching films like *Funny Valentines*, *Incognito*, *Love Song*, and *Rosa Parks* reminds me of those older Hollywood directors who were forced to make B movies but found ways to sneak their voices and their style into the genre film. Martin Scorsese calls them "smugglers."

Dash: That's the second time I heard that, and I love it. It's funny. I started teaching and I started making movies for museums, and I worked for Disney Imagineering, designing the African American Pavilion for Manassas, which was never built. But I also taught at the Indianapolis Museum of Art, a seven-month program . . . called "Smuggling Daydreams into Reality"! They were high school students. One was deaf, and he communicated through his sign language interpreter, who was also in the class. Another had Asperger's. All of the students, there was something going on in their lives. That's why I wanted them in the class. I wanted people who were struggling to find themselves, who they were and how they fit into the world, to be a part of this class museum experiment. And they created short films, and the short films were placed inside the gallery for several months. It was amazing what these children had inside of them. That's why we called it "Smuggling Daydreams into Reality."

Bilge: You could describe all your films that way: smuggling daydreams into reality.

Dash: Yes. Because you have to infuse what's already out there, what's been "approved." You smuggle elements, these tiny specifics of authenticity, into it. But you can't really tell anyone, because they will say, "No, you can't do that."

Filmmaker Interview: Julie Dash

Michael Glover Smith / 2016

Published on *Whitecitycinema.com* (November 18, 2016). Reprinted by permission.

Julie Dash's landmark 1991 indie film *Daughters of the Dust*, the first feature directed by an African American woman to receive a theatrical release, has been the subject of renewed interest this year due to the fact that it's a major reference point in Beyoncé's "visual album" *Lemonade*. *Daughters* has been newly restored for its twenty-fifth anniversary and will receive a one-week theatrical rerelease at the Gene Siskel Film Center beginning on Friday, November 25. I recently spoke to Dash about the film when she was in town for the Chicago International Film Festival.

Michael Glover Smith: Tell me about this beautiful new restoration of *Daughters of the Dust*. I read that you didn't properly color time it when it was originally released.

Julie Dash: Correct. We didn't have enough money to continue. Because back in the analog days, every answer print—you know, the whole answer print, answer print, answer print to release print [thing]?—we got to the second answer print, and that was $20,000. And it was like, "Enough!" I mean, at this point, let's get this show on the road! We can't go any further. It was the cost. And so that answer print did not look like the work print we worked on. The work print looked better.

MGS: Were you personally involved in the new restoration?

JD: We brought back in AJ [cinematographer Arthur Jafa] to sit with the people timing it and doing the scan. And—whoo!—we got it just in time. The original elements were starting to deteriorate. There was some shrinkage in some areas. They scanned it twice in 2K. We couldn't afford 4K. Once again! [*Laughing*] Here we go again!

MGS: It's great that it's getting rereleased theatrically.

JD: That was not even on my agenda. That came as an utter and complete, wonderful surprise. I just wanted it scanned and I just wanted a Blu-ray, you know? And we had it done. And then . . . *Lemonade* [Beyoncé's "visual album," which owes a strong stylistic debt to Dash's film]. And it was like, "Wow. This is wonderful. This is great stuff." And people were saying, "Well, what is *Daughters of the Dust*? What is this thing?" And I was like, "Yeah, we have it. We're planning to release it on Blu-ray." And then Tim [Lanza of Cohen Media] called and said he had a conversation with Charles Cohen. I hadn't met him yet, Cohen. And they decided: "Let's do a rerelease." I was like, "In the *theaters*?" [*Laughing*] When they started looking at the analytics and when *Daughters of the Dust* started trending on Twitter, it was like "What is this? Wow." I don't really see the precedent for this because it's not like it's *Lawrence of Arabia*.

MGS: But it *is* a seminal film!

JD: Yeah, but there's no precedent for it. The Shirley Clarke films? Yeah, okay. But, for me, it was just not on my radar to do that. And I was like, "Yeah. Sure!"

MGS: This rerelease makes me happy because *Daughters of the Dust* is a film that was really ahead of its time.

JD: It came at a time when everyone, in terms of independent filmmakers and artists and experimental filmmakers, we were all looking for new ways of telling stories. I said, "I'm going to create this griot story structure—like the way an African griot would recall and recount a family's history—and I'm going to write this." And everything was all good and hunky-dory and great. And then (when it was originally released) people were like, "Well, this is like a foreign film." And I think the wider general audience, they were more open to it than the established—how should I say it?—the curators of culture.

MGS: Including critics?

JD: Yeah. The curators of culture were saying, "This is a difficult film." Difficult? It's straightforward! They come and say goodbye, it's a picnic, and then they go on. It's the Great Migration, you know what I mean? The Industrial Revolution.

MGS: But it's not plot driven. It doesn't go from point A to point B to point C.

JD: Yeah, it's not *binary*. It's not "this then that." But don't they teach you in film schools not to do "this then that?"

MGS: Yeah, especially if you want to be an independent filmmaker!

JD: Why?! We have the binary already. And it's not something that, at the end of film, I say, "I was just kidding!" In anything that really has to do with another culture that's not Western, it's taken as something scary or something to be feared or something that's being subversive. No, I'm just saying, "Look, hey, man, this is what's out there." [In islands off the coast of South Carolina at the turn of the twentieth century] Muslims were still practicing their religion, there was West African religions being practiced, there was Christianity, there was Protestantism, all these things were happening. I didn't create this! It's there if you want to look at it.

MGS: And it's still there today.

JD: Exactly. Let's talk about it. These survivals, these retention patterns, let's look at them. People look at retention patterns in Roanoke and it's not scary. So look at all these islands where these people were pure African in many ways. It's like, "Well, we don't want to talk about that."

MGS: The film was also ahead of its time in terms of the subject matter because you're dealing with the aftermath of slavery, which was not a fashionable subject in cinema in 1991.

JD: I was dealing with the first generation of freeborn African Americans heading towards the Industrial Revolution. I thought that was a great idea. [*Laughing*] Instead of showing the whip marks on someone's back or something, I just made their hands blue. Everyone who was once a slave, their hands were blue from working in the indigo fields. And how is that subversive? I thought it was straightforward. People were saying "Why did you make it so difficult?"

MGS: It's not difficult, but it avoids formulas and stereotypes.

JD: That's what we're tasked to do, right? To find other ways of saying the same thing, to find visual metaphors of what we already know so it will have more of an impact and we'll go "A-ha!" Because, after you watch a couple slave movies, someone's getting whipped and you become anesthetized. But when you see someone's hands are blue, you go, "Oh shit! That was some rough work." And I just wanted people to see it wasn't just about picking cotton and someone blowing a harmonica. And so the music was totally different too. I'm really proud of John Barnes's score because he and I sat down together and talked about what's the sound of New World music. What came before jazz? He brought in an Iranian santur player, a Pakistani drummer, a Nigerian talking drummer, and Santeria, some Cuban singers and dancers. They were recording and dancing at the same time because they couldn't sing the Santeria songs without dancing.

MGS: You should've filmed the recording sessions.

JD: Who knew? Who knew? These were the sounds that we imagined these Africans heard during the Middle Passage because those slave ships were comprised of not just Americans; they were British, Irish, Dutch, Indian, Islamic. There were all kinds of people upstairs. It was three months. What did they do? They sang, they probably played flutes, they had drums. There was a sound that they heard. We created a New World sound comprised of all these different sounds and instruments just to make it totally immersive and different and to shock you into thinking new thoughts about historical events and issues.

MGS: I read an interview where you said this film was like science fiction.

JD: Yeah, they're "what if" scenarios. What if they heard it like this? Rather than just go the same old harmonica route, I was determined I was not going to have a harmonica or a banjo. You know that sound.

MGS: Yeah, it comes from other movies. I'm from North Carolina, and I can't stand to hear a fake southern accent in a movie. Actors doing southern accents always talk like they're in *Gone with the Wind*, but nobody talks like that in the South.

JD: *Gone with the Wind*! People from Mississippi speak different from people in Alabama and North Carolina and South Carolina. And you have the Gullah Geechee dialect, which sounds like Nigerian. The first time I heard it, I walked into a 7-Eleven, as an adult, and I walked in and these guys were talking, and I couldn't understand a word of what they were talking about. And they quickly stopped and went into English because everyone was always hiding if you were an outsider. My grandmother would even say a few things and you'd go, "What did you say?" They wouldn't share anything because they loved the fact that they had this information, but at the same time they'd been told over and over and over that to be a Geechee was to be the lowest of the low in African American society. If you wanted to insult someone, you called them "low-down Geechee."

MGS: It's probably not the same today, though, right?

JD: No. It has changed. A lot has changed since *Daughters of the Dust* too. Take a look at Charles Fuller's *A Soldier's Story*. Norman Jewison directed the film. It explains it all. It's set in World War II among Black soldiers. One of them was a Geechee who had to be killed because it was time that the Negro race uplifted itself and you couldn't have those Geechees around. [*Laughing*] Wow.

MGS: I'd like to ask you about the costumes. They're very elaborate for an independent film. Was it difficult to recreate period clothes on a low budget?

JD: We had people who sewed in Savannah, we had people sewing all over the place. I had access to a bunch of photographs that were housed at the Penn Center on St. Helena Island. If we had more money, I would've been able to make the hats that went along with it. They had black hats—this shiny kind of straw hat, but flat top and maybe a ribbon coming off of it or something. We just couldn't.

MGS: And those photographs were your visual reference for the costumes?

JD: Yes, and also to place them on the beach. Because when I originally wrote it I had them under a big tree—a little trope-ish—and I was like, "Oh! They're in the sand dunes?" So we shifted to the sand dunes. Just in Mill Valley a few weeks ago, I had several questions about the costumes. People kept saying, "Why are they wearing white dresses?" Once again, that goes back to *Gone with the Wind*. People are fixated, in a very myopic way, on how African Americans look in historical drama, and there's no reference point where you see them except if you look at—now they have so many historical books and you can see the pictures and they all had the white dresses on. They were seamstresses. So I made sure that all of the dresses that they were wearing, these Gibson Girl–like dresses, were at least ten to fifteen years older, late 1800s style rather than 1902. They were hand-me-downs. They were old and yellowing, some were kind of torn and raggedy. Because they only had two outfits: that would be their summer-slash-Sunday-slash-go-to-meeting outfit. And then you'd have your everyday-slash-work outfit. This was a special day. This was a celebration: It was coming together to say goodbye so everybody was dressed up in their Sunday-slash-go-to-meeting. And that's usually the same dress that you're buried in too. Same thing with the suits with the men: They were purposely done so it was like, "This wasn't made for him. He acquired this." And the kids really got raggedy. But a lot of people still have problems with the costumes because, in their minds, they're fixated on the "Mammy" dress and the headwrap, the do-rag, which is not even accurate. There's so much that's inaccurate but it's the standard, and so we're here to change all that. And I think it's more interesting to see things that are actually different.

MGS: The use of slow motion is incredible. Did you shoot that in-camera?

JD: Oh, you noticed it? Yes, we had a camera that was a prototype. Sometimes someone would be walking, then she'd wait, then it goes into slow motion [in the middle of a shot]. The speed-aperture control thing used to keep freezing on us. We had a hairdryer we had to keep putting on it because of the humidity down there because of the ocean. So it would shut down. But that variable-speed motor—it was called speed-aperture computer at the time—now they have it together, but it was a prototype at the time. That was part of the—I don't want to say "magic"—but of the voodoo of it, the science fiction. It's almost imperceptible: Someone's moving, and then the motion changes. It does have a visceral effect. It's like visual dubstep.

Daughters of the Dust Director Julie Dash Talks Filmmaking and Shaping the Black Female Image

Carlos Valladares / 2016

From *TheStanfordDaily.com* (November 20, 2016). © The Stanford Daily, Inc. All rights reserved. Reprinted with permission.

This December, a pillar of American cinema is being rereleased. *Daughters of the Dust*, the 1991 debut of independent director Julie Dash, has been restored and will be distributed by the Cohen Film Collection in theaters across America. In this era of Black Lives Matter, Beyoncé's *Lemonade*, Kendrick [Lamar], and the return of D'Angelo, the rerelease of Dash's film deserves to be greeted with cheers and trumpet blasts. *Daughters* is a seminal, visionary, challenging work of art—a masterpiece that every American should see.

The film traces the intergenerational trials and tribulations of the Peazants, a Gullah family who are the direct descendants of enslaved Africans. The Gullahs live along the coast of South Carolina in 1902, at the dawn of the twentieth century. Because of their geographical isolation, the Peazants have preserved the traditions, language, and arts (food, music, dance) of their African ancestors: the Ibo, the Yoruba, the Kongo. The film has a plot (the family is trying to move up north), but one that is presented in an off-center, nonlinear fashion. *Daughters* hazes by in dreamlike, color-filled shots, emotions, sensations. Dash—who has no cinematic parallel, whose only direct inspiration is the shared cultural heritage of all African Americans—keys in on the experiences of the Black women of the Peazant family. It's for these reasons (its laser-like focus on the lives of Black women, its avant-garde imagery) that *Daughters* has been seen as a major influence on Beyoncé's equally visionary visual album of this year, *Lemonade*.

Dash was part of the "LA Rebellion," a collective of predominantly Black filmmakers who graduated from UCLA's film school and who, in the late 1970s and early '80s, made a series of emotionally astonishing independent films (*Killer of*

Sheep, *Bush Mama*, *My Brother's Wedding*, *Bless Their Little Hearts*, and Dash's own *Illusions* and *Daughters of the Dust*) centered around the lives of African Americans, usually in the inner city parts of Los Angeles. Alongside directors like Charles Burnett and Haile Gerima, Dash forged a new independent aesthetic and a new direction for filmmakers of color who were shut out from fully realizing their artistic visions within the Hollywood studio system.

Daughters recently played in its restored version at the 39th Mill Valley Film Festival. *The Stanford Daily* sat down with Dash to talk about her film, *Lemonade*, depictions of slavery in film and much more. A living pioneer of cinema, Dash is engaging, lively, passionate—and has a lot to teach us about the direction in which cinema is heading today.

The Stanford Daily: How does it feel to have *Daughters of the Dust* receive the restoration and release it deserves after nearly twenty-five years?

Julie Dash: Twenty-six! And we shot in 1989, so that makes it even *longer*! Were you even born in '89?

TSD: No, I was born in '96.

JD: See, I. . . . Wow. Whoa.

So I'd be curious to know what young people think about it, because it was very experimental when I wrote and shot it back in the day. But it's all good. I'm very excited about the restoration, because now we get to see it in the way it's supposed to look. We just flat ran out of money when we were working with analog film, as opposed to digital. Back then, we had $20,000 for one answer print and didn't have any money for more. So we needed to correct the colors, to get back to the quality of the work print we were editing. The released film never looked like the work print. *Now* it does. It's in the digital space now.

I'm just happy, because I forgot you can look at the faces of the people, the robust colors.

TSD: Yeah—the only copy of the film I could watch was an old, faded, out-of-print DVD from 2001. Even in that quality, though, it blew me away.

It got me thinking a lot about the way we form a canon of "great films," and how that is totally dependent upon availability. Even now, filmmakers of color and female filmmakers don't have the same privileges as white male filmmakers have in terms of getting their films out there—

JD: Right, right—

TSD: —and the struggles to get *your* film out reminded me of another film from a Black female director, which is only now starting to get the canonical attention it deserves: Kathleen Collins's *Losing Ground*.

JD: I knew Kathleen Collins! And absolutely. She died way too young. I was in my twenties, and she had just graduated from the Sorbonne, was fluent in

French, had studied in French. And here I am, coming out of New York from the projects. And she's just here like, [*fanfare noise*], "Black Woman Filmmaker!" Before her, the other filmmaker to whom I looked up *also* passed away too early—Sara Gómez. She was a filmmaker at the Cuban Film Institute who did amazing feature films. It was a hard way to go for everyone. Neither of their films got distribution in their lifetimes.

TSD: It's a tragedy. Yours has, though, thank god. And certainly, with the release of *Lemonade* by Beyoncé—

JD: Haha, yes!

TSD: —it's put *Daughters* back on the map!

JD: Yes! Thanks to *Lemonade* and Solange [Knowles]. *Lemonade* is a triumph. Because I'm the type of filmmaker that likes to decipher stories. Now, yes, I like to watch things on television that are just straightforward. But then other times, I want more. And *Lemonade* was exactly that. And it was so culturally specific. I was like, "Oh . . . okay! I get you!" With the music, and the articulated movements that are very spiritual. It's very into expressions of ritualistic behavior. That's where film is going, I think. . . . Well, of course it is! It's *been* going that way. [*Laughs*]

TSD: In the case of both *Daughters* and *Lemonade*, it's a case of instinctual feeling and gut emotional response to pure and complex images, feeling something through the coded, culturally specific richness of the image. It isn't presented to you on a silver platter, with a note saying, "This is what it all means! Here is the easy answer!"

JD: It's visceral. Sometimes you know it viscerally, before your mind says, "Oh! I get it!" I like that.

TSD: Let's talk about the genesis for *Daughters of the Dust*. Who were you reading, which artists were you looking at?

JD: Okay—so the writers would always include Toni Morrison, Toni Cade Bambara, Alice Walker. The poets Nikki Giovanni, Sonia Sanchez, Jane Cortez. The films of Satyajit Ray, like the Apu Trilogy [1955–1959]. The [Soviet] filmmakers: [Sergei] Parajanov [*The Color of Pomegranates, The Shadows of Our Forgotten Ancestors*] and Andrei Tarkovsky [*Andrei Rublev, Stalker, Ivan's Childhood*].

For me, you don't have to exactly "know" the culture to get it. Sometimes, it's about the spectacle of being right *in* it, with stuff going on all around you, you start getting it little by little, and then you go, "Ah . . . yeah . . . ooh, I never thought of it that way!" That's visual poetry.

Daughters of the Dust is the cinema of ideas. I was always asking, "What if? What if an unborn child could come forward and help mediate a problem between mother and father? What if a great-great-grandmother could not physically travel to the future with her family? What does she do?" She offers her "Hand" [a talisman that the family matriarch always holds on to throughout *Daughters*].

Things just started falling into place when I wrote about the Hand that she makes. I didn't even know it was called a "Hand." But the concept of the Hand was: "Take my hand, take this compilation of the moss and the Bible that you love so much, kiss it, and take me where you want to go." The things I wrote just fell into place, naturally and spiritually. And it came out of my combinations: "Okay, let's pull in Islam, let's pull in Christianity, let's put in the moss." Let's pull all these things together, because it's *synchronicity*."

TSD: Yeah, it's like a masala, mixing cultural strands together—

JD: That's what it is! And that's who *we* are. And that's what this New World is. And it's especially reflected in the music of *Daughters of the Dust*. It's New World music. Me and John Barnes—the composer, who had only ten days to write and record everything, who went into this trance while doing it—came together and asked ourselves, "What *is* New World music?" In a Hollywood movie, they always try to put in some old harmonica or banjo. That's *not* it.

So what *is* it? Okay. Let's say you were traveling in the Middle Passage; below deck, what do you hear? Who was above? Some Irish sailors, British sailors—but you would also have Pakistani and Indian sailors, too. Iran. Persia. And so John put together this crazy team: a Pakistani drummer, an Iranian who could play the santur, a shakuhachi flute player (because the ship, at some point, must have stopped in Japan and picked up a shakuhachi). So we mixed all of these world sounds into "the New World sound." That's why the music sounds so different. We didn't use anything that Hollywood would use. Now, don't get me wrong: I'm not putting Hollywood down, but they just love to press the easy button all the time.

TSD: And your film isn't working on a simplistic level where it's neat, easy, tidy to get the first time. This is a film that is emotionally overwhelming, and that you need to watch again and again—

JD: Right, layers and layers. Because a lot's happening.

TSD: I was very moved and interested by the unconventional way you depicted a Black past, in particular the history of slavery in America. You don't use familiar images or tropes like cotton, the chain, the whipping scars. Instead, you bring up indigo, and the stain of indigo on a Gullah woman's calloused hands.

JD: Right. Exactly. You got it. Because my feeling is this: Having grown up watching *Gone with the Wind*, you see somebody getting whipped, you become anesthetized to images of slavery. Especially the sanitized ones, like in *Gone with the Wind* or in the old *Roots* from the 1970s.

But my question to myself was: What could I find to depict slavery in a new kind of way? Indigo! That was poisonous. Of course, in real life, it would have washed off by then, by 1902. But it was the *stain* of slavery, so I'm working with the metaphor. And it was the processing of indigo that initially made the American colonies so rich. Because every uniform in Europe was blue—where did that blue come from? Indigo. From Barbados and from South Carolina. Indigo and rice were the cash crops long before cotton, but everyone thinks "cotton" because everyone refers back to—what else?—*Gone with the Wind*. Cotton picking. The house mammy. Now, it wasn't necessarily to subvert the Hollywood images and models . . . but, *yes*—offering something new.

TSD: Do you have any advice for young filmmakers of color and female filmmakers trying to make films from ideas that are being rejected by producers?

JD: Nothing much has changed in that region. They just have to make the films that they want to make. It's always nice to go pitch a story—that's part of the growing experience too. But if they can't get money that way, they can always turn to Kickstarter, Indiegogo, whatever and wherever they can. Just start making a film that you want to make, even if it's a short. But don't let anyone *ever* tell you that there's no audience. Because that's a lie; just travel to international film festivals to see *why* that's a lie. That's where we started in 1979: Cannes, Munich, London. Across the world, there *are* people interested in the movies emerging filmmakers want to make.

You can't listen to the curators of culture. They make arbitrary judgments: "Oh, there's no audience. You can't sell that overseas. It's too complicated. This is not accessible." I was told after Sundance that *Daughters of the Dust* was not a real African American film . . . Well, who am I, then? Where did *I* come from?

TSD: Another problem is that the producers and critics evaluating these kinds of movies are predominantly white males.

JD: And if you show them things they don't already know, they freak out and go, "This can't be happening! I've never heard of Gullah or Geechee people. No one wants to see that. Gimme a good ol' fashioned slave whippin' film!"

But even if they're not that—Melissa Harris-Perry once told me, "You don't have any white people in the film." But it never crossed my mind! That was another film. If you have white people in film and you're kicking them and calling them names, they'll be happy, *because they're in the film*. But if they're not in the film at all, they're like, [*panicked expression*] "You don't like me?" It's like, "*No*, I was telling this story about these people on an island. You weren't over there!" You know what I mean? Those curators of culture—they were wrong about a lot of things, and they continue to be wrong.

But I always say, if you want to heal the ills of the world, it can be done through film. Anything and everything. If people see themselves represented in ways that they're inspired me, it doesn't have to be [*picks up nearby water bottle*], "He invented this Aquafina! So you should like him!" *No!* The real stories with depth and complexity. Characters with foibles and strength. If you see yourself on the screen, participating in all of this, you have hope of a future.

I grew up in the Queensbridge housing projects in Long Island. (Nas came from there.) Drugs, violence, it was one of the roughest projects in the city of New York. No one *really* saw themselves existing after age twenty-six. If you were thirteen, and you said, "Yeah, I guess I'll be twenty-six," you don't *really* have a clear or a future path. Me, I wanted to be in the roller derby. Why? Because back then—in the 1960s—roller derby queens were all the rage. They were mostly Puerto Rican and Black, had pink hair, big old scarves. And they had *agency*. Made a lot of money. Rough and tumble. I was like, "Yeah, I can do that."

But it's just all about seeing yourself not being pathetic. Or not being that hero that no one believes. Or not just being the *martyr*. I learned *that* from my daughter. She was like, "Don't talk to me about being like people on that wall. They're all *dead*." Malcolm X, Martin Luther King, Medgar Evers, JFK—all shot or dead. No one wants to be that. No one wants to see these dead people—and that's the end-all you're supposed to be inspired to be?

TSD: You know, it's interesting. You have such a diverse and wide range in your work. Like the other directors of the LA Rebellion, you work across different types of media: music videos, TV specials, Lifetime or BET movies of the week, educational one-hour videos, short films. And I was struck by an interview where you said that after *Daughters*, you had a lot of requests to keep making that same kind of story, as if to cash in on it.

JD: Yeah, they kept giving me these civil rights-slash-Klan movies. I don't think people *really* understand me. I like to do different projects. I'm a filmmaker, I'm a storyteller, and I'm always looking for new ways to tell a new story.

For me, *Daughters of the Dust* was science fiction. It was a voodoo movie. And an opportunity to show sci-fi or speculative fiction, which I've always loved, in a new way.

TSD: Afrofuturist, even!

JD: Yes! There were Afrofuturists before there were people on Twitter talking about it. There were Afrofuturists back in the 1930s . . . *hellooo!* And I was friends with the authors Octavia Butler and Nalo Hopkinson and Tananarive Due. Yes. I'd love to get money to do real Afrofuturist stuff. But people locked me in on *Daughters of the Dust*. I do different things. I even do cheesy stuff. Have you seen *Incognito*?

TSD: I haven't.

JD: [*Laughs*] Okay, maybe that's a good thing! It was another one of those sixteen-days feature films, you know.

TSD: You're part of the so-called LA Rebellion, a group of filmmakers who come out of UCLA in the 1970s and '80s to make these cutting, independent masterpieces. What was that atmosphere like, working alongside people like Charles Burnett and Haile Gerima?

JD: Well, I got there just as everyone was leaving, like Haile, Charles, Larry Clark. They were all pretty much finished, but they hung around for like a year. We got to view their films, and talk and interact with them. I worked with Billy Woodberry and Barbara McCullough. We were there for four years for graduate school. There was a lot of overlapping and working on each other's films. It was a great environment, because I graduated from CCNY [the City College of New York], then to AFI [American Film Institute] for two years. And at AFI, it was just so frustrating, and I used to hang out with the UCLA people because they were making films more radical. Larry would say, "I'm going into the desert next week, will you come and do sound for me?" "In the desert? Okay." I guess people are still doing that, but people were passionate about the stories they wanted to tell. They weren't traditional stories, but you wanted to be a part of it because you wanted to be a part of something, and you know you could learn and hone in your skills.

So it was just dedicated film students who lived at UCLA. Sleeping on the floors in the editing room. And everyone complained a lot: [*Mopey voice*] "I just want to graduate and get outta here, hate this place." But when you look back at it, you can see there was a collective of people working together. But we didn't have that name "LA Rebellion" given to us until years later. Clyde Taylor wrote a thing on us, and it was just UCLA filmmakers, different from the USC or AFI filmmakers, because they were being groomed to go right into Hollywood, and they did. My contemporaries at AFI were Mimi Leder, Amy Heckerling [*Clueless, Fast Times at Ridgemont High*], Marshall Herkovitz, and Ed Zwick [*Blood Diamond, Glory, The Last Samurai*]. We were all there at the same time, and they all went straight into Hollywood. There were no open doors for me.

TSD: You teach. What's the atmosphere like, to you, teaching on campuses today, as compared to what you went through at UCLA?

JD: When I came in to UCLA, it was posthippie and postprotests and radicalism. Everyone was still trying to find themselves, but those elements were still there. Hippie culture quickly turned to punk rock. It was fascinating to see people shift identities and be whoever they wanted to be. There was no criticism there, and when I saw someone like my friend Monona Wali, I'd think, "Wow. I've never seen a punk Indian before. That's so fascinating!"

Today, on campuses, post-Spike Lee, post-Ava DuVernay, a *lot* of people just want to be famous—which is not a bad thing. It depends on the campus I'm on. Some people—emerging filmmakers of color—do *not* want to be recognized as a filmmaker of color. Some of them do not want to be recognized as a "woman" filmmaker. And some just want to be famous. Some people, though, are really radical, like we were back in the day, in just wanting to tell stories.

But back then, there was no one that we could point to and say, "I want to be like this person." Now there are people you can point to, saying, "I want to be like Spike, like John Singleton, like Ava." People start honing in on those role models. They're now more clearly defined. When we were at UCLA, the idea, the *notion* of wanting to be a filmmaker, was kind of absurd. It was like, "Well, you're jumping head first into something where you have no future." And we were like, [*mischievous smile on face*] "Yeaaaaahhh . . . I have no future . . . yeah!" Gotta like that! Just like some kind of *Blade Runner* radical.

TSD: But someone has to forge the path, someone has to be the one to get it started, and you and Charles and Haile and all the other members of the LA Rebellion were the ones that dug that path.

JD: But we weren't thinking about being a pioneer, being a role model. We were just like, "We have no future. We can live with that." That's before you have a family or children. There was no pressure. With *Daughters of the Dust*, I didn't feel nothing but to sell this story. It was all some grand experiment. I was like, "Hmm, if I tell it *this* way, or *that* way. . . ." No pressure.

And that's what I tell my students. When you're in college or graduate or undergraduate school, stretch out. See who you are. Find your real voice. There's no pressure, you know? You just have to pay your tuition, which [*raises eyebrows*] is crazy now.

One of the benefits we had from the protests before we got to college was that I didn't have that kind of tuition bill. I did not have to pay $30,000 or $60,000. I'm a child of affirmative action. And it worked! So I didn't have those same pressures on me: "I have to graduate, I have to get a good paying job, I have to find a job at Universal Studios directing a big project." I was just like, "Well, good luck with *that*."

Being a filmmaker is still a political act. When people aren't buying what you're selling, or supporting you in advancing, you have to understand that it's because they're giving you a public voice. And traditionally those voices have been reserved for a very select few. Unless they know for sure what you're going to say, you have to toe the party line. And I think a lot of young people don't quite understand that yet: the power that blocks them, the power that they're reaching towards. And they can't understand why they're not getting work. It's a very powerful situation, and God bless you, and keep reaching for it. But . . . you know.

People say to me, "Oh, I have wonderful idea for a reality show." And you go, [*taps fingers*] "Oh. . . ." Why should *they* give *you* the opportunity to make millions without owning you? You're not related to them. I always tell people to read books and watch the connections. In that environment, everyone's related some way. Even if it's a fifth cousin, or whatever, it's prior relationships. Even today, when you see people all of a sudden spring forward, it's because they have the support. Someone's quarterbacking for them. They have an angel guiding them, and there's nothing wrong with that. But sometimes, that's just what they need. Ava's become an angel to a lot of people. With *Queen Sugar* [a TV drama created by Ava DuVernay for the Oprah Winfrey Network], she has, in six months' time, done more than Hollywood has done in one hundred years, by hiring Black women, Asian women directors.

Daughters of the Dust opens December 2 at the Landmark Opera Plaza in San Francisco and the Landmark Shattuck in Berkeley. Additionally, several of Dash's films are available to view on campus at Green Library's Media and Microtext Center. These include *Daughters of the Dust*, *Illusions* (1982), and a little-known but just-as-radical-as-*Daughters* short film called *Praise House* (1991), which can be best described as an experimental short tracing the history of African and African American woman through song, folklore, and dance. Scurrilous, active, a combo of African rhythm dance and a fluid God-like liquidy camera, "draw or die" is the moral of Dash's *Praise House* story, boldly explicating how Black women must create their own stories to combat the cartooned stereotypes that today exist of them in Hollywood. *Four Women* (1975), another dance short film set to the titular Nina Simone song, is available to view online.

Julie Dash on the Coming of Age of *Daughters of the Dust*

Stephen Saito / 2016

From *MoveableFest.com* (November 23, 2016). Reprinted by permission of The Moveable Fest.

Back when Julie Dash was a film student in Los Angeles during the early 1980s, she'd eagerly anticipate FilmEx, the film festival that brought world cinema to the city. As much as she'd look forward to the seeing to seeing the new films that might not come back to Los Angeles for months, if ever, the director of *Daughters of the Dust* was just as excited to see what was in the restorations section.

"I used to look at the old films like, 'Oh, they have a new print of *Lawrence of Arabia*! They have a new print of *Giant*!?!,'" recalls Dash, a day before a special screening of *Daughters* at FilmEx's antecedent AFI Fest. "Now, my film is in the restoration section and it's like, 'Wow, who knew?'"

Others might be saying the same thing to themselves, but for different reasons since Dash's first and (unfortunately) only feature feels so new that if one were to mention that it is twenty-five years old, you'd think not of the film itself, but of the vigor and verve that a filmmaker at that age would bring to it. While the film's influence is legion, seen as recently as Beyoncé's video album *Lemonade* where multiple filmmakers drew inspiration from Dash's subconscious-piercing, immersive visual style, especially as it pertains to the experience of African American women deeply conscious of the past and yet fervently pushing ahead towards the future, *Daughters of the Dust* remains a wholly original experience in following the Peazant family, proud Gullah descendants of West African slaves who have made their home on the Sea Islands off the coast of South Carolina, at the turn of the twentieth century, when the clan's tradition-bound matriarch insists on staying on the gulf while her granddaughters plan to migrate north to join others living there already.

The senses stirred by Dash haven't dulled over time—you can smell the gumbo served up by the Peazants for the dinner and feel the sand in between your toes as its characters ponder their place in the world, and it isn't an exaggeration to say watching *Daughters of the Dust* now is like watching it for the first time since Dash never created a proper release print for the film. (Using Agfa-Gevaert film stock from Germany, which the director felt illuminated Black skin like no other, the production could only afford two answer prints at a cost of $20,000 each to properly tinker with color correction—a process considerably easier and cheaper when it came time for the Cohen Media Group to do a full restoration earlier this year.) As the director says, "It looks exactly the way it looked in real life and it looks exactly the way that the work print looked like," the former detail hard to believe since she and cinematographer Arthur Jafa capture otherworldly sunsets and the beauty of beachside firmament generally untroubled by man.

Yet even as the film knows exactly what it is, the qualities that so ably pull viewers in are exactly the same that pushed the film industry at large away, leaving *Daughters of the Dust* to be rediscovered in film schools where its radical deconstruction of cinematic language, echoing the prose of African American authors Dash admired, could best be appreciated and the filmmaker to embark on a career where she'd become a professor herself in between gigs on TV movies and industrial films. While the world is surely a lesser place without the narrative features Dash could've made in the years since *Daughters*—she wrote a sequel to the film as a novel and is currently working on a documentary, *Travel Notes of a Geechee Girl*, about Vertamae Smart-Grosvenor, the definitive authority about Gullah cooking who passed away earlier this year at seventy-nine—it is one of the bright spots of this year to see the world finally catching up to her extraordinary debut, and for the occasion, the vivacious writer-director recently spoke about feeling all the love that's come her way recently, redefining narratives about African Americans, and the famous author who snuck her way onto the set of *Daughters* and wound up working on the crew.

Stephen Saito: The restoration of the film was particularly exciting to me since it's been very difficult to see it in recent years—a Kino-produced DVD has long been out of print. Was it a concern of yours that it had gone out of circulation?

Julie Dash: What happened was I loved Don Krim, the original owner of Kino International Films. He's the one who picked it up for distribution first. He's the one with the foresight. Then he passed away and other owners came in and when it came time to go digital with it, they weren't interested. It needed to be restored. So I pulled it from Kino International—actually to go with another company—and then Cohen Media stepped in and they started talking about the restoration they would like to do, and it was not only like saving the film, but we went back to the negative. We didn't copy the digital files from the DVD to

Blu-ray. We actually took the physical film and scanned it. It's incredible—you can see into the shadow areas, just like the work print.

SS: Let me get off the business stuff. . . .

JD: No, I love that conversation because when I think about it now, [Cohen Media Group] saved the film. Ten more years, the original negative with the splices—they'd start coming apart.

SS: When did you know this film had an afterlife beyond its initial release?

JD: Since it first came out, I've been traveling the world with it—Spain, all of Asia, all of Europe—just all over, and it was like, "Hmmmm, everyone here understands it and no one says, 'Where's the plot?'" And I think that has to do with the fact that people in other countries speak multiple languages, so they know how to code switch. Of course, that's something we do as African Americans because of the whole Du Boisian [double-consciousness] thing, and everybody that has parents that come from somewhere code switches. But sometimes middle America does not. They're used to five hundred television stations and everyone's watching the same thing. When the movie starts, you already know what's going to happen by the end. With *Daughters of the Dust*, you don't just know. People are speaking differently, they're looking different—it's just a whole mélange of things that are new, and I think it was like future shock for a lot of people.

SS: This most recent time I watched it, I was taken with the score, which feels as if it's futureproofing the movie since it's very much of its time in terms of sounding synthy, but anachronistic with the period you see on screen.

JD: Oh, John Barnes! We came up with this idea of what should it sound like. It shouldn't be that single harmonica or the banjo—usually [the sounds] that define those time periods, especially with visuals of Black people. And John said, they had many sounds—there were strains of Congolese sounds, strains of Arabic [since] they did have people of the Islamic faith in those islands. That's another thing that Hollywood never picked up on—when you go grab a bunch of people and bring them over, some of them were of the Islamic faith, but [filmmakers] just never bothered to go there. There are so many rich story materials that are available that I'm still chomping at the bit to get to because we don't need to tell the same stories over and over.

SS: What gave you the confidence to tell your story your own way? This doesn't adhere to a prescribed way of filmmaking.

JD: Because I had gone to so many film schools that each one was different. The first one was the Studio Museum of Harlem and in high school, I was shown Truffaut's *Jules and Jim* and De Sica's *The Bicycle Thief*. The neorealistic films were totally different than anything I had ever seen on television. It was like "What?!?" And you're seeing Akira Kurosawa's *Ikiru* and you're just like weeping, thinking, "I don't know what they're really saying—but I know his face, I know what he means," and I'd just never seen anything like that before. I went to undergraduate school at City College in New York [where] we had a lot of freedom and were learning how to make experimental films, and then I went to the Conservatory Fellowship at the American Film Institute—it was like goose-stepping, marching to make the film for television! [*Laughs*] You know, it was like oppression! They didn't want us to speak of David Lynch, even though he went to AFI. "Do not mention his name." "But we want to see *Eraserhead*!" "Do not mention his name." Then getting out of there, and going to UCLA for four years at graduate school, once again, [there were] no borders, no boundaries, and you have all of these filmmakers around you making all these different films and you're just invigorated by being in the bullpen.

Literally [at UCLA], they had editing tables surrounding [each other in] a room for the project ones, and all nine people [had their] sleeping bags next to their editing table because you didn't get a single editing room until you went up the ladder, so everybody's in the room and it's funky. [*Laughs*] But there's something about it that's like basic training [in the army]. You could just scoot with your little chair back and say, "I'm having a problem with this," and they'd scoot over to you and say, "Well, then, run it for me." It was wonderful. I don't think we knew at that time what we could not do.

That's the difference. There was no fear and no concern about what someone might think or say because it was about "How do we tell a story in such a way that it moves people for the better in some small way? So let's just keep arranging these items here and see what happens." We weren't even concerned with the outside world, much less Hollywood. We were concerned about the world because we were already going to film festivals and their films were much more complex. You don't want a single-layer story. You want something that's layer upon layer upon layer so then you feel it's a full experience. It's the gestalt of seeing the film that you come away with like, "Wow."

I think everyone stays inside the box because they want another job. We were young. We were arrogant. We were curious. We were trying to figure out how to tell a story in a new way. I remember there were conferences with not just Black filmmakers, but white filmmakers talking about "How do we tell a story in a different way?"—that whole artistic questioning of where we are and where we're going. *Daughters* I think was a part of that—do we always have to keep going back to *Gone with the Wind*? Come on.

SS: Was recruiting artists who weren't necessarily from the film world to be on the crew part of that?

JD: Oh, Kerry James Marshall, our production designer! He's up there now, and he was always a fine artist, but we figured he had the aesthetic sensibilities to bring this together—to oversee the art department. And there was also in his department Michael Kelly Williams, who's a great carver. And AJ [the cinematographer, Arthur Jafa] is up there, too—he was a film person; now he's doing something that's opening today in New York at an art gallery. They were all artists, and they had to learn the process of filling out the forms for films, so that everyone would be on the same page. But I wanted that kind of raw, authentic look, for [instance, with] Nana's chair and all those things. Not just grab a chair and put it there and let her sit there—[it was] "Let's rethink all of this. What would they do? How would they embellish? And where do you start when you start embellishing things?"

I had seen so many films of former enslaved people [where] you always showed the whip scars on the back, so I'm thinking, "How do you show it in another way?" They worked in the indigo fields, and of course, the indigo by that time would've washed off, but I bet for many years—just like when you drink those blue Slurpees, you have blue mouth—that indigo in its own way is a scar. It's a different type of visual metaphor saying the same thing, but in a different way to make you think, "Oh yeah, they worked with these dyes." And the other thing is every time we used to see a film, it was always picking cotton. Well, guess what? [*Laughs*] That was not always the case. It was rice and indigo well before it was cotton. So when you find out these things and you see people making the same visual tropes come alive over and over again, you're going, "What?!?" There's so much more.

SS: Over the years, I've heard literature was actually a bigger influence than other films.

JD: Of course, Toni Morrison, Alice Walker, Gloria Naylor.... Gloria Naylor actually worked on the film. She had just purchased a house on St. Helena Island when we were in preproduction, and she came by the production office and asked if she could work on the film. We were like, "That's Gloria Naylor. Are you sure you want to do that?" And because [an adaptation of her novel] *The Women of Brewster Place* was already on television, she said she wanted to do that. She just said she didn't want her name exploited and we said," Sure, we're not going to give you anything heavy to carry." She worked as a production assistant on the film the entire time. If you watch the credits, her name rolls by. But we never exploited her name, and we had Gloria Naylor on the set! She was there!

SS: Have you actually kept up a connection with the island?

JD: Yeah, in fact, my family lives down there, so I'm going for Thanksgiving. I go down there once or twice a year.

SS: So you knew about those amazing sunsets before shooting?

JD: Yeah, and the meadows and the marshlands.

SS: Did you have to wait for hours and hours to get some of those magic hour shots?

JD: What I would do, because the weather would change on us so often, is I always had a scene that I would shoot if the sea rolled back or the squall came in. We were shooting one scene when the sea rolled back, I knew that wasn't a good sign. [*Laughs*] I said, "Oh my god, it looks like a moonshot. Let's go shoot the scene with Mr. Snead, the photographer." If you remember that scene where he looks through and he sees the Unborn Child and he's out and he's not really there—that was one of those moments. The sea, for some reason, receded, and we were standing where the waves usually were.

SS: You've been working steadily in the years since, but this was your only narrative feature....

JD: Not because I wanted it to be!

SS: Since you teach, what do you tell students who ask for career advice?

JD: I tell them while they're young and emerging filmmakers that they need to use their authentic voice. They need to strengthen that and be proud of it. Then years later, they can either continue with that or then they can work as a filmmaker for hire. I've shot commercials, museum films, music videos, movies of the week—all those kinds of things that were nothing like *Daughters of the Dust* because I was a director for hire. I bring my expertise, my skills, and my vision to it—to a point, because most of those pieces have been written by someone else and I have to shape it in my own way, but they chop it back. [*Laughs*]

SS: If this is your only feature, are you at peace with it?

JD: Well, hopefully not . . . but I know. It's like, "Why weren't you able to make another film?" And to be honest, I think in many ways, it frightened a lot of people making those greenlight decisions. It was something different, it was something new, and they weren't quite sure of what it was and [wondered], "Is it a good thing or a bad thing?" A lot of people said it wasn't an authentic Black film because you have to consider the time it came out when a lot of urban films [came out with] guys shooting drugs, and I was a Black woman out there alone. There wasn't a whole sweep of Black filmmakers, so they focused on the male filmmakers who they could at least say, "This is a cautionary tale. Don't do drugs. They're not good." [*Laughs*] You know, it's like, "No duh." Those films were fine, but I needed more. And [the industry] said, "It wasn't that. And it's not *Sounder* or *Gone with the Wind*, so what the hell is it?" Because these people want quick answers to say it's like this, it's like that, and they felt good about hearing "it's like a foreign film." [And then it's] "Yeah, yeah, yeah, but we don't do foreign films."

Just as [when] you are a child, you have very provincial tastes and then as you grow up, you're able to drink wine and eat all these different cheeses and taste all these different flavors and appreciate them, I think the industry is like that in many ways, too. You have *Lemonade—Lemonade* kind of says it all. You can tell a story that's nonlinear, extremely visceral, confounding at times, but ya' like it.

[*Laughs*] It's really good. I really liked that. "What was that? What happened? I don't know, but ah . . . let me see it again." You have to be comfortable with other ethnicities to be able to do that. I watched Russian films and Romanian films [growing up] because of FilmEx, and I love to sit in front of a screen and be taken somewhere and [thinking at first], "Where am I? What's going on? Okay, got it. Oh, wow." And you carry those images with you the rest of your life and it's a good thing. You shouldn't be afraid of it. You shouldn't be fearful of anything different or new. There's a certain maturity that I think we've come to now.

SS: How'd you first find out about *Lemonade*?

JD: I had so many phone calls, and then my web manager said, "Your website shut down because it wasn't set up for that many hits." Then my daughter called and said, "Oh, now you're officially part of the Bey Hive." I said, "What are you talking about?" [*Laughs*] And then Ted Lanza, [who was restoring *Daughters of the Dust* at Cohen Media Group] called and said, "You've got to see it. I'm not going to say anything." And then I saw it and I'm just like, "Wow. This is something. I have to see it again." I played it again. Then I downloaded it. And the music, too! I love [Beyoncé], I love Solange, her sister—I just met Solange. AJ shot her videos for "Don't Touch My Hair" and "Cranes in the Sky," and they had an event [sponsored by] her company, Saint Heron, for him and myself in New Orleans [where] we talked about aesthetics and visceral filmmaking. It was wonderful. For like two hours, everybody in the community was just talking about making films that really get your pulse racing—you feel it here [motioning to her heart], and you don't know exactly why, but it's discovery. It's wonderful stuff.

Invisible Scratch Lines: An Interview with Julie Dash

Maori Karmael Holmes / 2016

Published in *Film Quarterly* 70, no. 2 (Winter 2016): 49–57. Reprinted by permission of University of California Press.

With the debut of *Daughters of the Dust* in 1991, director Julie Dash became the first African American woman to have a full-length general theatrical release in the United States. A graduate of AFI and UCLA and a fixture of the LA Rebellion movement, Dash had already directed three critically acclaimed short-form works—*Four Women* (1975), *Diary of an African Nun* (1977), and *Illusions* (1989)—before the film's release.

Daughters of the Dust is a story about the fictional Peazant family, set on one of the Sea Islands off the coast of the southeastern United States. The film opens on the day that many of the members of this Gullah family will make their way north to the mainland, participating in the first wave of the Great Migration. Nana Peazant (played masterfully by Cora Lee Day of Larry Clark's *Passing Through* [1977]) and her ways will stay behind. The film is seemingly a disruption to everything viewers have been taught about cinema. When first seen, for many, it's as if nothing is happening. Then you go back and begin to notice that actually quite a lot is happening in every second and every densely layered frame—its articulation of African Americana: the quilts, bottle trees, newspaper print on the walls, okra on the foreheads, the proprietary relationship to Black women's hair, the legacies of rape and lynching, the lure of Christianity and its promise of respectability.

At 113 minutes, *Daughters* is a protracted experience. There's no individual protagonist; instead, the family as a unit is deliberately centered. And the conventions of dramatic structure (exposition, rising action, climax, falling action, and denouement) are overruled; instead, the story continues. And continues. Toni Cade Bambara once wrote that "the narrative is not 'classical' in the Western-specific sense. It is classic in the African sense. There are digressions and meanderings—as we may be familiar with from African, Persian, Indian, and other cinemas that employ features of the oral tradition." The film had a brief theatrical run in 1991–92 and toured internationally to festivals and museums. In 2004, it was included in the National Film Registry of the Library of Congress.

Despite *Daughters* having long held the fascination of independent filmmakers and many other artists specifically interested in the legacy of Black cultural production at the turn of the century, its director has yet to obtain funding to direct another feature narrative. Dash has been working fairly steadily directing commercials, music videos, cable television films, and special commissions for museums. Her long-form, dramatic narrative films since *Daughters* have included *Incognito* (1999), *Funny Valentines* (1999), and *Love Song* (2000). She has directed videos for a range of musicians and has been filming a documentary on cultural anthropologist Vertamae Smart-Grosvenor for the past decade.

In April, *Daughters* (and Dash) unexpectedly entered popular culture at center stage upon the release of Beyoncé Knowles-Carter's "visual album" *Lemonade* (Jonas Åkerlund, Beyoncé, Kahlil Joseph, Melina Matsoukas, Dikayl Rimmasch, Mark Romanek, and Todd Tourso, 2016), composed of twelve music videos threaded together with Warsan Shire's poetry and allusions to Elizabeth Kubler-Ross's stages of grief. Beyoncé, who has long been fascinated with imagery of Black women in high-necked Victorian-esque dress occupying the center of the frame in her music videos, now (with her collaborators) expanded that enthrallment. *Lemonade* includes imagery of women in the sun in white dresses and veils, food preparation in wooden cabin kitchens, women in repose in swampy forests, references to Yoruba-derived spiritual practices, personal altars for deceased family members, and all of that water. Most strikingly, as in *Daughters of the Dust*, there are no white people in sight.

In 1993, film theorist Ed Guerrero made a prediction: "There is no doubt that, ultimately, over time, her film will get the popular reception that it demands. This will come about simply because *Daughters of the Dust* is engaged in the long, slow process of opening up new, liberated zones in the social imagination." And thanks to a magical storm of social media and the Parkwood Entertainment machine (neither of which existed when the film was released), Guerrero's prediction came to be. Within twenty-four hours of *Lemonade*'s release, social and legacy media were aflutter with references to the similarities of the project to *Daughters*. It was divine timing for the Cohen Film Collection's announcement of the film's 2K restoration and rerelease of Dash's film, which was already in the works; initially intended as a Blu-ray release, the restoration was quickly moved into a limited theatrical run in fall 2016 following its premiere at Cannes.

Maori Karmael Holmes: I've heard that *Daughters of the Dust* never looked how you had intended in the beginning.

Julie Dash: Exactly! It never looked the way it looked even during the editing process because, you know, it never looked as good as the work print even. Back then, we were editing on celluloid, and you go from answer print to answer print to release print—[but] we never were able to get to a release print, because each print was $20,000. We just never got to the correct coloring and we had maybe two printed, and that was it. Two answer prints. So now it's there, now that we're in the digital space, where you just dial it up.... Now, we're where we were supposed to be. And it's gorgeous. I'd forgotten how it looked. After twenty-five years, I'd forgotten how it was supposed to look.

MKH: When you saw Beyoncé's *Lemonade* for the first time, did you immediately think about *Daughters* or did it happen in reverse? Did people send it to you, saying, "Oh my god, look at this!"

JD: I have seen a lot from *Daughters of the Dust* in other films, so this was not the first time. When I first saw it, I was so enmeshed in the aesthetics and so excited by it. I was so moved by Serena, by the styles, by the mothers of the slain teenagers, that by the time they got to the tree scene, I was just floating. You know what I mean? It didn't really hit me like it did other people.... To me that's normal ... people being in trees, because actually my tree scene was an homage to Bill Gunn's *Ganja and Hess* [1973]. I figured it's all part of the continuum of the Black aesthetic.

MKH: That's really beautiful. I love that you position it this way. I hadn't realized how much cross-referencing and homage was happening between the works of the LA Rebellion movement until I saw Zeinabu irene Davis's new documentary, *Spirits of Rebellion: Black Cinema from UCLA* [2016].

JD: Yes, it's part of the culture. And part of a deeper aesthetic that's within us, that we've grown up with, [it's a] creolization of various styles and different parts of a Black aesthetic. When it blossoms forth in new work and actually transcends the work that it is "homaging," it gives further evidence that it is part of a continuum rather than some kind of "copy." It's more than that—because *Lemonade* transcends all its homages and takes them to new levels and new meanings. I'm glad to be part of the dance.

MKH: Not unlike a lot of people in my generation, I have watched *Daughters* a dozen times, read the text, watched the DVD extras with Robert Farris Thompson, and all of these things. I have always been curious: When you made the film, or were in the process of making it, did you have training in Yoruba aesthetics? I know that your family is from the Gullah region. Where did your cultural knowledge come from? Was it memory?

JD: Was it muscle memory? [*Laughs*] It was a combination of things, but I did a lot of research at UCLA. There were exhibits in the art department [back then] and at the Fowler Museum. I did research in New York at the Schomburg [Library], where I was able to look at initiation films made in Brazil. I was able to pull from my own family's background in the Lowcountry in the Gullah Geechee corridor. I went to the Smithsonian, National Archives, UCLA research labs. I was able to sit at the feet of Dr. Margaret Washington Creel, who was my adviser and was at UCLA at the time; Adrienne Lanier Seward, a folklorist from Indiana University; and Worth Long, a folklorist in Atlanta. I had a lot of mothers and fathers to be inspired by. That's where all of that came from. There was a lot of research and a lot of writing done.

MKH: Did you have any interest yourself in any kind of anthropological work or folklore?

JD: Yes. I think that if I weren't a filmmaker, I probably would have been an anthropologist with a focus on mythology or folklore. It all folds back into who we are as a people and the attempt to do a cinema that is authentic to who we are in this new world.

MKH: Let's talk a little about your new film, *Standing at the Scratch Line* (2016). I am curious what inspired you to create an experimental film. I've read that you've called it a "tone poem."

JD: I thought, if anything, it is a hybrid documentary drama. I was going to use this genderless suitcase, this traveling valise, as the protagonist, migrating north. It just shows you where my mind is—I thought it was a straight-up documentary! I read that it was labeled "experimental" and wondered: What did I experiment with?

My main goal was to show migration from the Lowcountry, which you don't normally see. You usually see migration from Alabama or Mississippi, all of these other places. I wanted to show Lowcountry environments: a lot of waterways, a lot of ocean, the marsh, the flooded areas. It's not just Charleston. I also included archival photographs of Savannah, Georgia Lowcountry, South Carolina's Lowcountry, and going a bit north towards the Lowcountry of North Carolina and the coastal areas.

Because it was so low-budget and so rushed—we only had a few days to shoot it—I figured, instead of trying to arrange [it] around a talking head, a historian telling us a story, maybe I could tell the story with a suitcase. I was going to actually ask Nikky Finney or Sonia Sanchez to do some original prose for it, but then I ran out of time. So I had to do it myself. And writing it kind of changed the structure of the story, because I started thinking about how departure and arrival in many ways mean the same thing. You're standing at the scratch line—do

I go or do I stay? And once you get there, whether it's a forced migration or not, it's still always the point of departure, because nothing stays the same. It started getting metaphysical in the end.

MKH: What an amazing coincidence to be able to link the histories of both Mother Emanuel in Charleston, which was the site of the tragic mass shooting in 2015, to the two hundredth anniversary of Mother Bethel in Philadelphia, the first African Methodist Episcopal [AME] church (and the oldest continuously Black-owned church in the United States).

JD: I actually show two churches in Charleston. I show Mother Emanuel as well as Mount Zion. I added Mount Zion because my relatives originally attended Emanuel and a lot of them are buried in the original old cemetery, but I also found out that my great-grandmother Emma Dash left Emanuel and cofounded Mount Zion! My father's funeral was at Mount Zion, my uncle Julius, everybody was buried at Mount Zion who wasn't buried at Mount Emanuel, so there were really close connections there. [In the film] I included my father, his older brother Saint Julian, and my great-great-great-grandmother Rosie, who was born a slave. They are [all] in the film. There's an image of an elderly dark-skinned woman, holding the heads of two young boys—they're just standing there—and that's my father and my uncle Julian (who wrote "Tuxedo Junction"; he was a tenor saxophone player). All of them migrated north. There's a lot of family stuff going on there, plus the Emanuel Nine, and the whole departures and arrivals thing with the massacre.

We thought that part of our history was done; no one could have imagined that, but it did happen [again]. And that's all connected to standing at the scratch line. Let's put a line in the sand and decide: Do I step over it or not? How do we go forward from this? How do we go forward from landing after a fourth migration? Do you just sink back into the water and die, or do you choose to live? So many of our ancestors chose to live. They stepped over that line, that invisible line in the sand where the water meets the solid ground; they stepped over it and chose to live.

I think we do that in life a lot. There are a lot of invisible scratch lines, but at the same time . . . I say, "Our deepest memories live at the water's edge." I know when I see people go to the water's edge, they're mesmerized. I don't think any Black person goes to the water's edge and thinks to themselves, "Whoop dee doo"—especially in the Sea Islands. We shot on Sullivan's Island, which has the plaque right on the beach . . . where the [slave-trader] boats pulled up, so it had a lot of meaning for us, and for me, especially. And if I just look at those waves, I'm reminded it happened right here, where saltwater meets solid ground. They had to choose to live or choose to die.

MKH: Did Louis Massiah [producer of the Great Migration series] know the history of your father's family in the AME Church? Is that why he suggested you cover Mother Bethel and Mother Emanuel, or did you suggest it?

JD: He suggested it. I didn't even know the deep details until I went to Charleston and we all stayed at my uncle's house. He said, "Well, you know your grandmother, your great-grandmother, etc." and I said, "You never told me!" And he said, "You never asked." And I said, "How would I know to ask?" This was all new information. So I went to Ancestry.com and I found all these people buried at Emanuel. I didn't know any of it. It was Louis and Reverend Tyler from Mother Bethel who, when we met with them, explained that a lot of migrants came from Emanuel and when they migrated, when they moved up north, the first place they went to was Mother Bethel. So there's that Gullah Geechee connection with Bethel. I never knew that before I had that meeting with them!

MKH: I think people always forget that since Philly is always touted as "the North," that slaves were here, too. As you know, during this year's BlackStar Film Festival there was a power outage; I found out a couple hours afterward, Tina Morton actually told me, that she had been at Penn's Landing and they were doing a dedication to enslaved Africans arriving at Penn's Landing and they had just put a marker in the ground when the power went out.

JD: I don't think there are any coincidences in life and it's kind of like people turning in their graves and saying, "Thank you for remembering, at the very least, remembering and honoring." I say in my film's poem: it's like cartographers mapping landscapes, because we shoulder these memories. A lot of people don't want to shoulder the memories and [they] say, "It was the past." When the lights went out, there was like a collective gasp. It was almost like an orgasmic sigh, because people were watching the performing at the water [in Roni Nicole Henderson's *{break}through* (2016)], and I think everybody was in the zone.

MKH: It makes me think of one of the lasting motifs in *Daughters*, in which Mr. Snead and his camera capture the image of the Unborn Child whom no one in the physical plane of the film can see. A mentor once told me that when she attempted to record images at Gorée Island in Senegal, although her camera was running, her footage came back blank.

JD: When I was doing my research for *Daughters* I had never heard of Dr. Lorenzo Turner. But in the university research lab at UCLA—and I don't tell many people this—I walk into the stacks and this book falls out. I pick it up and it's Dr. Lorenzo Dow Turner's *Africanisms in the Gullah Dialect*. I thought to myself, "Oh my god!" This was exactly what I needed. I didn't look that book up; it fell off the shelf, in the original blue cover. Things like that happen. They're like these little blessings, and that's when you know you're going in the right direction. I just sat and looked at the pages for a while. At first you kind of go Hollywood and think,

"Oh my god, this is creepy," but then you say, "Let's not go there. It's not creepy, it's a blessing." With the lights going out, I think that was a nod. Someone took a sigh and a long blink and that was it. You conjured it up, Maori! And it's all good.

MKH: I want to shift a little bit to talk about your career in full, where you've gotten to at this point and a little bit about things that you've been working on. Who are your filmmaking heroes? You said that you started to train as a young person in New York, and I was just wondering when you were getting into film, who were the filmmakers you were thinking about?

JD: There were actually three people. There was Jessie Maple, who had made a feature called *Will* [1981], starring Loretta Devine. But before her there was Sara Gómez, a filmmaker in Cuba, who had done a series of shorts, a documentary, and a feature, *One Way or Another (De Cierta Manera)* [1974]. She had attended the Cuban Film Institute, and she died very young. We didn't have access to her films until recently. Now all of her films can be found online. She was very important to me because she was a brown-skinned woman with a little Afro, in the 1970s. The image of her behind a camera was very important to me. She just looked like someone that I would have known having grown up in New York. Later on it was the films of Kathleen Collins, *Losing Ground* [1982] and *The Cruz Brothers and Mrs. Malloy* [1980].

MKH: Whose work are you thinking about now?

JD: For a time it was Mira Nair; I always really loved her work. And of course now it's Ava [DuVernay], Dee Rees, Gina Prince-Bythewood, and Nzingha Stewart. Before them, it was Barbara McCullough, the experimental filmmaker and animator who made *Water Ritual #1: An Urban Rite of Purification* [1979]. I remember when it screened at UCLA: At the very end, Yolanda Vidato, who was starring in it, peed and the audience went wild. It was bold, it was daring, and we got it!

MKH: How do you see your relationship to what's now called "the LA Rebellion"? Did you realize in that moment that you were a part of a movement? What's your relationship to that history?

JD: I realized that I was very comfortable there because I was coming out of two years of being a producing–writing fellow at the American Film Institute, where I was an outsider. I was not able to make a film, but of course I was able to work on everyone else's films. I was able to learn a lot and screen films that I had not screened before, and got to work side by side with a lot of foreign filmmakers.

At the time it was a very small class. There were only eighteen students in my class, and by the next year there were probably only fifteen or sixteen, so it was a very intimate setting. But at the same time, I was an outsider. All of my ideas were discarded. I was writing *Illusions* and *Daughters of the Dust* while I was at AFI, but they pooh-poohed [them]. I was able to work with some of the UCLA filmmakers like Charles Burnett, Haile Gerima, Larry Clark. When Larry was shooting *Passing Through*, I was the assistant soundperson on it.

By the time I got into UCLA, I came in with Alile Sharon Larkin and Barbara McCullough, [all in] the same year, 1976. I was there for a long time. Everyone took at least four years to get through the graduate program. Some people took five and six years, because you had to take time off to make money to complete your film. That graduate program was very long because we were working in film! It was celluloid and it was expensive.

MKH: And there probably wasn't funding for the tuition to MFA programs, the way there is now.

JD: No, because it wasn't trendy then. To say you were a filmmaker means you just got a blank look from people. They would correct you and say, "You mean, you're a photojournalist." And you would say, "No. Film. Motion pictures." And people would say, "Oh. Well, that's not interesting." Especially for Black people, because it predates Spike Lee. Until *She's Gotta Have It* [1986], people would ask Black filmmakers, "What are you doing again?" My family didn't even fully understand what I was doing. They just knew it was something with film, which they thought was crazy.

MKH: Many people don't realize that you have been working consistently for the past twenty-five years. Can you talk about the work you have been engaged with post-*Daughters*?

JD: I'm not offended that people always say that. Here's the thing. There was no social media. So I couldn't say "I'm doing this, I'm doing that" if I did a music video or television car commercial. At one point, I was designing an African American pavilion for Disney Imagineering. That was a great experience. And I've done a bit of museum work. I made a $1.5-million-dollar film for the National Underground Railroad Freedom Center [*Brothers of the Borderland* (2004)]. I think it's still playing! It plays every fifteen minutes.

You know, it's funny. With the movies of the week that I've done, people don't count them. But when you talk about Dee Rees, they'll count *Bessie* [2015] as a feature film she's done, or they'll say Gina Prince-Bythewood did *Disappearing Acts* [2000], and that was a movie of the week too. But no one counts my movies of the week, and that's part of the problem. I did *Funny Valentines* [1999], *Love Song* [2000], *Incognito* [1999], *Subway Stories* [1997], *The Rosa Parks Story* [2002]—that's five long-form works—plus the other work.

MKH: Why do you think you were never able to find funding to direct another feature?

JD: As I look back on it now, I think *Daughters of the Dust* may have frightened the powers that be. Because even when I was doing the long-form movies of the week, they would say, "Haha, just don't make it like *Daughters of the Dust*, haha." Hollywood producers felt that *Daughters of the Dust* wasn't for them. They felt left out. And I didn't notice it until someone told me, "You know, you don't have any white people in *Daughters of the Dust*." That never crossed my mind.

MKH: Isn't that amazing? People can watch Chinese films, Indian films, Iranian films, and put themselves in the world of the story. But if it's a Black American story, then, the industry says, "Where am I?" They can't relate.

JD: It means you must not like them or something.

MKH: You've been working on a documentary about Vertamae Smart-Grosvenor, one of your longtime collaborators. Can you talk about her role in *Daughters* and her role as a cultural figure overall? What I've read is that she was a much bigger figure than I think most people realize now, in terms of career and what she contributed. Can you talk about where the documentary is in production and what she's meant to you?

JD: So far, we have twenty-two people on camera. I think if there were no Vertamae and no *Travel Notes of a Geechee Girl*, there probably would be no *Daughters of the Dust*. I grew up being taught that you don't mention outside of the house that you're Geechee. And if someone calls you a Geechee, that's a reason to fight. She [Vertamae] identified as being a Geechee and even had it in print on her book. I got the book and as I'm reading, I thought, "Wow, everything she's saying sounds just like a relative!"

I didn't know her for many years, but just having that book gave me confidence and it also steered me in the direction of studying Geechee girl culture. When casting the film, I knew I had to get in touch with Vertamae. And not only was she interested in being in it, but also being a consultant. We also had another consultant, Ron Day, who translated my script into Gullah phonetically for the actors. He also worked as the dialect coach. You might recognize his name, because he went on to do *Gullah Gullah Island* [Nickelodeon, 1994–98] with his wife Natalie Day—they were part of *Daughters of the Dust* early on.

Gloria Naylor had just purchased a home down on St. Helena Island when we were in preproduction. So she came and worked on the shoot. She was there every morning at 5:00 a.m. like everyone else. We just promised not to exploit her presence or her name. She was there working like a production assistant because she wanted to learn film. After I finished the film, I did a novel [*Daughters of the Dust* (1997)], and Vertamae changed all the English dialogue into Gullah Geechee dialect. I still didn't know her whole story. But then I decided I wanted to do an oral history with her. So we started doing that, and that's when the whole story came out. My mouth hit the floor. She knows everyone in the world and everyone knows her. We actually have this Six Degrees of Kevin Bacon kind of game in private that we call Six Degrees of Vertamae. Here's a touch of it: Her first dinner party was for Yoko Ono before Yoko Ono was married to John Lennon in the Village. She knew Hugh Masakela, Miles Davis, Billie Holiday. She knows everyone. And they all have great Vertamae stories. Then we come to find out that when she was nineteen years old in the 1950s, she bought a one-way ticket to Paris. She didn't speak any French; she had just dropped out of high school, and she decided to become a bohemian. What woman, probably the age of your great-grandmother, [what] Black woman that you know, decides to become a bohemian in the 1950s?!?

MKH: Not anyone that carried it out. [*Laughs*] I'm sure my grandmother dreamed about it!

JD: I can't even picture it. That she would buy a one-way ticket and sail to Paris. And then she gets there and moves into a small hotel near the river Seine, which becomes known in time as the Beat Hotel—because of the bohemians and the American literary types who were living there. And who else was living in that hotel? Allen Ginsberg, William Burroughs, Robert Grosvenor, Harold Chapman, Jonathan Kozol. The first thing I said was, "*The* Allen Ginsberg?!" And she said, "Oh, yeah. We worked on a journal together." And she pulls out pictures of young Allen Ginsberg. She's there for two years, and it's all documented in photographs by Harold Chapman.

Then she comes back to the United States and she gets involved with the Black Power–Black Arts movement, [Amiri] Baraka and all of those people. And she has two children and everything, and then she divorces from Robert Grosvenor. Meanwhile Robert Grosvenor is the cousin of Jackie Kennedy Onassis! Needless to say, she knows every Black artist or political leader. In the middle of the 1960s she's looking for a job, so she starts working with Sun Ra. She becomes one of the moon goddesses. So she makes costumes and dances around with an *ankh* and they travel around Europe.

After that, she becomes involved with Bill Gunn and the Black cinema. By the time she comes to me, Calvin Lockhart had been her boyfriend; the list just goes on and on. At the end of the whole Black cinema thing, she segues into being a commentator on NPR—an award-winning commentator. She had so many wonderful programs on *All Things Considered, Morning Edition, Horizons*. Her voice is incredible. We found all the articles she had written for *Élan, Essence, Ebony*. She was a roving correspondent in Mexico with her grandson and a microphone covering the Day of the Dead and comparing it to the death of her grandson's father—who was Oscar Brown!

She has lived a remarkable, profoundly creative life and we need to honor that. It's taken us quite a while to be able to raise money. We did an Indiegogo [campaign]. National Black Programming Consortium gave us a production grant once they saw the footage: Quincy Troupe, Hugh Masakela, Danny Glover. And Nina Simone's brother, saying, "Did you know that she was best friends with

Nina Simone; the late Larry Neal, one of the architects of the Black Arts Movement; and Charles H. Fuller, who wrote the Pulitzer Prize–winning *A Soldier's Play* [1981] which became *A Soldier's Story* [1984]?" They were all teenagers together—Fuller, Neil, and Vertamae—in Philadelphia.

Her story is profoundly engaging, on so many levels, at the intersection of race, gender, height. I keep calling it "Being Young, Gifted, Black, and the Tallest Person in the Room," which I understand completely—I'm usually the tallest person in the room. It's a whole different life that you have. People don't ask, "Are you okay?" They figure, "You're big and big boned," you can take care of yourself." People treat you differently when you're tall.

MKH: Do you have a sense of when the film will be complete?

JD: We have more people to shoot and more money to raise.

MKH: When you look back at the work you've made so far, what has been an organizing thread? Have you had a manifesto or any kind of assumption that you've carried with you throughout each work? Or even that's revealed itself later as you look back?

JD: I chose a mission statement many years ago, it was this: that I was going to redefine how we see women of the African diaspora in historical drama. That's been my main focus. I wanted to show the culture of women of the African diaspora. I haven't done my Octavia Butler film, but there's still time.

MKH: Which Butler book do you want to do?

JD: I met her back in the early 1990s and all of her books were [already] optioned out. *Kindred* [1979] was optioned. Showtime had *Parable of the Sower* [1993]. They were tied up. I think Ernest Dickerson has *Clay's Ark* [1984] right now. But, pretty much any of Octavia's works, I would do. Or Nalo Hopkinson or Nnedi Okorafor or Tananarive Due. I love sci-fi.

Filmmaker Julie Dash: "#OscarsSoWhite Worked!"

Simran Hans / 2017

From *The Guardian.com* (June 4, 2017). © Guardian News & Media Ltd. 2024. Reprinted by permission.

In 1991, Julie Dash's *Daughters of the Dust* made history as the first film by an African American woman to receive a wide theatrical release in the United States. A hypnotic, otherworldly drama, it tells the forgotten history of three generations of Gullah—or Geechee—women, descendants of West African slaves brought to South Carolina's isolated St. Helena Island. Critically acclaimed upon its release, last year the film reached a new generation when it was the inspiration behind Beyoncé's visual album *Lemonade*. The film has been restored for its twenty-fifth anniversary and is being rereleased this month. Born in New York, Dash studied at UCLA film school in Los Angeles, where she became a key member of the LA Rebellion collective of Black filmmakers.

Simran Hans: You made *Daughters of the Dust* twenty-six years ago. How does it feel to be talking about it again?

Julie Dash: The conversation has been ongoing. Ever since we made it, we've been talking about it and showing it in various places around the world. I've found overseas they don't react like Americans, who want everything to be told with a Western sensibility. And certainly *Daughters of the Dust* does not do that!

SH: Beyoncé explicitly makes reference to the film in *Lemonade*. Did she have anything to do with the rerelease?

JD: We were already working on the restoration, but when Beyoncé's *Lemonade* came out, it just took the whole notion of it and propelled it out to a wider, younger audience. There's a new kind of curiosity that was not out there before. With such a renewed interest in the film, we decided to do another theatrical run.

SH: Did you meet Beyoncé?

JD: I have never met Beyoncé! But I was able to meet her sister, Solange, who sent for us—for myself and AJ [Arthur Jafa, cinematographer of *Daughters of the Dust*] and we did a kind of town hall meeting in New Orleans for her Saint Heron gathering [an event hosted by Solange's record label as part of the New Orleans film festival]. It was wonderful!

SH: The film was critically acclaimed and you haven't stopped directing since—you've made TV movies and documentaries such as *The Rosa Parks Story*—but you haven't made another feature. Why has it been so hard to get one off the ground?

JD: Well, easy question—how many times have you raised a million dollars? How many times do you have to do it? When we do that first film it's all on us, it's all or nothing, even though *Daughters* only cost $855,000, but that's the same as a million to me.

SH: Ava DuVernay, the Oscar-nominated director of *13th* and *Selma*, has called you "the queen of it all" and suggested your work was ahead of its time. Do you agree?

JD: It's always the money. I understand what she's saying, but it's not that I was before my time. It was that [female directors] didn't have angels, we didn't have anyone quarterbacking for us, we didn't have anyone shepherding us for the second one.

SH: How does that feel now that you're in a different position? Are you in a different position?

JD: I'm in a liminal state. It's interesting because I was so pleased and honored to have won a special award from the New York Film Critics Circle this past February, but I'm still knocking on doors.

SH: The filmmaker Barry Jenkins namechecked both you and Solange in a public letter he wrote about *Moonlight*'s influences. What did you make of his film?

JD: Well, I've seen it several times, and each time I'm always on the edge of my seat. There's so much tenderness in it. That kind of Black male tenderness is just not available in most places; you can't see it. It's gut-wrenching, but good gut-wrenching.

SH: In *Daughters of the Dust*, you're credited as producer, director, and screenwriter. Do you think of yourself as a director or a writer first?

JD: A director first. I started writing because I needed something to direct. [*Laughs*] You're the first person to ask me that, and that's the honest-to-God truth. Way, way, way back then, in the beginning, I wanted to be a cinematographer. But I was awful at it. I think I have the eye of a cinematographer, but my lighting sucks!

SH: How would you describe a Julie Dash film?

JD: I usually try to focus on the culture of women, trying to see what women are doing and how they're doing it and what makes it different and what makes it visceral.

SH: You once described *Daughters of the Dust* as a kind of sci-fi. Would you ever want to make a straight sci-fi film?

JD: Absolutely! I wrote [a sci-fi script] way, way, way back, in the 1990s. Originally it was called *Digital Diva*, but that got old really quick. [*Laughs*] You can't keep up with the future when you're writing sci-fi, so I went to the past.

SH: Last year, you were finally made a member of the Academy. How did that feel?

JD: Wonderful. I was very pleased because I applied twenty-six years ago and I couldn't get in, so #OscarsSoWhite worked, didn't it! And not just for myself, but for about 750 other people. It's never too late. I'm still very grateful, and I'm still working.

SH: Can you talk about your forthcoming film, *Travel Notes of a Geechee Girl*?

JD: It's a documentary based upon the life of Vertamae Smart-Grosvenor, who was a culinary anthropologist and Geechee girl. She was a famous cook, chef, novelist, and NPR journalist for many, many years. I met her and asked her would she be in *Daughters of the Dust*, would she vet it for me for the Gullah Geechee accent, and we just became best friends. She passed away last September, but you don't stop making the film. You soldier on, because it's her legacy.

SH: Food is also really important in *Daughters of the Dust*. . . .

JD: I come from a Gullah Geechee family and cooking was a big deal. I mean, everyone cooked—the men, women and children—and the thing was you had to prepare it the correct way. If you didn't know how to make rice, if your rice was too watery or too sticky, you were shamed!

SH: How does it feel to be an artist living in Donald Trump's America?

JD: Oh my gosh. Well, I'll tell you one thing—we worked for, like, a year and a half preparing the proposal for this big NEH [National Endowment for the Humanities] grant that we were trying to get and, as of this year, he's actively trying to dismantle that whole grant. That's how we were going to finance *Travel Notes of a Geechee Girl*, so in that regard I'm not a happy camper.

SH: What are you working on next?

JD: I don't know if I should tell you. . . . Well . . . I'm gonna be working on *Queen Sugar* next week. I was supposed to work on it last year, but we had scheduling problems, so [the TV show's creator, Ava DuVernay] said, "Next year, I'll give you two of 'em." I love the show, so it's like [*sighs excitedly*].

Controlling the World Within the Frame: Julie Dash and Ayoka Chenzira Reflect on New York and Filmmaking

Michele Prettyman / 2019

From *Black Camera* 10, no. 2 (Spring 2019): 69–79. Reprinted by permission of Indiana University Press.

In October of 2018, I had the pleasure of speaking with filmmakers Julie Dash and Ayoka Chenzira, both professors at Spelman College, to get their takes on the Black filmmakers and artists working in and around New York in the late 1960s and 1970s in an era we are calling the "New York Scene." Dash and Chenzira, born just a year apart, have each had extraordinary careers in filmmaking and media arts and both spent their early years as students in New York. Dash gained notoriety with experimental short films like *Four Women* (1975), *Diary of an African Nun* (1977), and *Illusions* (1982) and later with the iconic *Daughters of the Dust* (1991) and a host of other film and TV productions. As a young woman and a native New Yorker, she took film and photography classes at the Studio Museum of Harlem and would later go on to receive a BA from City College in 1974.

Chenzira, a Philadelphia native and dancer, pursued film and photography at NYU. Her earliest works include *Syvilla: They Dance to Her Drum* (1979); a groundbreaking animated piece entitled *Hair Piece: A Film for Nappyheaded People* (1985); *Zajota and the Boogie Spirit* (1989), which was the first animated film to combine film, frame-by-frame video, and computer animation; and a 35mm feature, *Alma's Rainbow* (1994). The women recall New York of this time as a space dominated by documentary filmmaking, which was cheaper and easier to produce and which captured the attention of young Black artists, writers, students, activists, and journalists who believed it could best address the sociopolitical anxieties of Black life. While both women worked in documentary filmmaking, each followed her own impulse to tell stories, often experimental ones, about women, and each began using filmmaking to cultivate her own artistic and cinematic potential. As the Black Arts Movement continued to evolve and theater and the visual arts remained pivotal spheres of influence, these women recall the nascent days of public documentary and narrative film work, crossing paths with the likes of Madeline Anderson, Gil Noble, Kathleen Collins, Bill Gunn, St. Clair Bourne, Roy Campanella II, Pearl Bowser, Kathe Sandler, Camille Billops, Fronza Woods, and many others.

Michele Prettyman: So thank you both so much for agreeing to do this. I know you're swamped with many things, so we really appreciate your time. In this *Black Camera* Close-Up my collaborator, Nick Forster, and I have been working to put together the archival puzzle of this network of Black filmmakers and artists, which we are calling the New York Scene. Since I was a graduate student, I've been trying to contextualize the significance of Kathy Collins, and Nick has been doing a lot of research on Bill Gunn, and in our conversations we realized that they were part of this large, interconnected network of people—some who might have been students, others were older professionals, but they were all doing interesting things. And so with this Close-Up we're really just beginning a conversation because a lot of the research that is really ongoing. So with this in mind, I just wanted to get the perspectives of both of you to help us understand what you were doing and what this world was like. So that's kind of the backstory.

Julie Dash: Okay, well, I could tell you I met Kathy Collins in the early 1970s. I think it was either 1971 or '72, and I was doing work study with Chamba Productions and with St. Clair Bourne in the Film [Center] Building on Ninth Avenue. And it was a very vibrant, exciting period of time where a lot of documentary filmmaking was being done. They were working on *Black Journal* as well as *Soul* (and Ayo can jump in). And Kathy had just had a baby and she was editing *Let the Church Say Amen!* [1974] for St. Clair Bourne, and she was very generous with her skills and crafts. That's what I remember. I would go into the editing room with her and she would show me things and I would hold the baby and it was just like a big family. It was just really very exciting, and that kind of sealed the deal for me in terms of wanting to pursue film studies. George Bowers, he was the editor, too. There were quite a few filmmakers around; it wasn't like a desert or anything.

MP: So, Ayoka, do the same thing. Set the groundwork for us for when you entered this space.

Ayoka Chenzira: So my entry into the New York film scene came from my work as a student at NYU. So when I came to New York I went to NYU to study film and photography. I got my degree in film, but it was during a time when there were four other Black people in the program and I think none of us were happy. And I remember going to the head of the film school, who at that time was a man named Haig Manoogian, who is very much revered even to this day in the film industry. But Haig and I did not get along. I thought he was sexist. Not really interested in the Black students or what we had to say. And I actually, prior to becoming a director, was interested in becoming a cinematographer, and I remember going to Haig to talk about this being my focus, and he was absolutely against it. (This will all make sense in a moment, but it's a little bit of a long answer.) And he and I got into, you know, a bit of an argument, and I decided that rather than arguing with him that I would see if I could spend another semester perhaps doing an independent study or something someplace else. And I ended up at Third World Newsreel with Pearl Bowser, Sue Robeson, and Chris Choy. The people there took me under their wing, and it's when I think I became very politicized around this idea of Third World Cinema and Black cinema, none of which was taught at NYU. Simultaneously, I am also dancing in a company with Syvilla Fort, who I ended up making my first documentary film about. So I was in this world of both film and photography and dance in New York, and as a result I met a lot of documentary filmmakers as well as people who were pursuing narrative film (I should say fiction), but more [people] on the documentary side. So it was not unusual to be in New York, where there are just a lot of amazing filmmakers who were interested in pushing back against the narrative that people of color basically didn't have anything to offer.

I can't remember the day or the place or the time when I met Kathy. It just seems as though she was always in my life. And as I've shared with you previously, she became my daughter's godmother. And when she was dying, she did not tell me that she was dying, but she called me one day to say, "I know you love all this experimental work, and documentary work, and these other projects, these animations that you have, but you need to be able to feed yourself and to feed my godchild. And so I want you to take my place at City College in the film program while I go on a sabbatical." And really what she was doing was setting me up to be there because, not long after, she passed away.

MP: So to go back for a moment. Julie, you said that that was 1971, 1972?

JD: Well, no, actually I didn't go back far enough. I started in '68 at the Studio Museum of Harlem, and I was studying cinematography and photography as well. And there were filmmakers all around us at the Studio Museum. Randy Abbott was our instructor, and it was an incredible time being there with artists, fine artists, and filmmakers. It was the after-school program that led to City College where I was in the film program. There was a pilot program the Leonard Davis Center. And that's how I got the internship with Chamba Productions for my summer work study.

AC: Were you at City College? When they had the Picker Institute?

JD: I was in the Picker Institute. I was in the first class of the Picker Institute.

AC: So, Michele, the Picker Institute is named after David V. Picker, who I think was like a third-generation Hollywood filmmaker; you can go and look him up. But the Picker Institute was really very important. City College has the first, or one of the first, film programs in the country.

JD: Yes.

AC: And it was started by the filmmaker Hans Richter. So Kathy eventually came in to be the director of the David V. Picker Institute, and that's what I took over when she went on sabbatical. But as you mentioned in your question, there are a lot of filmmakers who came out of that City College program. Ronald Gray. And I think Robert Gardner.

JD: Yes.

MP: So what time period—what year would this be?

AC: Well, actually, if we're talking about when Julie was there—Julie, weren't you there like the early 1970s?

JD: Yes, I got out of there in '73 and I graduated early, which was stupid because instead of getting a BFA I got just got a BA. I was so hot to trot to try to get out to LA because I had been reading about Charles Burnett and Haile Gerima making dramatic films, and I want [sic] to learn how to do that. When I graduated in February, I just went on.

MP: So one of the things that happens with Kathy Collins is that Ronald Gray is a student of hers, and he encourages her to start making features, is that right?

JD: Well, she was also very close with Bill Gunn. She did a film in his upstate New York house, *The Cruz Brothers* [1980] as well as *Losing Ground* [1982]. She was also very, very close with Phyllis Klotman at Indiana University.

MP: So a lot of Nick Forster, my coeditor's, research goes through Bill Gunn, who we mentioned earlier—can we go back to him for a moment? When did you first have an awareness of him and what he was doing?

AC: I actually met Bill through Kathy. Kathy used to have parties in her house in upstate New York and she would invite artists, intellectuals, writers, and Bill came to some of those events. And then, I think, after he's finished *Ganja and Hess* [1973], all the Black filmmakers or most of the Black filmmakers were invited to the first screening of the 35mm print, which was really breathtaking. I still remember the man running across the field; that will never leave my mind. [*Laughter*] So I met Bill through Kathy and going to parties with them.

JD: I was in LA by that time I heard about *Ganja and Hess* and saw it. Of course, I bit off a piece of *Ganja and Hess* in *Daughters of the Dust*. My homage is the tree scene with the legs hanging. I had never seen framing like that before and it was just so impressive. When he's arguing with Dr. Hess, you just see the legs hanging. That was the moment for me, it's like imprinted on my memory, like, "You know this works."

MP: So it's interesting to me that he is making *Ganja and Hess*, an obviously complicated piece that kind of defies genre, but he is working in a narrative way and later on Kathy's working in a narrative way. But, Julie, you said that LA, for you, was where some of the interesting stuff was....

JD: I wanted to learn how to make a dramatic film. I was working more in a documentary format on the East Coast. So I went out to go to UCLA and actually ended up going to AFI first, for two years. Then UCLA for four years.

MP: Back to *Ganja and Hess* for a minute. Ayo, you said it was breathtaking. Do you remember what other people's reactions were?

AC: Well, first of all, it was an invitation-only screening, so it wasn't a screening that was open to the general public. I don't remember the location, but wherever it was, the screen was very large and it was obviously very sophisticated storytelling. And I would say that because I think one of the things that happened on the East Coast side is that we became very interested in documentary filmmaking because you've got these cities that are walking cities where you see people every day. And so the injustices are very much in your face. And it's also a time when you have the remnants of a lot of uprisings. You have somebody like Gil Noble, for example, and what he was doing with *Like It Is*. He would be somebody who is very important to acknowledge.

JD: And he took classes with us at the Studio Museum. He started out as a host-slash-commentator and then he became a filmmaker.

AC: That's right. That's right. And so you see a lot of documentary work coming out of, I think, the immediacy of living in a place like New York. And you have a lot of people who have formal training and some who don't. But everybody is committed to "the people," if you will, and trying to figure out how to visually right wrongs. So when you saw Bill's *Ganja and Hess*, it was breathtaking—one, I think, because it was visually interesting to look at, and [also] because it wasn't so self-conscious in its making. I think it's one of the first films that I saw where I felt that the filmmaker had a real freedom and commitment to talk about anything he wanted to talk about in any way that he wanted to talk about it. There were no boundaries around what "Black" was, or is, or what it could be, or what it should be. And so that made it very, very exciting to see this work step outside of the space where, in some ways, we weren't allowed to operate, with a very different lens. Julie, can you tell Michele the story about when you were studying film at the Studio Museum and you wanted to make the film with the pantyhose?

JD: Yes, well, actually, that was *Four Women* [1975]. There was pushback by male documentary filmmakers on *Ganja and Hess*. I didn't go to that screening, but I heard the rumblings about it. I was not motivated at the Studio Museum of Harlem because they were looking for agitprop. And that was being supplied. There were only two females in the workshop, myself and Myumbi, another young lady from the projects where I grew up. So I wanted to do a dance film based upon Nina Simone's "Four Women," and of course people were saying, "Why would you want to do that? How does it 'save the people'?" We were at the tail end of the Black Arts Movement and people were still going by those seven lessons or rules....

AC: The Nguzo Saba.

JD: Yes. And I wasn't hitting any of those check marks or rules.... [*Laughter*] My dance film starts out in the womb of Africa, and people weren't thinking that way inside of the Studio Museum of Harlem in the film program. They would want to do, you know, the most righteous documentary ever. There were lots of docs being made about Baraka, Malcolm X, Black martial arts, and stuff like that. So, no, I didn't get to make that film with a woman emerging from a womb out of pantyhose fabric until I shot it when I was at AFI and then I edited and finished it at UCLA. And my professors at UCLA, the main one said it was "chaotic." [*Pause*] And I was thinking about this.... It was just at the museum, at the film festival at the Smithsonian, and people actually thought it was made in '78, '79, and I actually shot it in '75.... It was a long time ago, before music videos and all of that. So as a people, as a culture, we were working within the strict confines, during that time, of making films relevant to your community and not coloring outside of the lines.

AC: So I think too, Michele, two things. I would say, if you look at some of the women documentary filmmakers on the East Coast one of the ways that we were pushing back was to make films about women. The other thing that comes to mind is that if we're going to talk about filmmaking during this certain period, you're going to have to look into where the grant money was coming from, because whomever the funder is . . . the funder has expectations. So if the narrative is that Black life has been in turmoil and we've been omitted from the screen and we want our stories told and we want our heroes on the screen, then you'll get a certain amount of money popping up for documentary work. So, you know, if you wrote a narrative or a proposal for experimental filmmaking, nine chances out of ten, it would be harder to get money from a place, unless it was a place, for example, like the Jerome Foundation. So the making also represents what was available in terms of funding and how funders were also guiding the narrative.

JD: Right. And also institutions like the Studio Museum of Harlem, what they would allow to squeeze through. The Studio Museum was fully funded with film and all kinds of equipment. We started out with the spring-driven Bolex cameras. They were financed as a result of the riots that happened in Harlem in 1966. By 1968, all of a sudden, they had all this film equipment, which they later took back, by, I think, '73. Yeah. They shut down the program and never started again. So I don't know if that was part of the mission statement of what we were supposed to be doing, but most of the projects began and ended really quickly, and no one was really finished with anything. You could just shoot, shoot, shoot every weekend and go out onto the streets, 125th Street, shooting "Reclamation Site #1," shooting Kenyatta speaking on a soapbox, or Micheaux's bookstore. You would just shoot, shoot, shoot without really completing anything. And I remember, I think it must have been Madeleine Anderson, who came through the Studio Museum, and she was teaching us editing techniques and teaching us how you could make a story: a beginning, middle, and end out of anything and everything. But people really weren't allowed, they weren't given the space or the opportunity to create beyond a myopic scope.

AC: Yes. You had to save the race in some way in your film, and I would just say—you know, Michele, I'm talking about this in hindsight. You know, I sort of have the arrogance of hindsight, where I can say, "here's what was happening." But I will say that I think that that period was also very important because time after time when you turned on the television you really did not know what "the people" were thinking. So when the uprisings happened around the country in the 1960s, white journalists weren't going into what would be considered "hot" areas. They were looking for Black people to go in. So, you know, Al Santana became a camera person at one of the networks and other people got their start as well. First we didn't have any access, then there were the uprisings, and then suddenly they were looking for Black people who would go in and get the stories.

JD: Right. I remember two of the Young Lords members became newscasters. . . . Felipe Luciano. He was one of the "Last Poets." He became an "on-camera" news reporter. And Pablo Yoruba Guzman.

AC: That's right. Yes, that's right. So it's not that it wasn't important. It's really just explaining what the environment was like. And quite frankly, you know, explaining it in hindsight. It is also a time when you have Black people really wanting to create and shape things for themselves. So if you lived in New York, for example, and it's December during the time of Kwanzaa, everybody is in their garb. It was a time when people were still trying to figure a lot of things out. So it did fit very much on top of what was happening in the world of fiction, which, in terms of storytelling, was much broader and more interesting. But that kind of work was not really being pulled into filmmaking easily and readily.

JD: Remember the movie *Will* [1981]? Was that Jessie Maple?

AC: That was Jessie Maple.

MP: Talk to me about her.

AC: So I did bring her to Spelman. We gave her an award a few years ago. Jessie is considered the first African American woman cameraperson, and she has a book that she self-published, *How to Become a Union Camerawoman*. She talks about how the union members who were giving her the test—because you've got to be able to take apart a camera and put it back together and do other things, and these are 35mm cameras—would hide parts. Basically, they sabotaged her, and she ended up suing and won.

JD: Oh wow, I didn't know that whole story. I remember seeing *Will* projected at a private screening.

AC: Well, Jessie and her husband Leroy have made films together for a long time. They've made several features. They also purchased a brownstone in Harlem that became the place to go see Black independent film.

MP: I did read about that. Was she someone you knew of? Was she connected to this group?

JD: She was older than we are, right?

AC: Yeah. Jessie's a little older than us. She was kind of in the circle and not in the circle simultaneously. So when I say that, I'm talking about from an exhibition and distribution standpoint. Her films would sometimes be exhibited as part of the Black cinema circle. And then she'd be brought out as "one of the first of the Black women feature filmmakers," and then she'd disappear for a while. But she and Leroy had a long history in Black independent cinema in terms of making and exhibition and quite frankly, they stay on the road exhibiting her films.

MP: What other figures from this moment are important in some way that we should be including in this larger narrative?

AC: I would say Monica Freeman.

JD: Yes, yes.

AC: Monica is somebody who really took me around and under her wing for a while, and she was friends with Betty Blayton Taylor (a founding member of the Studio Museum of Harlem), who was an artist that had a building up in Harlem where the downstairs was devoted to teaching art. And somehow I met Betty and Monica there. But Monica knew a number of the filmmakers. I think she was the person who introduced me to Roy Campanella Jr., who was in New York at the time. And she did a film on Valerie Maynard, the sculptor.

JD: Yes.

MP: Ayoka, go back for a minute. So you went to NYU, and at what point do you become faculty at City College?

AC: So I become faculty at City College in 1984. I think I started as an adjunct in '84 and then by '86 I'm in a tenure-track position. So I went from NYU and I still hung out with Third World Newsreel for a while and then I decided to go to graduate school and I went to Columbia University Teachers College. And at that time I was very interested in art and education. I had this idea of taking Black and brown children around the world and exposing them to the arts—all forms of the arts, you know, film, dance, theater, music—as a way to think about life differently than what I thought was being taught in higher education. So I did my graduate work there. I think shortly thereafter I must have gone to work for the Black Filmmaker Foundation, which was a place that was very instrumental in the distribution and exhibition of Black independent cinema.

JD: Right. And that's how we met.

AC: Yes. And so a lot of us know each other from the conference that the foundation organized in New York. In fact, it was the first time that a lot of Black filmmakers from the East Coast and West Coast and in between actually met each other. So Julie and I have known each other since that conference. [*Laughter*]

JD: Since 1977.

AC: Yes.

MP: And at the time, who was the director, was it one of the Hudlins?

AC: Yes, Warrington Hudlin was.

MP: What would you want people to know about how this time shaped you and your work?

JD: It was just an exciting time. It was like learning things that I'd never even considered. Every day was something new, whether it was technical [or] about foreign film; it was like a magical time. And you'd be surrounded by all the old heads. And one of the things with Kathy, I remember that she was thirty years old and she looked really great. I remember thinking, "My God, she's thirty and she looks so good." And she spoke fluent French and she had studied at the Sorbonne in France, and I was starstruck having just come out of the Queensbridge Projects in Long Island City and I'd never even been on an airplane in my life. And here is this beautiful young woman with a baby who knows how to edit and speaks French if she chooses to. And they were vegetarians and that was another new concept. Everything was new, and everything was wonderful.

AC: So I think, for me, it was a very magical time. It was a time when, regardless of what genre you were working in, you were experimenting because you really didn't know. You were really trying to figure it out. *Hair Piece* [1985] is me figuring out animation. But with Kathy, one of the things that was so exciting to me about her is she could be extremely critical. She had a razor-sharp tongue, whether she was speaking French or English. And she could be—let's just say, she could be very, very strong in her opinion. Kathy was one of the first people that I ever heard be critical of the work of Toni Morrison and some of the other women writers. She was very rooted in the fact . . . I mean, we never talked about science fiction or alternate realities. But she was very clear that she did not like, for example, to see Black characters—for example, in one of Morrison's books there is a character that is born without a navel, but Kathy didn't like these presentations of Black people that put them in a position where they were not fully human. And she was so critical of writers who did that, because she felt that people already saw us as not being human and that it was simply adding to that narrative. And

I remember we were sitting down having a talk once and I was just so surprised, because the idea of being critical—and you know, I'm like a kid—but the idea of being critical of these people who would become the warriors not only in their specific arts field, but the warriors for Black people. It's like, "Oh, you mean you can criticize these people?" [*Laughter*] It was quite an eye-opener.

But to answer your question, for me, I've never been wedded to a genre. I've been wedded to what's on my mind, what's in my heart, and what is upsetting me. And then trying to find out some answers as I work. And so after I made my first documentary, I didn't go back to documentary work for a very long time because I thought it was too confining. My next work was animation, and it gave me, in part, a form of control. Control over every single frame and also control over my own time. And after that I just began to explore other things. So I've never been wedded. It's like I'm more wedded to my own curiosity than I am to a specific genre.

JD: And that's a great way of putting it, you know, discovering the wonder of controlling worlds within the frame. Yeah, that's it. That's the thing.

MP: Do you see this time as a movement? How would you characterize it?

AC: I definitely think it is, but I don't think that the people who were doing the work were thinking about it like that. I think we were just trying to figure it out—where is the money going to come from, where are the people going to come from, whose house can I use, who has the wardrobe that I need, who has an antique car. I mean, you're trying to figure it out, but you're not thinking of a conscious movement where you have a manifesto and, you know, you're moving forward. Perhaps some people did; I was not part of that. So I would say, Michele, that as a writer and a researcher, this is one of the things that writers and researchers do. They find something and then they pee all over it. And part of that is labeling. But there are enough people (in this time) who made really important work. By the way, a lot of the work the museums are now just starting to buy because they are looking in their collections and seeing that there is a big gap. And so now they're starting to reach out to Black filmmakers, saying, "Do you have a print?" "Can we buy?" And some people know where their films are, and some people don't. But it was definitely a very important time.

While Dash moved on to LA to attend the AFI and UCLA and began working with the now famous collective of Black filmmakers termed the LA Rebellion, Chenzira remained in New York through the 1980s and 1990s as a professor at City College, where she cofounded the MFA program in media arts production in 1996. In recent years, both women make Atlanta their home and have directed episodes of the TV southern drama/phenomenon *Queen Sugar* helmed by Ava DuVernay and Oprah Winfrey. Chenzira is now the division chair for the arts and chair of the Department of Art and Visual Culture at Spelman, where Dash was recently named a Spelman College Distinguished Professor in the Arts. Since the early years in New York, both women continue making films and have left powerful footprints around the world.

Michele Prettyman (formerly Michele Prettyman Beverly) is assistant professor of media studies at Mercer University and a scholar of film, media, and African American visual culture. Her current research explores the spiritual and metaphysical possibilities of Blackness, the work of Kathleen Collins and Black independent cinema, hip-hop and visual culture, and the visual culture of the South. Her work has appeared in *Black Camera* and *Callaloo*, and she contributes an essay in the anthology *The "Lemonade" Reader*. She is also a contributor and advisory board member for *liquid blackness*, a research project on Blackness and aesthetics.

An Interview with Julie Dash

Carina del Valle Schorske / 2020

From *The Believer*, no. 133 (December 1, 2020). Reprinted by permission.

I spoke with the legendary director Julie Dash by phone in March 2020, during her spring break from teaching at Spelman College, when both of us were staying home after events we'd planned to travel for were canceled. We were just cresting the wave of coronavirus rumors, a breath before the devastating flood of the global pandemic. I'd forgotten—since I so rarely speak on the phone—how the human voice, keenly heeded, archives its own history: Dash, sixty-eight, grew up in the Queensbridge Projects in Long Island City (where Nas was raised too), and her voice is warm and forceful, full of New York music. But there are other musics layered underneath. Every summer when she was young, Dash would visit her father's family in Charleston, South Carolina, and hear relatives speaking Gullah dialects without knowing that was what she was hearing. "Nobody explained it to me," she said. "I found out on my own."

Dash has a genius for research, and for her, confusion is not an impediment but a productive point of departure, a spiritual practice, and a source of creative excitement. In an early interview, she rhapsodized about her first adolescent encounter with film cameras, in a workshop for high school students at the Studio Museum in Harlem: "All this equipment, and I was allowed to touch it, play with it, and be confused by it—and then make the decision to master it." Dash would continue to explore new territory, from the documentary techniques that dominated New York filmmaking in the 1970s to the narrative and lyrical techniques she learned at the American Film Institute, in communion with Russian montagists, Third World Cinema filmmakers, and her peers in the movement that came to be known as the LA Rebellion.

Dash's early short films testify to the restless range of her imagination: *Four Women* (1975) is a choreopoem set to Nina Simone's melancholic ode of the same name; *Diary of an African Nun* (1977) is an adaptation of Alice Walker's short story about a woman wrestling with colonial religion; and *Illusions* (1982) tells the story of a white-passing Black professional attempting a Hollywood career behind the camera in the 1940s. Each film seems to follow the form of the protagonist's psyche.

Daughters of the Dust (1991), Julie Dash's first and only theatrical feature film to date, also seems to unfold like a dream from the minds of the women who populate it. The film's immersive intensity is evidence of the mastery she acquired in her medium through her willingness to be guided by the unknown. In *Daughters*, multiple generations of the Gullah Geechee Peazant family are poised on the brink of the Great Migration, arguing about what to keep and what to leave behind from their complex syncretic culture. Dash's long takes show how history is made through the mundane rapture of repetition—ring dances on the shoreline and green wheels of okra sliced into a cooking pot.

Daughters of the Dust made Julie Dash the first Black American woman director to have a general theatrical release in the United States, and in 2004, *Daughters* was included in the National Film Registry at the Library of Congress. In 2016, the Cohen Media Group restored and released a twenty-fifth-anniversary edition of the film to wide acclaim, allowing new audiences to make the connection between *Daughters* and the swampy lyricism of Beyoncé's Black womanist utopias in *Lemonade*. Like the Unborn Child that narrates the film, *Daughters* teaches us a new relationship to legacy: a dream of the future, disguised as a ghost of the past. If Dash has supreme patience for what she doesn't yet know, she is rightly less patient with an industry, and a public, that can't see the value in being decentered: racially, historically, or aesthetically.

After many years directing music videos and commercials, Dash helmed features for television, including *Incognito* (1999), *Funny Valentines* (1999), *Love Song* (2000), and *The Rosa Parks Story* (2002). Presently, she is at work on a much-anticipated biopic of Angela Davis, forthcoming from Lionsgate. But even when working to represent iconic figures like Davis or Rosa Parks, Dash is always alive to what remains misunderstood, cryptic, and hidden in plain sight about the lives of Black women. This conversation finds her back at the library, schooling us in the finer points of decolonial communism, and listening hard for the low tones in rap ciphers and the walkie-talkies of Navajo Code Talkers.

—Carina del Valle Schorske

I. No Explanation Necessary

The Believer: I once heard Stephanie Smallwood say she views Toni Morrison as a colleague, a fellow historian of slavery. I notice that at the end of your short film *Illusions*, Mignon, your protagonist, says, "Your scissors and your paste methods have eliminated my participation in the history of this country, and the influence of that screen cannot be overestimated!" As a filmmaker who's worked on a number of so-called period pieces, from *Illusions* through *The Rosa Parks Story*, how do you view your own position in relation to historians?

Julie Dash: When I think about it, I don't have an original thought within me. History is all there: I just dig it up, unearth it, make it available. It's in the books; it's in the journals and oral histories from primary sources. It's in the film clips from the turpentine camps in Zora Neale Hurston's early quote-unquote "documentary films." It's all there: everything that's in *Illusions* and also in *Daughters*. I followed the bread crumbs and made those stories visual from the point of view of a Black woman.

BLVR: You've said you might've been interested in working as an anthropologist if you hadn't gotten involved in filmmaking.

JD: Yes. Absolutely. That interest comes from combining research with the ethnographic films we had to make at UCLA. And then it just starts merging. I learned that Zora Neale Hurston was an anthropologist alongside Margaret Mead and Ruth Benedict and Franz Boas—Boas was their teacher, you know—so I was like, "Oh, man, this is interesting." Research is cheaper than film: you could spend years in the library! I still love the library. I was so sad when they moved the UCLA research materials off campus. You have to put in an order for a book, you know: send it over in two days. I like just browsing the stacks. You never know what you're going to find.

BLVR: There's an improvisational element that you can't take away, really.

JD: Right? And that's how I found out about the *Wanderer* [a slave ship—one of the last—that landed at Jekyll Island, Georgia, in 1858]. There was an ancient catalog of late-nineteenth-century magazines from New York, and that's where I got that little snippet from [for *Daughters of the Dust*], because, of course, all of this was before Google. That's why we hung out in the libraries.

And there was a secret underground service run by research librarians—I believe it was called Hoot Owl. I believe it may have been in San Francisco or something like that. You know, that was during the early days of the internet, and the *Whole Earth Catalog*—it was this big book that had everything you could think of.

I don't remember where I got the number [for Hoot Owl] from, but I remember being told, "Do not abuse it. You will thank them. And you will not call with every little question in the world." How did I remember that? I mean, this is from the 1970s, the Hoot Owl number!

BLVR: Both Hoot Owl and the *Whole Earth Catalog* seem to have a mystical quality—the sacredness of knowledge.

JD: Exactly. It was like some secret society thing.

BLVR: Well, it's important to archive all of this—the changes in research methods. I've been thinking about your novel sequel to *Daughters of the Dust*. Your protagonist, Amelia, is working toward her degree in anthropology and returns to her mother's home island to conduct fieldwork.

JD: Funny you should mention that novel, because I just decided that if I could ever find my book contracts—I think they're in storage in Los Angeles—I'd like to have it made into an audiobook. I've been listening to Toni Morrison's audiobooks at night to help me go to sleep.

BLVR: The ultimate human music.

JD: Exactly. It's her voice and it just lulls you to sleep. I'm listening to *Song of Solomon*, and she's talking about Milkman and Guitar. I read those books so long ago, I didn't realize how great they were.

BLVR: The density of her novels reminds me of the density of *Daughters*, how any given shot is so layered. You're going to catch—and miss—something new every time.

JD: I mean, it's all fresh and new, even with the reread, because I'm a whole different person.

BLVR: Back to Amelia: It's hard for me not to see her as a kind of alter ego for you. First of all, she's a New Yorker, and she's got her little camera. . . .

JD: I thought you were going to say—

BLVR: That Amelia is Zora?

JD: Yeah, that's why it's set during the Harlem Renaissance—but it doesn't take place in Harlem. We had to find out the real details, like who had fellowships back then? Where could you study anthropology? Okay, Brooklyn College—so actually, the Amelia character was reversed-engineered to be like Zora Neale Hurston, and then I had to find out what kind of camera she would have had. But you're right: I'm in there, too, with my own Gullah Geechee thing. Because we'd go down there [to Charleston], and if we asked our family a direct question, we wouldn't get an answer—we'd get a long story that maybe had something to do with the answer. Everything was hidden. Camouflaged. But that's because they were indoctrinated not to explain stuff—or speak in the Gullah dialect—because they were considered the lowest of the low. I don't know if you know this or not, but the little girl who played the Unborn Child in *Daughters of the Dust*? I didn't use her voice to narrate the character, because her mother had told her, "Never let anyone hear your dialect." And so she had the perfect look, but she would not speak to me out loud. You know the other little girl in the film, with the hairstyle that we call "trees"? Who's on the beach all the time? We brought her up to Atlanta to do the final narration. She had the Gullah dialect and was not ashamed to speak it.

BLVR: That's heavy. That's like the reverse plot of *Illusions*, where Esther, a Black performer, is hired to sing for the white actress on screen in a musical number.

JD: Yes.

BLVR: Beyond your own novel, I know you've always looked to literature for inspiration, even when you're not directly adapting something like Alice Walker's short story "Diary of an African Nun," which you did in 1977. You were just talking about Morrison. I'm curious to know what Black women writers, especially of your generation, have taught you, and what you've taken into your work from those sources.

JD: Okay. So what I learned from writers like Paule Marshall, Toni Cade Bambara, and Alice Walker is that there's an audience for writing from your heart. Some things don't have to be explained, because we already know them. And that flies directly in the face of the advice you get when you're writing for commercial films. Because people are so used to being spoon-fed: you have to explain every single thing to them, otherwise they're angry. And my response to that has always been, "Well, you have five hundred different television stations. Just go watch television, where you know what's gonna happen before the opening credits are rolling. You can tell what's going to happen by the music."

I love the work of those ladies because I love foreign films. I like to have a new experience. Like when I was at the Studio Museum in Harlem early on, watching, you know, the films of [François] Truffaut, [Yasujirō] Ozu, Sergei M. Eisenstein, Akira Kurosawa, and Satyajit Ray, I didn't know what was gonna happen next. I had to keep my eyes on the screen and keep reading the subtitles, and go, like, "Oh, I get it. Ohhhhh." And it was a real complete experience, as opposed to going into the theater, watching a commercial film, sitting there, and by the time you're in the parking lot looking for your car, you can't remember what the film was about.

BLVR: Before you moved to LA, I know you started out making documentaries in New York, but got frustrated with the form because your family never wanted to come downtown to your screenings unless it was a narrative feature. What do you think your family was hungry for that documentaries couldn't or weren't offering them?

JD: Well, they were more familiar with the "voice of God" type of documentary: *And here we have the river, and it flows* . . . you know? The form wasn't allowing people to speak for themselves. Documentaries are so compelling now. I mean, they're really meshing with dramas, the way they're being edited.

BLVR: You've cited the Cuban filmmaker Sara Gómez—who had a syncretic approach to documentary and narrative techniques—as an early influence.

JD: Do you know what's so interesting? I saw Sara's face, and I saw stills from her productions. I read about her, and then the next thing I knew, she was deceased. But that was before DVDs and YouTube. If you wanted to see someone's film, you had to see it projected on 16mm or 35mm. So I just saw stills from her productions, and photographs of her directing, behind the camera. I remember she had a short-cropped Afro and big eyes and I just was like, "Oh my god, she's directing movies!" That was enough for me. She was my inspiration when I was at the Studio Museum in Harlem and early on at UCLA: We knew she existed. Therefore, I could exist. She mattered so much. I didn't get to see her films until maybe thirty years later, and the Spanish was not subtitled yet. I saw a pirated version of *De cierta manera*. I think someone else finished editing it for her. I am not sure what she died of. It wasn't, like, diabetes—

BLVR: It was asthma.

JD: Asthma?

BLVR: Yeah, she had a fatal asthma attack. Pretty tragic and probably preventable.

JD: Yes. That's something.

II. Solar Power, Death Rays, and Fax Machines

BLVR: Now that there are multiple generations of Black filmmakers at work in the industry, I'm wondering what the opportunities for exchanges with younger filmmakers have meant for you.

JD: Well, they have their own voices. As artists, we want to, say, reimagine or redefine something. So the younger filmmakers have their particular things they want to speak to, and we have ours, and that doesn't mean there's a conflict between us. Nothing is in conflict at all. I know a lot of them are looking at Afrofuturism. I was being interviewed by a young documentary filmmaker, and she asked me if I had heard about it. I said, "Well, actually, *Daughters of the Dust* is an Afrofuturist film." And she said, "Oh, I never thought of it that way." I said, "Yeah, like the Unborn Child comes forward as a character from her mother's womb." That's speculative fiction.

BLVR: And it's the technology too. Mr. Snead comes with all these newfangled portable cameras that seem to become ritual objects in the Sea Island context, capable of perceiving unseen futures—

JD: Yes! And the kaleidoscope he brings.... So these are conversations that we need to continue having. Afrofuturism is not the *word*. The *phrase* might be something new, but the exploration has been going on since the 1930s with the solar power and death rays and fax machines in George Schuyler's novel *Black Empire*, his satire of Marcus Garvey's movement.

BLVR: Even Du Bois has Afrofuturist writing, like his short story "The Comet," from the early twentieth century.

JD: Some new issues are front and center now. Identity has always been up front, you know. But LGBTQ issues, and sexual harassment with #MeToo—all of that is very *now*. Whereas for us, it was more about the diaspora, you know, being connected, being part of a continuum of activity—of music and science and everything that came about in the African diaspora. Less about the individual, less about the self, and more about collective memories, collective history. I'm not saying one is better than the other. It's just the way it panned out.

BLVR: Yeah, that's interesting. I mean, I do see *Moonlight* as a very diasporic and collective film, even though it's also putting a queer love story at the center. Like, there's that amazing moment at the beginning when Little is sitting with Juan at the beach and Little asks Juan where he's from. And he says, "Cuba," and the kid looks really surprised. And Juan says, "There are Black people everywhere."

JD: Yeah. *Moonlight* was amazing on so many levels because it had to do with the Caribbean diaspora; it had to do with cooking as healing, with having a meal together; it had to do with just . . . Black love—Black *male* love; and it had to do with overcoming. And so many things didn't turn out the way they normally do in films like that. I was watching it at the London Film Festival, and I was on the edge of my seat, because I was saying, "Oh god, is there going to be a drone hit on the two of them in the restaurant?" I mean, usually with Hollywood films, queer Black love just doesn't end well. And when the drone hit never came, I was very pleased. I was so pleased that I was actually stunned, sitting in my seat. I was like, "I'm emotionally worn-out."

BLVR: I want to ask you a few questions about technique and process. I once heard you say you fell in love with film more for the mechanics than the art of it, at first. Is it still a tactile thrill to work with film now that the tools have changed and so much of filmmaking is digital?

JD: It's not quite the same. It started to change once I became a member of DGA, the Director's Guild [of America]: then I could no longer edit my films; I had to use a union editor. So I retreated from that, and now it's more about the writing and creating and reimagining and reframing, but still . . . you're absolutely right. It was the tactile that drew me in. You know, I was in high school, and we were in competition with boys all the time—and the boys was all, "You can't load this camera, you can't do this, you can't do that." And it was like, "Ohhh, let me show you how I can."

I'm teaching now. I have a chaired position at Spelman College, and so I'm able to express my mechanical imagination through my class, focusing on the composition of the frame—constantly going over imagery and lighting and stuff like that. I do miss having filmstrips around my neck, editing. But I love the fact that now you can have so many alternate edits of your work—I mean, that cannot be denied. We're using Premiere Pro. Editing with digital files is faster, better, cleaner, less expensive, all of that. But slicing film together—that was something else, man. You know, we had marks on our arms all the time from the Rivas 35mm splicer. We were all cut up because of the single-edge razor attached to it.

BLVR: When you're first starting to kind of get your head in a film, is there an element of it that usually comes first for you? Like a color palette, or . . .

JD: I read the script to see if it's resonating with me. I go back and read it again and start visualizing things, and then I start creating look-books or decks, inspiration boards, which also may include a color palette. But I want to be fluid with it because it's one thing to create something on your desktop and then, on location, it just doesn't work. You have to be willing to adjust. I'm pulling images from all over the world for my decks. I don't know how I'm going to use the images or even *if* I'm going to use them, but it's something to start from.

BLVR: So it starts sort of as an associative collage.

JD: You have the right words for it. Yeah, associative collage.

BLVR: You've talked before about being guided by a womanist vision in your filmmaking. And I'm wondering if you've thought kind of explicitly about what defines a womanist aesthetic for you in terms of style and sensibility.

JD: Well, I know for sure that people have said that in *Daughters*—in most of my films—I have a different type of gaze for Black people, for Black women and children. In most films, they do not go as close up as I go with the camera, for example, braiding women's hair. I don't pull away. I go closer because I'm used to seeing that, so I'm not doing the *National Geographic* thing—shooting *those people* from a distance. And there are other subtle elements that are just always there that I want to show. Composing shots and building scenes for the visual language of film is kind of like writing poetry with images: You want to be able to say something using the words that everyone knows, but the *phrasing* is different.

III. Come by Here

BLVR: Can you talk about some of the projects you have going on right now?

JD: Absolutely. I have my documentary that I've been working on, and I can't wait till school is out so I can finish shooting it. The film's about Vertamae Smart-Grosvenor—*Travel Notes of a Geechee Girl*. She was a culinary anthropologist.

BLVR: It seems like she did a whole range of things in her life. That's what it's like when you have to keep moving and trying different industries that may or may not be ready for your work. You have to be creative about how you express yourself.

JD: Yeah, she lived the artist's life. She knew just about everyone, from Jackie Onassis to Larry Neal, playwrights and politicians—there's a picture of her in Jimmy Carter's Oval Office. Just unbelievable. But that's the life of a culinary anthropologist who's also a chef, you know, so she would cook for various people, and they would introduce her to others: We have footage of her in the kitchen at Muhammad Ali's training camp. David Bowie, she knew. We connected on *Daughters of the Dust* when I asked her to be in it, because I knew she was from the region and she spoke the Gullah language. And she just reminded me of a relative, but a relative that would finally tell the truth about what went on in Gullah Geechee culture. Then I'd take the information back to my own family and they'd say, "Oh yeah, we know that." Well, why didn't you tell me? My grandmother would say something to me in Gullah, and I'd be like, "Say what?" And then she'd just wave her hand at me like, *You don't get it*. It was all a big tease.

BLVR: Can you understand Gullah better now?

JD: There's several layers to it. I can understand someone with a heavy Gullah Geechee accent, but when they go right into it, it sounds like complete non-English, like Nigerian. When we were down there shooting on St. Helena Island, the actors mentioned it too: They would go into a 7-Eleven and maybe there'd be two guys talking at the counter, and they saw we weren't from the region by the way our eyes would glaze over. Then they'd switch up. Code switching. Everything is camouflaged—it's a survival technique.

BLVR: That reminds me of the way some people have responded to *Daughters of the Dust*—like you have a film dialect they can't understand. Of course, not all your films have that same opacity. I'm wondering how you carry that love or interest in opacity to other projects that are more straightforward in a narrative sense.

JD: That's why I'm doing *Travel Notes of a Geechee Girl*—Vertamae uses camouflaging wonderfully. And then finding out what it all means, finding out that there's so much of the Gullah Geechee dialect in everyday English language, almost a thousand words. Like everyone knows what *goobers* means—you know, the peanuts they sell at movie theaters. *Goobers* is a Gullah word derived from the West African *nguba*, meaning "peanut." And whenever anyone goes on a camping trip with the Girl Scouts, they're singing "Kumbayah," right? That means "Come by here." That was what the Gullah slave people used to sing around the campfire. It was all: *Dear God, come by, hear me, come and get me up out of this*, and it just came off as "kum ba yah." Now, even in corporate America, people say, *Well, we're not going to have a kumbayah moment here*. So now it just means things are warm and fuzzy—you know, singing together. The real meaning's gone missing—whitewashed, absorbed into mainstream America, and lost to African American history.

BLVR: That's so interesting. I've been trying to do a little research on the Indigenous languages of the Caribbean, and again, there are so many words that are part of our collective American vocabulary: *canoe, hurricane*. And it's like, of course! Our language is made by the people who've lived here, who've moved through here. Despite it all.

JD: Yeah. *Barbecue*, too, right? *Barbacoa*, or something like that. It comes from *barbacoa*.

BLVR: I know you've been working on the Vertamae project for a long time, but I'm wondering what it's like to return to the documentary form after working in the narrative form for the majority of your career.

JD: It's such a sweet relief. I just need time to do it. I really, really enjoy it because we can do what we like. Unlike with the studio films—they're so concerned that people won't understand. For instance, with the Angela Davis biopic: She eventually joined the Communist Party, but not the Communist Party USA. She joined a *faction* of the Communist Party called the Che-Lumumba Club. Now, Americans don't even know that there were factions of the Communist Party—it's all the same to them. The media promotes an image of a sickle and hammer, and that's all we really know about it. So if you're going to talk about the Che-Lumumba Club in relation to a feature film about Angela Davis, then you have to know who Patrice Lumumba was! And then you also have to know who Che Guevara was in the world at that time. Angela Davis recognized their importance.

BLVR: But the result is a kind of lie.

JD: It's a lie, yeah, because the sickle-and-hammer people on the East Coast actually didn't acknowledge the Che-Lumumba Club until Angela Davis was on trial for her life, and they realized she would be great publicity for the Communist Party. And then they jumped in wholeheartedly to support her defense. So many things have to be made clear.

BLVR: Absolutely. And so, by contrast, is the relief of working on the documentary film more about working *independently* than it is about preferring the documentary genre?

JD: Exactly. It's a minefield.

BLVR: Beyond these negotiations, what has the research process for the Angela Davis film been like? Is it based on her autobiography?

JD: It's based upon the autobiography, yes. And she's still alive. So I'm able to sit with her and talk with her. She's been active in so many places. She was active in France. She was active in Germany. She's talked about life in Birmingham, growing up on Dynamite Hill, where the bombs were going off constantly. We only have two hours in which to tell the story, so that's the challenge. She's very open—you know, her major, before she switched to philosophy, was Romance languages, French literature. So she understands that there will be dramatic scenes to help move the story forward.

IV. The Joy

BLVR: It seems you've always been embedded in a community of really close creative relationships: writers like bell hooks, Angela Davis, and Toni Cade Bambara (may she rest in peace); dancers like Martina Young, the choreographer and star of *Four Women*; actors like Barbara O; fellow filmmakers like Arthur Jafa—

JD: Right, or production designers like Kerry James Marshall, who brought so much to the visual style and structure of *Daughters of the Dust*. I mean, he was just making stuff in his workshop. He had a whole wall of images that he pulled, and we'd go through them. We were wondering, what did the indigo plantations look like? Because there are no photographs from the Sea Islands. And so he suggested we look for images of the places where they're still processing indigo in West Africa, and we recreated those ancient types of mounds. Everything had to be built. Like, the chair that Nana Peazant was going to be sitting in had to be totally organic. Michael Kelly Williams [the film's art director] took an old chair that he had started to repair and created this *Game of Thrones*–type thing, but with branches and twigs. And then Kerry and Michael built the ship's figurehead floating in the muck and mire. All the paddles we used when they were going upriver: He carved all those out himself. Everything was created because we couldn't just get props from a props shop—it was all based upon the collective memories of the people living on those islands. So we had all of West Africa to think about in terms of artifacts, because the people came from various ethnic tribes in West Africa, right?

BLVR: It's almost like a ritual: the film set itself, the work of conjuring those objects.

JD: Absolutely. Absolutely.

BLVR: Where do those objects live now? Do you have any of the objects that were made on set?

JD: No, we were so broke afterward that everything that was put in storage was auctioned, or it's still down there. We gave the house that was built to one of the actors in the film. He probably used it as a shed on his property. Because it's built old-style, you know?

BLVR: Have you maintained a relationship to the Sea Islands over the years?

JD: Well, yeah—I go down every couple of months because my uncle is in Charleston; he has the homestead down there. And all the family's buried there. Between Charleston and [Johns] Island. We were shooting on Hunting Island, and we'd go do our banking on the mainland. Now that place looks like, I don't know, Calabasas [in California]. It has its own outdoor mall, the whole nine yards, you know? There's a lot of talk about that because they're pressuring people to give up their property down there: It's all being lost to taxes or to "family" just appearing. It's all this million-dollar beachfront property that was unmanageable back in the 1920s—no one wanted to be down there, because they didn't have air conditioning. Swampy, mosquitoes. But now they're building hotels and condos. They changed city laws so your house has to be elevated a certain number of feet, because it's low country, and for a lot of folks, sitting your house up on cinder blocks is just about the best you can do. But if it's not elevated *properly*, they take your property. Or if your relatives migrate up to New York or Philadelphia, if the old people die and the land isn't *tended* for a certain number of years, they just take it. They have all kinds of scams.

BLVR: It's the same strategy, really, all around the world. This sounds like a direct description of what's going on in Puerto Rico right now. Given all this worsening exploitation, what's keeping you inspired these days?

JD: My work: I have several film projects in various stages of development. Also, I'm interested in how people are thinking about everyday objects in the world and how to use and reuse them in different ways. One thing I noticed that's really picked up: You can find bottle trees online and order one from Amazon. We had Kerry James Marshall make our bottle trees based upon the deep research we did in the Sea Islands. And now it's part of the culture to have a bottle tree with blue bottles in your backyard. When you read around online, they'll say, "Oh yeah, bottle trees, they originated in Texas and this and that." Oh my god. Okay. It's been, like, thirty years, almost thirty years since *Daughters*, and now you can get a little bottle tree to put in your window. I laughed when I saw it on Amazon.

BLVR: Wow. You have to laugh to keep from crying.

JD: Get you a little bottle tree! I'm on spring break all week, just writing other Afrofuturistic things. . . .

BLVR: What kinds of Afrofuturistic things?

JD: Well, I have a project called *Cypher* that I've been working on for years, about an encryption specialist.

BLVR: Oh yeah! Is this the one that used to be called *Digital Diva*?

JD: Yes, it is. Yes, it is. Oh my god, you do know stuff.

BLVR: I try to do my homework! Encryption is such a theme in this conversation, because we were talking about—

JD: The code switching and camouflaging. Yeah. It's a natural progression to go toward encryption. And the ciphers used in hip-hop.

BLVR: At the beginning of *Illusions*, doesn't Mignon pitch an idea for a film about the Navajo Code Talkers, who developed a combat code language in World War II?

JD: You know, I came upon footage of the Navajo Code Talkers while doing research for something else in the 1980s. And it was like, *what*? They never taught us this in school. Eventually they made a Hollywood movie about it where a Code Talker had to be sacrificed. That's the white male gaze on things—like he was so valuable they were gonna put a bullet in his head if they thought he was about to be captured. What kind of shit is that? "We love you. You hold the magic potion. You hold the formula, so you may have to die if you share it with anyone other than us." Colonialism. A little bit of that is in *Cypher*, flashbacks about the Code Talkers. People are saying, "But, JD, don't you think people will be confused?" I'm like, "No."

BLVR: And also, isn't it okay for people to be confused? Some people don't know. And even if some people are confused because they don't know, they can learn. Why would you want to give up the potential to inspire somebody to learn?

JD: What's the joy?

Without Living in the Folds of Our Wounds: A Conversation with Julie Dash

A. E. Hunt / 2020

From *The Notebook* (June 2020). Reprinted by permission.

Nearly thirty years ago, *Daughters of the Dust* ruptured the fixed line of film history. It was the first film directed by a Black woman to see theatrical distribution in the United States. It fit neither the Black history Hollywood co-opted, nor the modern Black story they allowed (urban peril). *Daughters of the Dust* portrayed a day in the life of the Gullah Geechee community off the coast of South Carolina through their circular perception of time, a past, present, and future that run concurrently. Nana Peazant, the old matriarch, urges her successors to cling to their roots, to hang on to her, as each body holds both "the last of the old and the first of the new." The younger generations plan to run up the river north, leaving behind Ibo Landing, home to centuries of their ancestors. An unborn child narrates from the future and dawdles through the present day, 1902, while Nana clutches the ground by the gravestones.

Writer-director Julie Dash does not frame the dispersion of the Gullah community as purely tragic or Nana's old ways as purely outmoded. Their differences are not so plain that either side doesn't understand and still appreciate the other. Nana is exhausted by the new ways pervading the old, but she accepts it as hard, inevitable, and beautiful. The divide is never inflated to the kind of conflict often perpetuated in movies. *Daughters of the Dust* is inimitable, like all things that rupture a fated course. It has not been replicated to this day.

Dash is one of the preeminent figures of the LA Rebellion, the Black anti-Hollywood movement that came to fruition at UCLA film school between the 1960s and '80s. Since her first short films (the venerable *Diary of an African Nun, Relatives, Illusions,* et cetera), Dash has continued her fight to widen the scope of Black film in an industry that spends itself to narrow it. No one would fund the next Julie Dash feature film; executives were scared by what they didn't know from record to be lucrative. There was no reference for anything Dash proposed, nothing to mollify their cowardice; so they retreated to the racist track record at the industry's base. But Dash didn't relent. She directed the TV movies *Funny Valentines, Incognito, Love Song,* and *The Rosa Parks Story*; a $1.5 million immersive film exhibit, *Brothers of the Borderland*, commissioned by the National Underground Railroad Freedom Center; short films; documentaries; and commercials. Today, she's finally in development on her second feature film, an Angela Davis biopic, fighting the same fight to make it right.

On Juneteenth, Julie Dash talked to us about the racist, capitalistic, and ineffectual model of the film industry that tries to hold her down, about how perceptions of her seminal work *Daughters of the Dust* evolved over time, and her hopes for reform going forward.

Notebook: Are you doing anything for Juneteenth?

Julie Dash: Not in the daytime, but I'm doin' somethin' for the West Coast, so that doesn't happen until later tonight because of the time change. I'm doing a film program. So tell me a little about what you're doing.

Notebook: There've been so many "Best Black Films to Watch Now" lists, but little interest in reaching out to hear from the filmmakers on that list, so that's what I'm doing.

Dash: I do understand. "This is my favorite. This is my favorite." It's all so subjective. It's lovely, but. . . . [*Laughs*] If I were to make a favorite list, it'd be all foreign films, even today. [*Laughs*] But let me not go there on Juneteenth.

Notebook: Just four years ago you said, after watching some films on TV for Black History month, that a lot of popular Black films were still repeating that same "Jane Pittman" ending. Do you still see that today?

Dash: [*Laughs*] Did I say that? Sounds like me. But not with Ava DuVernay's films, no. I think everything's changing since the murder of George Floyd. I think Hollywood is taken aback and they're saying, "Oh we didn't know, we didn't know!" That's what I've been telling you! All the memos I've been sending! [*Laughs*] Hollywood has been making films, even if they're Black films, through the eyes of white producers for their white viewers. So our films were like Barbie dipped in chocolate. [*Laughs*] Why can't we say what we want to say? Why are we being censored all of the time when it's something so benign, when it's just something to do with our culture or history? It's just like the thing with Trump saying he'd never heard of Juneteenth. Why!? [*Laughs*] How could you even say that out loud? How can he be so insensitive and ignorant? This is something that Black people have been celebrating since Juneteenth! Since 1865! He could have said, "I don't know [what it is], tell me." But no, he had to take it to another level and say, "I just made it famous by saying I never heard of it." It's just so myopic, and he's not the only one.

Hollywood can be just as myopic. Even with the Black producers and executives that they have. The Black executives, for the most part, follow exactly what the higher-ups say. You go sit in an office, and it's the same thing over and over. They're all eager and say, "My door's wide open to you," but when you talk to them about something they've never heard of or don't understand, they almost treat you like you're a threat. They love putting out misinformation that's just infuriating. They want to reimagine our history and say it's the next best thing. The historical films, I know those filmmakers, and it's just like, oh my god. Oh. My. God.

Notebook: Which is something you've explored since your thesis film *Illusions*: the distortion of the film industry and the real world going hand in hand.

Dash: Filmmakers like myself, Charles Burnett, Billy Woodberry, they're not hiring us because we have a different story to tell. It's almost like there was a blackout against film school graduates. They wanted people who were actors or comedians—and I know I'm going to get in trouble for saying this—but they wanted people with no film background, no historical background, people without the level of education we had. So the producers tell them to follow the bouncy ball. "This is what's going to happen in history. You take so-and-so and she runs through the woods," et cetera. It's like, what the fuck? [*Laughs*] "Excuse me? Is that Frederick Douglass over there?" No connections, everyone's an individual. It's like Ayn Rand's history: individuals. Like, let's give him the Academy Award for this individualistic, existential take on slavery. What the fuck? [*Laughs*] What. The. Fuck.

Notebook: I've encountered a pattern in the reviews of *Daughters of the Dust*, *The Glass Shield*, and even *Moonlight* (*The New York Times*), where white film journalists are surprised these films had a unique stylization and weren't shot as cinéma vérité. There's something patronizing in that surprise.

Dash: That's from the point of view of white privilege. I've been asked by journalists why I hadn't made a documentary about the Gullah Geechee people first. Uh, because I wanted to make this film! There are plenty of documentaries about it. Basically they're telling you, "Do not tell me anything that I do not know. You have to educate me first." I have to educate them so that they can understand the movie. Maybe this movie was not made for you, have you ever thought about that? I'm trying to take the conversation to another level. It's not just that it's for all Black people or people of color; it's not a sophomoric conversation we're having. But they don't want to allow that and are offended by it.

Another thing is that, because I did *Daughters of the Dust*, I'm supposed to be this Earth Mother that only does these historical dramas with swirling dresses. It's like, no! I'm a filmmaker, fool! [*Laughs*] I wanna make sci-fi! I write westerns! I write stories. But I got locked into this. It's just very myopic and anticreative, the people they have in charge of these things. They think you have one story. It's very weird for us, but it's been going on for many years. And then with Barry Jenkins, they wanted his second film to be more like *Moonlight*! [*Laughs*] He's already said that, sang that song, did the dance, and now he's onto something new.

Notebook: Your experimentation with frame rate and shutter speed is a throughline in your shorts, TV movies, music videos. In *Daughters of the Dust* the technique often indicates when the past or future are interacting with the present.

Dash: Yes, but also it's almost like a brain freeze: Remember this. This is important. This is a snapshot. The girl looks over her shoulder. This is how I'm going to remember her. We were using a prototype computer for doing that on the beach, but now you can do that in post real easy. [*laughs*] You can change the frame rate and stuff. But the cinematographer Arthur Jafa and I had talked so much about how things would move. It's kind of like a dub version of things. We didn't even have the verbiage for it; we just knew the music and the response we wanted from the audience.

Kerry James Marshall was the production designer, and now Kerry blew up! [*Laughs*] AJ's big too because he won the Golden Lion last year [for *The White Album*]. He's gonna be directing a film soon.

Notebook: You and Arthur Jafa compared making *Daughters of the Dust* to playing jazz, but did you prearrange the structure of any of the concurrent past, present, and future?

Dash: It organically evolved while we were down in preproduction. We'd find locations, there'd be silence, and you'd look at another person and nod. Or something would happen while we were shooting a scene. I would nod and we knew exactly what to do, whether to continue shooting or to pan over to something else. We were so in tune to the environment, the story, tone, and tempo that that's where the "playing jazz" came from. Jafa said that years ago and now a lot of people say it. [*Laughs*] We were crazy then, but now it's like okay. We were crazy with the dub version of the motions. It kind of puts people into a meditative state. They're out of it, and then they come into it, segue out, come in et cetera. We were just playing with all kinds of ways to enlighten the senses with images and sound. For the music, John Barnes and I hired a Nigerian talking drummer and had him tap out "Remember me. Remember my name." All kinds of little things we added to resonate, and I was able to do all of that because it was an independent film. If it was a studio film they'd say, "I don't know. There's no reference to it! You can't do that! It will take us out of the focus!"

In all honesty, I've done like five movies of the week: *Love Song*, *Incognito*, *Funny Valentines*, *The Rosa Parks Story*, and those things would come up every time I tried to infuse it with more resonance. So you have to do it silently, without letting them know; otherwise they'd try to stop me from making the film. I once got a fax to my trailer that said, "Stop making it so beautiful. This is not a feature film, it's a television movie." Why do they do that? There's no answer to it. If you dig deep first, they'll say they didn't do it, and if you persist, they'll say, "I was just kidding." Why would you send someone a fax saying that? That happened on *The Rosa Parks Story*. And there was more crazy stuff than that. It's cultural. It has to do with legacy. They want me to make the film that's in their head, not the one that's in mine.

I'm running into the same things with the Angela Davis biopic, which has been in development for over two years.

Notebook: How's that going?

Dash: It's going. It's good to make the movie. But it's so hard for them to grasp who she really is. It's hard for them to grasp that she was trilingual—she spoke English, German, French—and that she's known all over the world. Some of it has to do with the youthfulness of the development people. All they know is Angela Davis on the poster, wanted by the FBI. They want to rush to that. But it's like, "No, man, she was in Paris with the Algerians, she was in Germany." "That's really not important." Are you fucking kidding me? She was in Helsinki for the World Youth Peace Festival in 1963. Years later she became part of the Che-Lumumba club of the Communist Party. "Why do we have to show that?" Because it's not a part of the regular Communist Party.

It has to do with the way people are educated in this country. They don't learn the truth; they learn a cursory knowledge of history, that's their foundation, and you can't challenge it. The woman has an autobiography from the 1970s, edited by Toni Morrison, it's sitting right there, and they'll tell me, "Let's just focus. Let's just get her to Los Angeles." It's a blind determination to tell the story that's played inside their heads since they've been children.

Notebook: Did you ever run into Angela Davis at UCLA or see her speak there?

Dash: Yeah! I met her in the 1990s. We were outside of Paris doing a film panel—we went on a television show together. She has a huge following in France, so to eliminate France from her life in the movie—she spent years over there. One of the things that had the most profound impact on her life was that she knew the four little girls who were blown up in the [16th Street Baptist] church during the civil rights movement. I don't want to get too deep into that, but some *amazing* things have been said about that. [*Laughs*] Let's stay out of that because my best producer would have a fit if I told you. [*Laughs*]

Notebook: How do you think the accessibility of cameras and social media makes today's Black Lives Matter movement different from other revolutions in history?

Dash: You're seeing what people have been saying for years. The lynching never stopped, there's just new ways of lynching people, although people were lynched last week. I'm in Atlanta, fourteen or fifteen days after George Floyd, a guy is shot as he's running away. Didn't you get the memo? The protestors are just around the block and you did it anyway? The mindset is so profound. "This individual who's sleeping in his car should die because he won a tussling match with me." I don't think he even gave it a second thought. It's like a video game. They have the gun, and you don't.

Notebook: And to do it shamelessly into camera...

Dash: The police will take care of them. They might get a little bad publicity, but they'll be back on the force somewhere and probably get a promotion. White fragility, that's what the whole Trump rally was about, people lining up days in advance to get COVID. [*Laughs*] "You can't tell me what to do, I do what I want. I'll come out there three days in advance!" You've got three days extra to get COVID! [*Laughs*] It's damned and determined, "I'm American and this is my protest, because I've been emasculated by the Black Lives Matter protest at the boulevard leading up to the Whitehouse." [*Laughs*] It's hilarious. I love it.

Notebook: People walked out of *Daughters of the Dust* and *Illusions*. What do you think happened inside those individuals when they left the theater?

Dash: [*Daughters of the Dust*] was thirty years ago. What was in the theaters then? It was Ernest Dickerson's *Juice*, Matty Rich's *Straight Out of Brooklyn*.... All of these films were bucketing *Daughters of the Dust*. I had someone tell me it was not an authentic African American film because, in their mind, we were out at the plantation picking cotton. It had to be a movie about that or an urban thug. There was nothing in between, you could not even visualize it. *Daily Variety* wrote a review saying it looked like a buncha people runnin' around with Laura Ashley dresses on. It actually became offensive because I wasn't pointing the finger at anyone; it was just about what this family was doing. "How dare you not call me white! How dare you not talk about race! How dare you not include me in your film! How dare you do something beautiful with Black people." That's that white fragility. It's weird.

So years later, I just have to tell you, movie critics have come back to me and apologized. They said they were wrong at the Sundance screenings. They gave *Straight Out of Brooklyn* a standing ovation while I was on stage with Matty Rich. *Dust* got Best Cinematography and *Brooklyn* got the Audience Award Jury Prize.

Notebook: How long did it take them to come around and apologize?

Dash: Twenty years. I think they had been talking about it amongst themselves too. *Daughters of the Dust* had ruptured their reality of what Black film was and could be just like Charles Burnett's *Killer of Sheep*. When I first saw *Killer of Sheep* I assumed it was a female filmmaker because it was so soft and tender. So there are a lot of assumptions.

As filmmakers at UCLA we were encouraged to explore. Our job was not to make a television episodic while we were there. Everyone! It wasn't just the Black filmmakers; it was the white filmmakers too. We were all trying to explore new ways of telling a story. We worked on each other's films and we challenged ourselves. Then when we got outside people were insulted by us trying to tell new stories. People were actually angry. It's like, "Why are you mad at me?" [*Laughs*] It's tough to talk about. [Charles Burnett] told me he was working on some show and the Black actors were disgruntled when he showed up on set like, "Why is he here?" Giving him a hard time. What's going on here?

Then we went to some awards presentation, and I was sitting next to Charles. A Black director was going on and on about how he didn't go to film school, how he didn't need film school because he "made films from the heart." Afterwards, at the cocktail reception, I said, "Charles, what is this anger about film school students?" It was at a time that the LA Rebellion was getting a lot of press. Having come up through AFI undergrad and UCLA grad school, we learned that there was no competition. If there's any way to help each other, we would. We worked on all of each other's films. As artists, the only competition you have is with yourself. The challenges you put before yourself, the tasks you want to see completed. There's no such thing as competition. It's not in our worldview.

People always ask me, "How do you feel about so-and-so doing this film and you're not?" Well, it's wonderful. It's a miracle any Black made film gets made. It's just a miracle. You don't steal each other's work, you can't be in competition with others, you just have to do your own thing. We have that understanding, but a lot of people do not; they pit one person against the other. It's the antithesis of making art. People say, "Well it's a matter of art versus commerce." Not really. Calling it *art* doesn't mean it won't be profitable or travel the world.

Notebook: Some of the LA Rebellion filmmakers have said they tried to stretch their time at UCLA so that they could keep making films with the school's resources, as the industry outside felt so futile. Did you do that?

Dash: I don't know about trying to stay longer. Years later I walked into Melnitz Hall and recognized the smell. I had an anxiety attack because I remembered it. It's kind of a funky smell, knee grease and body odor from people editing. It was like, "Oh my god, I have to get out of here." [*Laughs*] It's that time in life where you have relationships, you break up, you're working as a receptionist or a caterer—you're doing everything to make your film. It's very traumatic. [*Laughs*]

Once you're done, you're done. So I wouldn't say we were *trying* to stay, it was like we couldn't get out of it. It was like being incarcerated. Self-incarceration at Melnitz. [*Laughs*]

Notebook: Are you still trying to get some of the films you've been trying to get made, like *Digital Diva*, off the ground?

Dash: We changed the name to *Cypher*. Now I'm with CAA [Creative Artists Agency], and we're revisiting a lot of the things that I wrote a long, long time ago. I have these young Black agents now, so they're very excited about it. That's a whole other story, Black Hollywood years ago. In many ways there were certain executives who fought so hard to create their own Julie Dash, their own Charles Burnett in their eyes. They didn't want us; they wanted someone of their own creation, and they did create these people. Those people are all working.

Every damn thing changed when Ava DuVernay came on. She switched from being a publicist to a filmmaker, out there with the *Queen Sugar*. Everything changed because she allowed all of these women to flow through—she called them "sugar babies"—to the DGA. Now everyone's trying to act like they've been inclusive over the years. No! No! No! If anything they promoted Black males, but not Black females. There's a bunch of Black female executives who completely close their doors to us, and I think you know who I'm talking about. They'd say publicly, "Black filmmakers never pitched anything to us." Well, I have names, dates, and places that I can't count.

They were not interested. They came from business and tried a risk management thing. "Who can I promote that's going to help me make it in this business?" Their calculations were wrong because they didn't understand why we existed. They were going to drive a culture that they predetermined as important. "Pimpin'? Push that. Thugs in the street, get that." They were trying to get ahead of the curb from behind the curb. The people that were ahead of the curb, they wouldn't have. But it's like Mother Nature didn't like that. [*Laughs*] They were only successful for a beat in time because they miscalculated. Now they're trying to have Zoom meetings with Black women talking about inclusion, but it's like, "No, baby, you were the ones shutting the doors. [*Laughs*] You've been the head Negro in charge and *now* you're saying this?"

Notebook: Are you hopeful for the future with the massive push for systemic reform happening now?

Dash: I am hopeful, because we're seeing wonderful LGTBQ+ programs, Ava DuVernay. Things are expanding and opening up, and all these people who made wrong calculations are kind of on the fringes now. I hope they learn that it's not up to one individual to determine culture, what's hidden and what's not. I'm glad on many levels. Scaring young filmmakers from doing anything like

Daughters of the Dust because they'll be marginalized and not be able to make hip movies—just because that was my case does not mean it will be so in theirs. It was a shock to the system. This is thirty years later. Young filmmakers need to push boundaries. That's their job as an artist and a filmmaker.... Thank you so much for having me here today.

In the Director's Chair with Frances-Anne Solomon and Julie Dash

Frances-Anne Solomon / 2020

From *CaribbeanTales-TV.com* (July 5, 2020). Transcribed by Philip Kassabaum. Reprinted by permission.

Frances-Anne Solomon: Let me introduce our guest, my friend, and an amazing filmmaker and wonderful women: Julie Dash. Julie Dash broke through racial and gender boundaries more than twenty-five years ago with her Sundance Award–winning film *Daughters of the Dust*, for which she also received a special award at the New York Film Critics Circle Award in 2017. She was the first African American woman to have a wide theatrical release of a feature film and is one of only three African American women with a feature film inducted into the National Film Registry. She's written and directed films for CBS, BET, Encore, Starz, Showtime, MTV [Films], HBO, and OWN. She directed *The Rosa Parks Story*, which earned her two NAACP Image Awards and nominations from the Emmys and the Directors Guild of America. She's also directed a number of episodes of OWN's *Queen Sugar* series. Julie is presently the distinguished professor of the Department of Art and Visual Culture at Spelman College. Let's take a look at some of her remarkable work.

FAS: Hi, Julie.

Julie Dash: Hi, Francis-Anne, how are you doing?

FAS: It's wonderful to see you.

JD: It is always good to visit with you.

FAS: Yeah. [*Laughing*] So how are you?

JD: I'm just, I'm fine, all things considering, you know, I'm fine. There is a lot going on, um, but I am encouraged by the youth, Black Lives Matter, and the diverse representation on the streets changing things here in the United States. It's encouraging.

FAS: Great, that's wonderful. So let's start at the beginning. Where were you born?

JD: I was born in New York City. On Long Island City, to be exact. I was born and raised in the Queensbridge housing projects. It is a little community right under the 59th Street bridge connecting Long Island City to Manhattan.

FAS: And what was it like growing up? Like, tell me something you enjoyed about growing up.

JD: Um, playing basketball because I was tall. [*Laughing*] Skating. In the summers, I do remember how the kids would act out scenes from movies on the street. Usually, it was some kind of James Bond movie [*laughing*], you know. We would learn the dialogue and act it out, you know, on the streets.

FAS: And so, what, what, were your most important memories of growing up, would you say?

JD: Wow, um, friends, family. [*Pause*] Cooking. My family is from the Gullah Geechee culture and so they had a very specific way of preparing meals and celebrating. And at the time when I was growing up, I was actually a little uncomfortable with people knowing how different we were. Because, you know, like, in the mornings, most kids were eating cereal, cold cereal, bacon, and eggs. And we were eating fish roe [*laughing*] or some kind of fish dish with grits. And so, I was a little—a little embarrassed by that back then. But I appreciate it now.

FAS: And tell me, um, what, what made you think that—I know that for myself, there was nothing in my environment growing up that told me that I could be a filmmaker. What made you think that that was something that you could do? Like, what lead you to that place?

JD: Well, the same—as with you, there was nothing in my environment that, um, that really led to me studying film or becoming a film maker or writer. I just kind of—in high school I stumbled into a cinematography workshop. I went with a friend. We thought it was a still photography workshop at the Studio Museum in Harlem. And it turned out to be cinematography and they started showing us foreign films and I had never really seen foreign films like that before with subtitles and everything and I was hooked. You know, and after two weeks of being in the workshop we realized it was not still photography; it was motion picture photography that we were studying. Uh, still in all, I just thought it was, you know, a place I would like to go, you know, on school nights and weekends. But I had no plans on becoming a filmmaker because I did not even—it was not on the charts, you know, no one I knew was a filmmaker. I mean, you know, it just wasn't something—it just wasn't something I was aware of. You know, I was like most people growing up. I thought the actors were making up the lines as they were going on. [*Laughing*] I did not know there was a script written. So I had a lot to learn.

FAS: So what was that moment when you said, "Okay, I'm going to go and study film making and become a film maker?"

JD: It was, uh, I know that I was at the Studio Museum of Harlem, and we had an editor come to visit us and she talked about, I think it was Medline Anderson, and she was talking about reality within the frame and reality outside of the frame. And how you could—we couldn't control everything that was going on in our lives, but we could control the reality within the frame, and we could change the reality and we could change life. And at that moment, I realized that yeah, I'd like to take control of the reality inside of a frame, you know, if I could. I'd like to tell stories.

FAS: That's amazing. And was that the moment when you kind of found your vocation? . . . Would you say that that was the moment when you thought, "That's what I want to do with my life?"

JD: Well, not quite yet, because I was still stumbling through wanting to be a cinematographer. I was the worst at lighting. You know, you had [to have] a special skill that I just did not have. And after high school I went to undergraduate school at the [City] College in New York, and I majored in film production and television. And uh, I was focusing on writing and documentaries at the time, and then I decided that I wanted to learn how to write dramatic films and learn how to a make dramatic film. And so, after graduation, I went out to—I relocated to Los Angeles and attended the American Film Institute as a producing–writing fellow, conservatory fellow, back in the day. And then after that I decided to continue on. I wanted to direct some of the things that I was writing. And so I went to UCLA's Graduate School for four years, and I got a master's degree in directing motion pictures and television.

FAS: Wow, I'm really in awe. Because having grown up, I'm sure, in much the same way, without any encouragement. I am just, um, I am actually amazed at how single-minded and clear you were about your intentions and what you set about accomplishing very young. That's amazing.

JD: Yeah, you know, it was just [that] I just came up with a mission statement and, you know, I think at the time they told us everyone had to go home and write a, you know, one-paragraph mission statement. And I was determined at the time to reimagine and redefine how African American women are depicted on the screen. Because the films I was seeing at the time, you know, bore little or no resemblance to the women I know—the African American women in my family, who I grew up with. And I just said, "Well, I wanna make a film like a Toni Morrison character, like, you know, Toni Cade Bambara's characters, you know, who speak to me so, and Alice Walker characters, who speak to me so intimately," but I was, at the time—we weren't seeing that on the screen.

FAS: Amazing. That's incredible. That's incredible. So I'm going to go on to talk about the voice. So what would you say, following on from that, what would you say your voice is? Um, what makes you decide to tell a story? I mean, perhaps it's self-evident at this point.

JD: Well, I would say what drives me is historical projects and just the amount of stories that have not been told about us, about our families, about our condition. And they all don't have to do with race. They are all of these intergroup relationships that are just ignored and, you know, like Hollywood goes in cycles. You know, they'll do social activists' films. They'll do, you know, comedies, and then they'll do romantic "rom-coms." But we seem to be on kind of like a treadmill trying to pattern films, Black films made after what's trending, when in reality, coming from a tradition of people who created jazz, we have a whole bunch of new stories to tell that perhaps do not follow those patterns at all. You know, people, everything that we do is ancient to the future, and now, you know, they call that Afrofuturism and . . . I'm loving it. Because, you know, we are part of a continuum and as people—as the descendants of people who were enslaved in this country—we're constantly holding onto the past and to the future as we, you know, juggle the present. So . . . there [are] just so many wonderful stories to be told. That—*that* drives me.

FAS: Absolutely, no, I agree with you one hundred percent. What specifically made you want to make *Daughters of Dust*?

JD: Hm. Let's see, um, *Daughters of the Dust* was something that was a—came from a whole bunch of different ideas. You know, I started thinking about it while I was a student at AFI, you know, and Ingmar Bergman came and spoke to our class, and I was watching his films, and I was looking at so many different foreign films and they were, you know, complex, lots of residents, multilayered. And our films about Black Americans just seemed to be so simple. You know, "Uh, look, me, see, do, from A to B to Z." And I said I want to do something that involves our culture, our story, our traditions, our religion; that is complex. In fact, it may be so complex that [it] is viewed as a foreign film itself.

FAS: Absolutely. I think that's what's so amazing about that movie is just how layered it is and how nuanced in all kinds of ways. You feel like you've never seen these images before.

JD: In many ways, it's ancient to the future. It's Afrofuturistic. It's what if. It's speculative fiction mashed up with history. The events and issues of history.

FAS: Wow, wow that's incredible. Um, *The Rosa Parks Story*. What was it that you wanted—why did you want to tell that story? I mean, it's a very familiar story. Obviously, it hasn't been told enough, but what was it that you saw in it that you wanted to convey to the audience?

JD: The reason I worked on that story was directly due to Angela Bassett; she asked for me. She asked them to interview me to see what I could do. There was a script that was written by Paris Qualles, a wonderful script. And I just worked with Angela as well as with Miss Cicely Tyson, and we reimagined some things; we rewrote some scenes. We told her life from the point of view of her being a woman, an African American woman first, and then an activist. Uh, because she's already—everyone knows the story. She's a, you know, civil rights icon, the mother of the civil rights movement. But what about her? What did she want? What do we know about her? What did she do in her daily life? What was her relationship like with her husband? So that's the story that I wanted to tell, a very personal, intimate story. Um, and we did. And it was wonderful working with them. I mean, yeah, of course. You know, Angela Basset, Miss Tyson, they're, like, incredible.

FAS: Absolutely. And that is what comes across in that story. She is very much an ordinary, an ordinary person going about her life, you know, in a very personal and intimate way; it's wonderful. Thanks for sharing that.

JD: We also wanted to show that . . . it had nothing to do with her feet hurting. That's a myth that she didn't get up because her feet were hurting. She didn't get up because she was working with the NAACP on bus cases. And prior to that, she was working on rape cases. And so she was an activist—she had a long career of being an activist as well as her husband, too.

FAS: Wow. Yeah, that comes across. So tell me about character development. We've talked, you know, obviously the characters that you create are nuanced, complex, three dimensional. It's such a relief from the way that you see that Hollywood has tended to represent us, or just generally the film and television industry generally, as thugs, bad guys, slaves. You know, but you really broke that a long time ago in a very powerful way. So how did you create the character of Mignon Dupree? In *Illusions*, which was, I mean, that was in nineteen what? That was in 1982 that you made that film? Was that your first film?

JD: No, but it was, it turned out to be my thesis film in college, my college thesis film. Yeah, there were so many things I want to say about how we're represented in film and why and how film is used as a tool for propaganda. And then, you know, being in, you know, graduate school and finding out that, yeah, the studios were propaganda machines churning out movies during World War II to inspire hope and joy and everything in the community. But at the same time, you know, there was no Black person working on a studio lot, you know, not even in the janitorial services. So I have my character Mignon Dupree go inside as kind of like a spy and whatever . . . to learn everything she can. So she could, you know, come out and, you know, start her own film company stuff. People always say isn't this highly self-reflective, but I wasn't thinking about it like that at the time. It was just like, "How do you get an African American woman into a film studio? She has to be passing for white." So does that mean that she's ashamed of being Black? No, not at all. She's simply just, you know, like—they didn't ask, and she didn't tell. She didn't say anything, but of course you have the character of Esther Jeter, a singer who comes in and looks at her. And you know, we could tell each other. And she says, "Oh, they can't tell you Black?" And she says nothing. So, you know, it just kind of makes a lighthearted joke about it. But it just, I just wanted to tell different things about the period, about the development of films, about the history of filmmaking and the importance, and to lay down a predicate that this is what we need to do and why.

FAS: Absolutely, amazing. In terms of technique. Most directors—people say that most directors have something that they do, techniques that are their signatures, you know, that evolve as part of their art. Some people say that mine is how I use archives, but what would you say is your signature or, well, one of them?

JD: Attention to detail. The tiny specifics of things that I like to build. Shots of very close angles on things. . . . Within each scene. I like to tell two bits of information, not just the obvious, but something else is embedded within it. And I have fun with that. So you may not get it on the first screening, but you definitely get it when you walk away the second time. You go like, "Hey, wait a minute." You know? We have fun with that, you know. So I think that's one of my voices. I always wanna tell, at least, to give the audience at least two pieces of information that drive the story forward within each scene. Now you'll say, "Specifically, which one?" But I do not remember. [*Laughing*] I do not remember.

FAS: Well, you got to remember one. I mean, what I can tell you is that it's definitely multilayered; these are complex images. So much is going on in the frame at the same time. You're kind of, you're stunned by the novelty of the imagery and the way that things are laid in it and the time. Like, you don't rush things either. It's careful, composed, layered, and emotional and personal.

JD: But that's not all of my films. . . . *Daughters*, yes. But, like, with *Love Song*, with Monica, it was like, chop, chop, chop. That's because it was on MTV. Yeah, so. But still, I try to give out two pieces of information but it's moving a lot faster. So each film that I make has its own history to it, its own tone, tempo, and texture. I just like exploring and playing with different things. And sometimes they work out, and sometimes they don't. [*Laughing*] But at least I try.

FAS: Well, it is very smart.

JD: We do try.

FAS: Yeah, absolutely. And you've done a lot of music videos. That's a good segue. How did—you actually have answered this already—but how does your technique change for a music video? Like, what would you say?

JD: I haven't made a music video in a long, long time because the whole music video industry has changed—but it was fun. Because I was able to use equipment that I, you know, normally couldn't use. And, you know, you would be shooting for a day or two and you could just go all out. And it's wonderful working with the musicians. With that talent that those artists [have.] One of [my] best ones I think was with Tracy Chapman.

FAS: Yeah, it's gorgeous. It's so beautiful.

JD: Yeah, and all she asked was that she wanted to have a blue curtain in the background. I said, "Uh, okay." [*Laughing*] And we created a juke joint set, you know, when she sees the guy to the side doing the jerk, you know. Like he had on a white belt and it's just like she's singing about "give me one reason to be here." [*Laughing*] You know, you find yourself in a situation where, you know, you think it's gonna be cool and it's just like, "What?" Everything is going wrong. We actually cut out a shot. I had a big hunk of raw meat being sliced for sandwiches, you know, [not] knowing she's a vegetarian. But she said no, I couldn't use that. But that went along with "give me one reason to be here." You know, it's like, "Oh, God." So anyway, that was fun. And Dianne Reeves was in it too, she's the lady getting done up and made up. Yeah, that's Dianne right there.

FAS: It's lovely. It's really lovely. And you had fun doing it.

JD: Yes, we had fun, yes.

FAS: So is it important to you that your work be female focused? Is that something that you insist on, or what's your relationship with that?

JD: Well, it's like, that's what I'm drawn to. Yeah, it's not that I won't watch a film that is male focused or whatever. And I have been offered many films and I say, "You know, like, why don't you take it to this person or that person or the other." I mean, time, life is [too] short. There's so many of our stories that we need to tell that I've been trying like for, you know, like nine years or so to do. You know? And I know you did a World War II drama about women in the service in the UK. And I've been trying to do a story about the Six Triple Eight Postal Battalion. These [are] 850 African American women who served overseas during World War II. There's a no brainer. That's a wonderful story, a wonderful story! Nine years. No takers. I have, you know, another one called *Colored Conjurers*, about a family of traveling magicians traveling the Chitlin Circuit, doing magical tricks. A wonderful story. I have a reparation story called *Dry Bones*. It's about Deadria Farmer-Paellmann who sued for slavery reparations in New York City and actually had laws changed. So many stories to tell and so little time, and so that's why I'm focusing on our stories about women of the African diaspora.

FAS: Well, fantastic. What are you working on now? Do you want to talk about that?

JD: Oh yeah, uh, [what] I'm working on now? I'm in development with Lionsgate on the Angela Davis biopic. And that is a tremendous story. Um, the script is still being written, and we've been working on it for some time, but it's all good. The end result is going to be—it's going to be wonderful. Angela is an incredible human being, activist, scholar, intellectual, humanitarian, and I just don't know of any other Black woman alive today who has accomplished as much as she has. Or who has touched the lives of as many people as she has. So her story needs to be told, and it's going to be really powerful.

FAS: And what is the angle you are taking on her? You were telling me a little bit about that earlier.

JD: Well, she was born and raised in Birmingham, Alabama. And at the time it was nicknamed "Bombingham," Alabama because of all the houses that were being bombed by the racists. And she actually lived in a segment of the town that was called "Dynamite Hill." It was called Dynamite Hill because so many houses were dynamited there; they were blown up. So looking at the photographs and talking to her and reading her biography, I said to myself, "Well, this is just like the children of Aleppo" that we see and we feel so much for, when we see the children of Aleppo sitting within the rubble." But we don't have that same connection, that same emotion to the children of Birmingham, Alabama. Why is that? Well, because you never see it on television. You never see photographs of it, and you never see it in feature films. And so I want to start this film out as the same thing as Aleppo. Let's look at these little Black girls, boys and girls who in the middle of the night are standing around in the rubble because their house has been bombed.

FAS: Wow. Well, thank you for your work.

JD: Thank you.

FAS: It's incredible talking to you and hearing your thought processes. Let me think. So we have some questions. I'm gonna hand it over to my producer, Vanella. So over to you.

Vanella: Hi. Good afternoon, ladies. Great discussion. We do have a few questions from our audience. The first one comes from Endio. He says, "As a Zimbabwean actor, I want to see more dignified portrayals of African people without compromising on quality. What do you think can or must be done to update the narrative?"

JD: Everything. [*Laughing*] You know, I mean, the narrative so far has been overshadowed, and the engine that drives it is systemic white supremacy of all things that have to do about our Black lives. So it's not just one idea, one story, or one moment in time or time period. It's' everything. There needs to be a total overhaul. And we need to be driving that engine, powering that engine, and at the wheel and telling our stories. And I know we've heard that phrase "telling our stories" a lot. But, you know, just like Black lives matter, Black cinema matters equally. Uh, because Black cinema lives within your head, within your memory.

It, you know, it can either traumatize you or uplift you and inspire you, and we need all of that because we have certainly been traumatized.

FAS: Absolutely. Yeah, and it's about who makes decisions and who makes decisions about what films get made and how much money we get to make it.

JD: Right. And what can be said in these films. Because we just won't have a film that's been neutered. You know, you would have a historical drama and it's just like, it plays out like [*pause*] something that is just a costume drama with Black folks in it. That's not helping us.

FAS: Exactly, no, I couldn't agree more. Vanella?

V: Yep, we have another question. This is from Elizabeth. She says, "What was it that made you, Julie, feel like you had to get degrees to learn how to do filmmaking? Many white male filmmakers pride themselves on being self-taught or without formal education."

JD: Well, you have to understand, that's a very good question. Number one, when I came up, when I was in school in the late 1970s and '80s, all the way to the '90s. That was the only way I could get my hands on equipment. We didn't have digital film then. We didn't have—you couldn't just slip a memory card in. You had to buy the film stock, you know, $400 for two minutes, you know, of film. Institutions and film schools were a place where you could have access to the equipment, as well as the raw film stock. And then also I was curious about filmmaking once I got hooked into what I was curious about—the history of film worldwide. And at UCLA I was able to study African American, I mean, African cinema as well as Latin American cinema, Asian cinema, the cinema of Germany. So I have a general interest, and so that's what kept me in school. It wasn't like I felt like I had to stay in film school for so long. But I was being pulled by a dream of being able to get the information about the psychology of colors and how to put together a ethnographic film, how to put together a documentary, how to put together a narrative film, and then after getting all that information, then I decided with *Daughters of the Dust*, how it's going to do my own film, which violated a lot of those rules in stone that have to do with telling a dramatic narrative story. But I felt that was the way that film had to go.

V: Okay. We have another question. This is from Rachel. She says, "Miss Dash, what is the process like for getting your films produced? *Colored Conjurers* and *Dry Bones* sound like amazing films. Why do you think it's taking so long to get these made? Thank you."

JD: Thank you. Okay. I think it's taking a, well I know it's taking a long time because filmmaking, just like everything else has to do with legacy. *Dry Bones* has to do with reparations—reparations for African Americans. There have been reparations for Asian Americans for, you know, the Japanese internment camps.

And there have been films made about that. A few but not enough. But it has to do with our stories. And [*pause*] the producers, Black and white, aren't really feeling it. Maybe they are since last month, but prior to last month, no, they weren't really feeling it because it has nothing to do with their present day. And they were like, "Ah, reparations. That might not really work out." *Colored Conjurers*, it has to do with, you know, it's so funny. When I pitched that story, people try to correct me. They say you mean Black musicians. They could understand musicians. "No," I said, "No, magicians, you know, conjurers. You know, hand tricks." And they go like, "Oh." So, they can't place it. They can't source it because they haven't seen photographs, films, books, anything about Black magicians and so therefore its censored, just erase it. It's like, "Oh, you know, you have anything about some contemporary story? Do you have anything about a rapper or something like that or someone who's selling drugs?" Why? Because they can source that. You know what I mean? They can parse it. They can't parse a lot of the different stories that have gone untold for a very long time.

V: Okay, we have another question from Adriana. She wants to know, "What's driving the resurgence of reboots, remakes, and revivals in TV and film, more so in the last few years, especially when there are so many other original stories to be told?"

JD: It's primordial. A lot of people and these producers [are], you know, venture capitalists who make these films and who produce them. They know the story already; they've seen it before. So they're more comfortable doing a remake, reboot, a retread than trying something new. And I say it's primordial because it's like telling a story around the open campfire. Which comes from, you know, Neanderthal days. You know, everybody wants to hear a good story around the campfire. They want to hear the story told over and over and over. "Maybe a little twist here, a little twist there, but...." Those are the kinds of things you learn in film school. That, you know, people they want to see what they've already seen. They wanna know what's gonna happen before it happens.

V: Okay, this might may be—you may have answered this sort of in that question, but this is from Mendi, and she says, "Do you think that film drives conversation as a powerful medium?"

JD: Absolutely. Film not only drives conversation, it drives politics. It drives awareness and drives culture. It drives religion, it drives social activities. A film can change, one film can change the world. It can be so revolutionary that it changes the world, and we've seen that recently. We've seen it with Ava DuVernay's *The 13th*. We've seen it with *Black Panther*. I mean, literally, those films caused a culture shift in a very good way. They make people go, "Oh. Ah-ha." You know, and you want people to have those "Aha" moments. That's what you need. That's what we need. That's what we want.... But, I mean, back in the day, the saying was, "Film is the most powerful medium of the twentieth century," and that's why all of the films that were being made during World War II out of the Hollywood studios had a signal corps officer assigned to their development departments, because film was the most powerful medium of the twentieth century. Now we're in the twenty-first century and we have digital films that you don't have to carry the big reels of film around the screen. You could, you know, beam them down from satellites to a thousand different theaters. And so it's even more powerful. And so just like the internet, it's controlled. Monitored. The stories that are told are monitored. And I'm not saying that there's any big conspiracy or a cabal, you know, sitting around going, you know, twisting their mustaches saying, "Oh, we're not gonna do this film or we're gonna do that film." I think it's just something inside of people who are making and greenlighting a film that say, "Uh, meh." They, you know, that "meh" is very powerful.

V: We have one last question. This one is from Joanne. She says, "If you were to make *Daughters of the Dust* today, what would you do different?"

JD: I would probably do many things differently because that was twenty-five or thirty years ago. I've grown. I know more. And so, it would probably be even more dense than it is already. [*Laughing*] I, you know, there's no way that—it's just like a painter who paints a picture or someone who writes a novella. If they go back twenty-five or thirty years, it's not gonna be the same. And I would not try to make it the same. And I could actually see, I actually do see errors in *Daughters of the Dust* that I would never go back and change because that's my voice from that time period. That's the song I was singing then.

V: Well, thank you, everybody, for your questions. I hand it back over to Frances-Anne to wrap it up.

FAS: Yeah, I have one last question. Have you ever made a film that you regret making or made a film that you didn't want to make?

JD: Oh, my gosh. Oh, actually. Yes. It was something for Showtime. It was part of an anthology, and I had the best cinematographer in the world, Matthew Libatique, who was—he'll kill me if I tell 'em what it was. [*Laughing*] And we found out after we finished shooting it, or *while* we were shooting it, that it was executive produced for Playboy Incorporated. I was like, "What?" It's supposed to be, you know, when you know, they pushed the whole women-centered thing, but really it was about sex. You know, hard R-rated sex. And it's like, "Ew," you know.

FAS: And how do you feel about that now?

JD: Well, it's not on my reel! [*Laughing*] Yeah, but you find out, you know, you find out things then, you know. I was eager to make that film. I was eager to be a part of that group of women, you know, participating with the anthology of films. But then we found out that the agenda had nothing to do with women's empowerment. It had to do with, "Let's get 'em naked," you know. Yeah.

FAS: Okay, cool. All righty. So, thank you, Julie. It's been amazing. Yeah. What a, what a gift.

JD: Thank you so much for having me here today.

Race, Rebellion, and Resilience: In Conversation with Julie Dash

Kameelah L. Martin / 2023

Interview conducted January 16, 2023.

Kameelah Martin: Today is Monday, January 16, 2023. I am Kameelah Martin, editor of the collection *Julie Dash: Interviews* for the University Press of Mississippi. It is my pleasure to commence the final conversation with the iconic and legendary Julie Dash.

So first, thank you for accepting my invitation to discuss the project, to reflect on your legacy, and to ensure that you receive your flowers while you are still here with us.

Julie Dash: Like, the clock is ticking! [*Laughs*] No, no, no, I appreciate that. I really, really do. Thank you.

Martin: When I was invited to do this collection, I agreed with the press that there needed to be a definitive source on the body of your work. And so that is really the impetus for the project. But I also wanted this to be a love letter to you, a deep dive into your career, into your film, and an appreciation of what you have given to the world. And so that is the tenor and tone of this final interview. So we'll jump right in!

As you know, some scholars have called your style a type of "Black feminist narrative" approach to filmmaking. From your earliest works such as *Diary of an African Nun* to *Four Women* and *Daughters of the Dust*, you have unapologetically fused your filmic work to the tradition of Black women writers and storytellers such as Alice Walker, Nina Simone, Paule Marshall. You have worked closely with Gloria Naylor, interviewed Octavia Butler, and your dialogue with bell hooks on the making of *Daughters of the Dust* is one of the most cited interviews, just to name a few examples, and as a trained literary scholar myself, I have long argued that you sit squarely within this tradition of Black women writers and storytellers. Not only with your films, but also with your debut novel *Daughters of the*

Dust: A Novel, that came out sometime after the film. How have you received the intellectual adoration of these Black feminist scholars?

Dash: Wow! Well, I was friends with bell hooks. So that helped right out. You know, a friend introduced us. She used to come over to the house when we lived in Atlanta back in, I guess in the 1990s. Yeah, that's why I met her. And I was also friends with Octavia Butler. . . . All of that helped, you know. I mean, I looked up to them. I looked to them for counseling and advice and analysis and critical thinking and all of that. And including Toni Cade Bambara, you know, like I used to just be frozen sitting around next to or near her just listening and watching and waiting. I guess all of this kind of happened pretty organically. It wasn't like I sought them out. But I still, of course, you know, when I was coming up, when I was a student at the American Film Institute, and I used to be reading [them]: Alice Walker, of course. Toni Cade Bambara's *Gorilla, My Love*—that had a *huge* effect on me when I was in undergraduate school. And Toni Morrison. And I always, you know [*laughs*] . . . this is gonna sound silly. But when we in a dormitory as undergraduates, we used to act out Toni Morrison's dialogue. You know, we had the discipline on the dance or something from Sonia Sanchez . . . the "Malcolm died this thick lip," you know . . . blah blah blah. "Violets like casting it to echo me." [*Laughs*]

Okay? So this was like in the 1970s and '80s. So we didn't have this [representation] on the screen. We didn't have this available to us, but it lived inside of our hearts, in our minds, of course. So much so that for me as an emerging filmmaker, that's all I wanted to see. I wanted it, I had the hunger to make films with that kind of dialogue and plotting and structure. . . . Including what, even up to you know, *Beloved*. . . . Like I've said so many times when I first read [it], I had to get up and go in the in the bathroom and get a towel [to dry my eyes]. It's laid across my lap, and here I was reading [while crying]. Yes, it was like [that]. I would read. You know, Morrison was such a writer that you, you don't know *how* she came up with the sentence structure, the complex sentences. You [would] find yourself just looking at, holding the book in hand and looking off into space. [And it's] like, "I *know* these people. I *know* this feeling. I *know* this situation. How does *she* know that? How does she know about the Deweys?" Because growing up in New York City and the Queensbridge housing project, we used to go upstairs to Miss Edward's house. She would take care of all the kids. Well, until your parents came home from work—everybody was a latchkey kid.

And I swear I knew the "Deweys"! Who's that over there? This one out there. [There were] three of them. [Miss Edwards would say,] "Whatever your name is,"—you know they called people by the same name, and everyone was a "Dewey." I just found all of that to be so invigorating and remarkable, and magic that she *knew*. [Morrison] had the spice of life, you know, she knew what to write that just really, really mirrored your life, our lives and our community . . . the way we thought, the way we pulsed—all of these things. And I just really wanted to make film reimagining how Black women are seen in historical dramas as well as contemporary dramas. That's what I wanted to do.

Martin: Absolutely. Absolutely. That's beautiful. I want to continue to talk about Black women writers and this idea of storytelling, particularly stories of Black women. And I want to get into the weeds a little bit and talk about your novel because nobody talks about your novel. I've been doing all of this research on your career, and hardly any prior interviews address your creative writing.

Dash: Most people haven't read it! So let me let me back up a little bit and explain.

So when I agreed to do [the book], they gave me a double book deal. I wrote it under the name "Geechee Recollections" because it's a *continuing* story of *Daughter's of the Dust*. A whole lot of people haven't read it because they think it's the novelization of the movie, and it's not.

Martin: It is *not*.

Dash: It was never my intention to do a novelization of the movie, but Dutton Signet Books decided on their own (the marketer is within the company) that that's what they wanted because of name recognition. And that's what they did. We tried to fight it as much as we can, and they just said, "Look, buddy, at the end it's already copywritten and at the Library of Congress with the ISBN number. It's *Daughters*." I was really humiliated, because the first thing people would ask me was, "Why did you name it [*Daughters of the Dust*]? Are you, you trying to get mileage off of your movie?" No, it's because the marketing department didn't think Black people would understand what "Geechee Recollections" meant. [That's the] absolute truth.

And the second novel, which I broke up into three parts, and . . . I don't even know if I can talk about it now. They paid for [it] and everything, but they didn't want [to publish] it.

Martin: Oh, wow! So there's another Julie Dash novel out there!?

Dash: That was during a time when. . . . It's a trilogy, and it's a "perfume trilogy," and they wanted something more . . . "street."

Martin: Oh?

Dash: [Something more like] "my gangbanger's boyfriend" or "baby mama" talk . . . so I don't know.

Martin: There is a whole market for what they call "street lit" out there. That is fascinating.

Dash: They told me the exact size they wanted [the book] to be to fit into someone's purse so they could read it on the subway. Well, it was like, and I was writing something too long and too big. They said, "Nah, nah, nah." I still have it. I was working on it this morning, you know! I was working on edits on my day off and stuff like that. [*Laughs*]

Martin: Well, that's beautiful, that's beautiful. Well, I have taught the novel several times over the years, and I just think it is fascinating and underappreciated. It really highlights why you fit into this Black woman's literary tradition quite well.

Dash: It was carefully edited by Ms. Deirdre Melayne! [She would look at it and] say, "What?" Because I kept moving out of the third person into the first person, like with scripts. It was humbling. It was terribly humbling, but, you know, I learned so much. And I still slip in and out, and I know that I need a great editor to work with. Because [film and books] are two totally different platforms. So . . . maybe *that's* why they didn't want the new one. [*Laughs*] I don't know, but I've also written treatments to adapt that [second] book into a second film, a follow-up film. I have never been able to get financing on it, either. Let's just say.

Martin: Understood, understood! The book is still in print over twenty-five years later and was recently recorded as an audiobook in June of 2021. Congratulations on that, by the way! I need to go back and listen to it. I still have my original copy, but I want to hear it read aloud, now, performed by . . .

Dash: By Bahni Turpin, who played the part of Iona in the movie [*Daughters of the Dust*].

Martin: That's right!

Dash: That is right. We knew her voice, and this is what we decided we wanted and that this was what we were gonna do. And so we did it. Yeah.

Martin: That *is* exciting. The novel does follow the story of the Peazants as we look to that next generation after leaving Dawtuh Island.

Dash: The novel is, you know, I am clearly basing it on a kind of Zora Neale Hurston journey . . . the anthropologist who goes back and investigates the family. And the family is like, "You don't be coming down here studying me. You can come and visit, but I'm not here to be studied."

Martin: There *is* this really interesting tension between the Northern, if you will, Peazants who come back to the island, or Amelia, anyway, who comes back to learn more about her family. And it's sprinkled with recipes and remedies and rituals. It's dense with what Toni Morrison would call the "interiority" of Black lives, and I think that's one of the most beautiful things about the text. Why was it important for you to tell this part of the Peazant saga, particularly Amelia's discovery of her Gullah Geechee roots?

Dash: Because there are many levels to it, like I said earlier. It's me controlling my Zora Neale Hurston experience because I study her a lot and her work with Boaz and Ruth Benedict and all of them. As an anthropology student, I get to put a camera in her hands and send her down to do an official study. It's to investigate a little bit more, in a more linear way—because, of course, *Daughters of the Dust* was nonlinear—a more linear way of chronicling the history of the people of what they call the Low Country. Now, when I grew up it was just called the Sea Islands or coastal communities. It's like, okay. [*Laughs*]

Amelia goes down on the train. [The novel] talks about the time period, there was the *Plessy v. Ferguson* thing, and so you have her on the train. And I just wanted to show also how difficult it was to get there back then. Because people say, "Well, I didn't feel like I was on the island." I was just shooting down there [in the Low Country] last spring because I was doing a movie for the International African American Museum that's scheduled to open soon. They pushed the date back; it was supposed to open on the twentieth of this month. They pushed the date back again.

But anyway, you know, and so I'm down there with a crew, and people kept saying, "I don't feel like I'm on an island." I said, "You know those conduits and all those little bridges we went over?" This piece of land is not connected to where the hotel is. There were lots of little islands, and they weren't really connected until the late 1920s. Many folks who were born on John's Island . . . they [were] not connected to Charleston. You had to ferry over. It was a big deal depending on where the island was situated.

They remained isolated for a very long time. I wanted to show that isolation. And there are just some wonderful, *wonderful* things about the Gullah Geechee community that I didn't get a chance to really get into [in the novel]. And I'm still learning. My father used to take us down there [as children]. But I'm *still* learning things that are amazing, like the history of the Jenkins Orphanage Band and choirs that toured Europe back in the day. Just wonderful stories. I shouldn't talk about somebody else's film, but now that Gullah Geechee is a more recognizable name and phrases, now, all of a sudden people are taking it and trying to turn it into something else. There's a horror movie coming out called *Geechee*, for instance.

Martin: Oh, that's . . . that's so unfortunate.

Dash: Now I haven't seen it yet, so I shouldn't be talking about someone's film but . . .

Martin: But the appropriation of that term is problematic. It is absolutely problematic.

Dash: I've taken so many pitching meetings in Hollywood, out in [Los Angeles] and stuff, and often they're always looking for exposés. "Tell me something different about the African American community. Tell me something different about being Gullah Geechee." [In response, I say,] "Well, we rice every day." [The studios are like,] "No. What else? What else is there?"

Martin: That is interesting. I recall a time when, hearing this from my grandfather, who is eighty-nine years old, and who was in the Air Force stationed in Savannah for a time. He talked about how the term "Geechee" was derogatory. It's really interesting that we've come such a long way from that connotation of the term and the communities connected to it. But then someone else is going to reappropriate it and suggest that perhaps there is still this sort of sensationalism or a less than honorable connection to be made to those communities. So that's problematic.

Dash: Well, when I was growing up my grandmother, my father's mother, said "Don't let anybody call you Geechee. But never you mind, never you mind." And they'd sit around and be speaking in the Geechee dialect and loving them some Geechee stuff. And teasing, "Oh, you just an old Geechee." Geechee this, that, and the other . . . but don't let anybody *outside* call you a Geechee.

When I did my corporate paperwork in Georgia back in 1988 or '89 in preparation for shooting, because, you know, we shot in 1989, you know. I named my production company Geechee Girls Productions. I got a call from a clerk. . . . It was a Black woman's voice who just want to let me know, [in] a very nice kind of loving way, that Geechee was a bad word. I said, "Oh, no, it is not, ma'am; I'm a Geechee, my parents are Geechee." She said, "Well, well, then, just letting you know that a lot of people consider it a bad word." And then I thanked her and hung up. That was as [recent] as 1988 or 1989.

Martin: Let's talk a little bit more about the differences between writing a novel—creative writing—and writing for visual media.

Dash: Okay, it's very simple. In film, scripts [answer the question] "What do you see?" What do you see? What is happening? What's the action? How do we see the plot unfold? How do we see . . . what are the tiny specifics that you can see within each scene? What are you telling [the viewer] in each scene? How do you depict those bits of information to drive the story forward?

In a novel, all [of] this is in [characters'] interior thoughts. You could speak from multiple points of view, multiple voices if you're dealing with third-person past [tense]. It's just totally different.

Totally different.

I see a lot of novels today being written in the first person. But then you're limited when you choose that method of first person. You can't parallel cut like you could do in film . . . you can't parallel cut to what someone is doing over there—loading a gun or whatever. They are just two very different ways of exploring, and a film script is more like a blueprint for visuals.

It does not read very interestingly sometimes, but that doesn't mean it's not a good script. And then therein lies the problem when you have producers who are used to seeing more of a verbal narrative in the text and they want dialogue.

That's very on the nose and direct where people are saying things. You don't have to say it in film. You can show it. They don't want to read the description. They just want to know what each character is saying, and that's how and why a lot of films just talk, talk, talk, talk, talk. Because people are just standing there talking about what they see, what they feel, what they remember.

And plus, always calling out the person's name! Listen when I tell you, no one calls a person by their name when they're having a conversation with them, unless they're calling them from across the street. [*Laughs*] But you see that a lot, because you have a lot of producers who need that in order to track the story. That is the difference between some great visual storytelling and something that reads like a magazine article. Magazine articles get made more frequently.

Martin: Let's segue and talk a little bit about *Professor* Dash. You have held several faculty positions over the tenure of your career, notably faculty positions at Wayne State University and College of Charleston. I'm still upset that we didn't seal the deal and keep you at the College of Charleston! I heard about that when I when I arrived in 2017 and thought, "Oh, you all fumbled the bag!"

Dash: I remember I really did the College of Charleston because I wanted to spend time with my uncle. I still have family there. I thought, "I'll do a year there, and I spend a year with Uncle Johnny." I still go down to visit Uncle Johnny. The family house is there.

Martin: How wonderful! There is also Morehouse, Howard University, and of course, currently, Spelman College. You are the Diana King Endowed Professor in Film, [Filmmaking,] Television, and Related Media. When considering your legacy, I think it's important to take a holistic approach and delve into all the ways that you are contributing to your discipline. Tell us about your evolution as *Professor* Dash. How did you first find your way into college teaching?

Dash: Let's see. Well, I did a lot of speaking engagements, and I've always been asked to [consider doing] a residency. The first residency was at Wayne State. I think that was 2013. It was real cold. It was real cool, and it was with graduate students. I got to Detroit, and I got a chance to work with Juanita Anderson, Jiah Khan, and especially Juanita Moore at the African American Museum there. We did many projects together while I was there. I was at the university, and then we did something called the Elders Project where we decided that [since there were] all these pro programs and projects initiatives for children—and my mother had recently died—how about we do something for elders?

We had a major luncheon for elders. And we gave a prize to the oldest person arriving. She was about 104 or something like that. We had it into rotunda. We had a beautiful, beautiful luncheon with the poet laureate there, and it was just wonderful. We always said we were going to do it again, but that it took a lot, and it was part of my residency budget to do this huge thing. I got to work with the museum, which I always love working with African American museums. I did a short film, large-scale video projection thing with them.

Then I went back to LA, and then I was at a film festival, and Haile Gerima was there. Haile, the independent filmmaker who was part of the LA Rebellion in the years prior to my arrival. We were in the same hotel, and he's pacing up and down. I asked, "What are you doing?" He says, "I'm getting my exercise." He said he was trying to figure out what to do, because he wanted to go on sabbatical. But he had a class at Howard, and he couldn't just walk away from his class. But he wanted to finish his film. He wanted more time to edit his next film.

He said to me right then in there, "I want you to come to teach my class." I said, "I can't. I'm at Morehouse right now." I was at Morehouse in the Cinema, Television, and [Emerging] Media Department.

And so we worked it out. It was gonna be one day a week. So I actually did both. I did [class] at Morehouse, and then I [would] fly the next day to Howard and then have my graduate class and then I['d] fly out. It was kind of like a game. It was kind of fun.

So then that's what got me to Atlanta from LA. I was Airbnb-ing it. I had a great class of graduates and undergraduates to it. It was wonderful. [Howard] asked me to stay. I was like, "No, no, I'm just doing this for Haile, and I gotta get back." I'm still in touch with my students; I email them all the time. They, of course, graduated. Now they've been to festivals around the world. Cannes and everything. I always push them, "Go, go, go!" They've interned at Sundance and at the Black House.

Then headhunters were after me, for, like UCLA and USC. And they kept offering [positions]. And I was saying, "Well, all I have to do is fly back home." But then, at the same time, we got an offer from Spelman. It's a Black women's college. It's across the street from Morehouse. [I considered my access to the] Woodruff Center, Woodruff Library—all of these things [at my disposal]? This is where I belong. I belong at Spelman. Okay, okay, because I could speak to them frankly. I could tell them about my experience. I could teach film and documentary and film history as it pertains to Hollywood. I have a class called "Hollywood in History" about how African Americans and people of color are treated in Hollywood films from the beginning, from *Birth of a Nation* on to *The Green Book*.

And it's a very lively class, and I enjoy it. And then I also teach documentary film production. We intend on opening it up to narrative film once our new arts building is completed, and that'll be in about two years. But right now, it's documentary film because they can hit the ground running and just use documents. Just tell us about yourself, your community. What are your voices? We want to hear the intimate details of their voices. And it's good for me, and it's good for them. So that's why I chose Spelman.

Martin: That makes absolute sense. I'm not surprised to hear that. What is it that you want to impart to your students about film? How do you approach teaching them about film and media?

Dash: Well, first we start out with the basics, you know, step by step on how do you make a great documentary film? What are the elements that you need to do this? Because it just seems all-encompassing to people. [They say,] "I want to tell story, but I don't know how." Okay, *this* is what you do. You have the first kind of interview, second kind of interview; you have *cinéma vérité*. B-roll. And this is how you use each of these six elements to put together a cogent story.

And you also want to make it visual. The first class we have with them is a yearlong class, and they develop two projects. The first project is a three-minute project, and the second project is a five-minute project. Those are like small bite films. It's not like they run off and [must] make a thirty-minute documentary about missing children. That's too much. So [I approach it] step by step.

And then, after they learn storytelling and counternarrative, all of that, all the elements of making a great film . . . then the next year they go into learning how to use better cameras, lighting and sound. And by this time, we know who wants to remain in the program or not. because a lot of people say, "Well, I didn't think it was going to be all this. I'm not interested in this. I really would rather do reality TV or go into women's studies because I don't want to have this pressure on me to produce, direct, and edit three-minute films." By the end of the fall semester, we usually have one or two people dropping out, and it's best for us, and it's best for them to go on to what they really, really think they can accomplish in their remaining three years at Spelman. We don't [accept] freshman. [Our students] come in as sophomores in the documentary film program.

We're promoting excellence. We're promoting having our graduates in the program, in the major, come out with a portfolio of work. Having them come out knowing how to budget a documentary, how to write a documentary, how to create a lookbook, to present their documentary with the colors and the palettes, and all of the necessary things needed in addition to the film treatment or the proposal. It's a comprehensive, intensive three years as a major. And I only teach majors because I find that people who are minoring in documentary just want to see *if* they want to make a documentary. I could be spending more time with those who know exactly what they want to do, and they want to push forward and advance.

Martin: So how do you balance teaching and filmmaking? I can't imagine what that's like.

Dash: [*Laughs*] Well, actually, that's another reason I chose Spelman. Spelman has been very gracious to allow me to have the opportunity *when* an opportunity is presented to me to do something that's meaningful and impactful they allow me to take a brief leave of absence. My first leave of absence was for a few weeks to when I shot two episodes of *Women of the Movement* about Mamie Till Mobley and her journey to find justice for her son by returning to Mississippi. We were down there for about a month, during serious COVID, doing production. And then after that I did *Our Kind of People*. So that was pretty much the fall [semester]. It was just about three weeks [left] when I came back. I get someone to sub for me. And then, I also did, last spring, I did *Reasonable Doubt*, which was a lot of fun. It's a courtroom drama. And then after that I did the Met Gala. But school had ended. We end about April 30, so I was able to go to the Met Gala. Met meaning ... I did the two rooms at the Metropolitan Museum of Art. One was dedicated to Anne Lowe, the Black designer, and other one dedicated to Madam Eta Hentz, which I, of course, populated with Aphrodite and Eartha Kitt.

Martin: Wonderful, wonderful, wonderful! Last question about teaching. If you were teaching a course on Black feminist visual narratives, who would be on your syllabus? Whether screening or reading.

Dash: Okay, so I had to teach something like that at Morehouse. But of course, Gina Prince-Blythewood. Of course. Neema Barnette, Euzhan Palcy, Ava [DuVernay]. Mira Nair, even! She's Indian. They're just so many [to choose from] at this point! There are just so many that are wonderful. It used to be [that] on one hand, you could choose [Black women filmmakers], but not anymore! And it's so much to talk about it. It's really exciting how things have opened up.

Martin: Absolutely. Let's talk LA Rebellion and Black, independent filmmakers. We know that you're associated with a group of Black, independent filmmakers coming out of UCLA, which is also my alma mater. I did my master's there. Go Bruins! This group is known colloquially as the LA Rebellion. How valuable was it for your development to be in creative space with other Black filmmakers who were experimenting and redefining what Black film could be?

Dash: It was not only helpful, it was *essential* to developing who I am and who I became because there were a lot of young, courageous filmmakers. And I just always have to say not everyone was Black. . . . It was just a group of independent filmmakers who we were all looking for new ways of telling a story. Not that we were gonna abandon the old ways of storytelling, but you know, let's see what other way that we could use to tell a story, and especially stories about people of the African diaspora, and our communities, which we felt weren't being represented the way they were supposed to be represented in film and television.

So we didn't have that moniker, that name "LA Rebellion," at the time. [*Laughs*] That was later, and people say, "Well, what do you think about it?" It is like, okay . . . whatever. We were just underground filmmakers. At the time there were a couple of articles written on us, and they called us "film outlaws." And that was because we were like, "No, no, no, no, no. I'm not doing this story. I'm not telling that story. I'm going to tell it my own way. I'm going to tell it the way that speaks to me, and speaks to the people I know, and [that] I want to represent." You know, my mother, my cousins, my aunt . . . the way *I know* them to be. Not the way *you know* them to be. Because you don't *really* know.

We were arrogant. [*Laughs*] We tried new things and some things worked. Some things didn't. I have two MFAs [master of fine arts degrees]. And coming out of AFI [American Film Institute], you know, as a screenwriting fellow, at the time, I was taught that you can't have *two* people narrating. And I did that with *Daughters of the Dust*. I had the eldest and the unborn narrating the same story. And I actually did start writing *Daughters of the Dust* while I was at AFI. But it "could never be done" because I was "violating all the rules." But those were the rules that spoke to me. That was *my* voice. Being in places like that, where they try to nudge you to do some kind of slice-of-life story that's not a slice of *your* life but a slice of *their* life . . . [only] populated by people of color . . . but I wasn't doing it. And so I found a lot of freedom being around the filmmakers at UCLA.

Martin: In past articles you've talked about the way that you and your UCLA peers worked together. Did they offer any constructive criticism to you on your early projects? And did any of that feedback make it into the final cuts of your early films?

Dash: There was constructive *and* destructive! [*Laughs*] Okay, let's get into this. *Always* there were . . . gender issues. There were always gender issues. Some of my ideas were accepted or encouraged, and some of them weren't. And everyone was going in these different directions. So I worked on a lot of their films. They worked on a lot of my films. They didn't understand what I was doing. Like, with *Illusions* they were saying, "Well, why don't you change the name?" Some people were saying, "That's just so on the nose." Or "Why don't you have more Black people in *Illusions*?" Because there was no one!

Martin: That was kind of the point of the film, right?

Dash: There were only two Black people. . . . "[You should] add a janitor." In my research there *were* no Black janitors. So that was that. I made a film on a stage which was very different. I wanted to be like that quirky kind of *Sullivan's Travels* (1941), that kind of 1940s fast-talking [film]. I wanted people to think it was made in the 1940s when we were doing it. The sound is kind of *quite* awful. But that's the sound we could afford. But anyway, moving on from that. Well, what made it into . . . ? I remember when I was editing *Illusions* . . . at some point I was even editing in my apartment. I just got an editing machine and brought it there. Charlie Burnett used to come over. And he was very supportive. He said, "Just make the film that you want to make." Because everyone has an opinion and deservedly so. Everybody's opinion is cool. But you take in opinions and then you just make the film you want to make. Of course, I heard comments like, not just with *Illusions*, but also later with *Daughters*, "It seems so female oriented. Where are the men?" Well, I'm speaking from the *women's* group. [The men are] over there, and usually it's the other way around. And it makes some people uncomfortable.

All my films have made people uncomfortable. I think you know, even when I did a short [film] called *Praise House* with the Urban Bush Woman—a dance troupe out of New York—some people said they found it frightening because I had them dancing inside of the graveyard. In the cemetery, where I come from ... my family goes to the cemetery and we clean the cemetery, pull weeds and stuff like that. The cemetery has never been anything [to fear]—and I had to learn to call it the *cemetery* because I grew up calling it the *graveyard*. We learned to be very comfortable around and in the graveyard. That was like, "Oh, let's go visit Mama. Let's go visit with Uncle Julian." Then we drive down there and you bring your rake and you're just cleaning the graves. Keeping it tidy. But for other people it's "Ewww, you were in the graveyard! Don't touch me!"

Martin: Those are some interesting cultural dynamics there. I, too, call it the graveyard and never thought anything of it. I guess it is, actually, a cemetery.

Dash: But some people will correct me. I said, "Yeah, we were in the graveyard." "You mean *cemetery*?" It's like, "Right. Whatever. You know what I mean."

Martin: Have you all in the LA Rebellion continued to collaborate? Have you all reflected collectively on your impact on filmmaking?

Dash: Well, just because you asked. . . . I guess that's why this interview has been pushed so far back. I went to Lisbon, Portugal, in November. They were celebrating the LA Rebellion.

Yes, I was there with Ben Caldwell, Charles Burnett, Billy Woodberry, who now lives in Lisbon. We got to do a lot of flashback talking in the way back machine. Especially when we started crunching the numbers. So now I think everybody has kind of a stoic view of it, looking back. Like watching Charlie's *Killer of Sheep* (1978), watching Ben Caldwell's *I and I* (1979), or Billy Woodberry's *Bless Their Little Hearts* (1983) and plus watching his newer films, documentary films. We *did* do quite a bit of work, huh? Yeah, we did that.

But we have to take it in. It must all be put in perspective because with the newer generation of filmmakers every generation has their own creative challenges and tasks and independent voices. We can't lay what we were trying to do on top of what people are doing today. We have to appreciate and listen and watch and see what they're doing. And just try to continue to make films. We [say] that they have a thousand ideas, and we were kind of stymied once we got out. We were not embraced by producers. Not Hollywood *or* television. We kind of remained independent. Not so much today. [They] grab people from here and there.

It could be because we studied so much. We studied films from Asia, Africa, Latin America. [We studied] the psychology of film, the psychology of color as it relates to film projection theories, and all of these things. Some people say, "Oh, well, you guys are like eggheads, you're too cerebral." But that's the way I think. Now, you know, because I do understand that film is hypnotic. I *do* understand you could change your whole army or generation of people with a with a single film, with an idea. We *do* understand that all films are propaganda. So [the question is] how are you going to use your visual rhetoric in relation to that? What are the visual metaphors that you're thinking about using to open your film?

Now, I'm not saying at all that everyone has to go to film school because that became a thing for a while. People saying, "Well, I'm not going. . . . I didn't go to film school, and I *still* made a movie." That's what's so great about what we did. And if [someone asks], "Do you think I need to go to film school?" I always tell young people, if you have the opportunity, take it.

It doesn't mean you won't ever make a great film if you don't [go to school]. But if you have the opportunity, make yourself available to it.

Martin: I want to talk about your legacy. And first I just want to acknowledge that you are still very much a living, breathing, and *working* filmmaker.

Dash: Yes! I show up at film festivals all the time. And people walk up to me and ask, "Are you still making movies? [*Laughs*]. That's why I'm here."

Martin: And undoubtedly you have much more to give to the world. But you've personally produced, to this point, a body of work that has made an indelible mark on the culture, if not the industry. So [let's start] with *Daughters*. . . . It has been around and with the people for over thirty years, now. And it recently was digitally remastered. It has been part of the National Register of Films since 2004. Its influence spans generations. It is a cult classic, to be sure, and your most recognized film.

Dash: It also just recently made number sixty out of one hundred of the best films ever made.

Martin: A new accolade that I wasn't aware of! Well, thank you for sharing that!

Dash: That's from an international critical list. Not domestic. *Sight and Sound* [magazine] does a list every ten years. They do a list of the one hundred best films ever made. And I made the list this year, and it came out number sixty.

Martin: Wonderful! Congratulations on that.

Dash: And I have two films on the National Film Registry. *Illusions* and *Daughters*.

Martin: You are correct! You haven't been shy about the struggles to get your films made, however, and so I want to ask: In 2023 do you feel a sense of vindication with all the cultural significance *Daughters* and some of your other films have garnered? Do you feel vindicated for some of the struggles you experienced early on?

Dash: I don't know if that's the right word. I think that we make films because we're storytellers, and we want to tell a story in a different way, a different structure. We have something to say. So I'm not really looking for outside approval because that's not the way I came up as a filmmaker, as an artist. Maybe some people are measuring. I would love to have the opportunity to get financed, to make more films and do more television. But I'm not weighing things. I'm only in competition with myself, as the old saying goes. On this film I want to accomplish this [specific goal]. On that film I want to accomplish that [specific goal]. I just finished a twelve-minute film for the International African American Museum in Charleston, South Carolina, where I was able to accomplish something else. Each film for me is so personal. Each film for me has different history and meaning. Maybe I'm not aggressive enough to get out there and pitch stories in a certain way. I'm not trying to build on the numbers or the budget. I'll make a twelve-minute film. Then I'll make a 120-minute film. They're stories. They're pieces of important art. . . .

Martin: I follow you. The story and the creative process are more important to you than the exterior accolades.

Dash: Right? So I got to work with Bradford Young on this twelve-minute film. He's one of the best Black cinematographers living right now. And so that for me was [the icing on the cake]! When they said Bradford Young is going to shoot, I was like "Yesss!" So like with Bradford Young, oh, my god! There are perks, like, "Yum yummy. This is delicious! I get to make a film with Bradford Young in the Sea Islands of the South where my family is from, and I get to create a little narrative drama about a ritual called seeking." . . . [That is what excites me.]

Martin: We're looking forward to the debut of that film here in Charleston! Would you say that the industry has been easier to break into in the latter half of your career? What challenges remain for you, and what has been easier to navigate?

Dash: No. For me, personally, the industry has not been easier to break into. But now that you have young Black producers, female producers and directors . . . they pull me in beyond those the gatekeepers. Kerry Washington's new series that came out in the spring called *Reasonable Doubt*. . . . She got that show after *Scandal*, and she produced this show. She brought me on. Angela Bassett is the reason I was able to direct *The Rosa Parks Story*. Alfre Woodard is the reason I got to direct *Funny Valentines*. They asked for me directly, and that's how I got the job. I was never picked from a pool of potential directors. Never, never, never.

Every single thing that I've ever done is because someone said, "I want her. I want Julie Dash to do it." And then I go do it.

Martin: I think that that speaks volumes about your work, your creative vision, and your reputation in in the industry. At least among a certain community.

Dash: Yeah. Well, that's good. Every time I go to these big public events everyone is like, "I can't wait to work with you," and then you reach out to them afterwards, and its crickets. All of these big-time producers—they've all said, "You know we want to work with you. Our doors are always open." You call up or knock on the door, [and they're] not available. That's the situation. That's what the situation has been, so I just try to do the best work I can. I think I've lived a good life. I have a chance to work with a lot of great people, you know, have a great family. Have a grown daughter. I have a grandson, you know. I'm good.

Martin: We love you, though. "We" being Black women. I can't say that enough, and I can't help but notice all the projects that you just named, when you were called in, you were called in by other Black women. I just want to acknowledge that. We "cape" for each other, and I think that's a beautiful thing.

Dash: That's true, absolutely. [*Laughs*]

Martin: Which brings me to Beyoncé and *Lemonade*. Her visual album pays homage to you and *Daughters of the Dust* in its imagery, but also in the way that it focuses on telling a different story about Black women by offering a different version of the South from a very Black and sacred perspective. How did it feel to see the cultural impact of your work come alive in such a public way? We're talking Beyoncé and the tremendous platform that she commands.

Dash: I was like, "What?" Someone had to send me a link. Let me tell you what happened. [*Laughs*] Oh, gosh! . . . It was not that long ago. About three or four years ago, I got a call from my website manager who said, "Your website has crashed, and we think it's because of *Lemonade*." I was confused. They said, "Well, you have to see the film, but it's not released yet. You have to have the private link," and we finagled around and got a private link, and I started watching it. I was like, "Oh!!" I was [hanging with my mouth open] for forty minutes. "This is so good! This is wonderful." The next day people started asking me, "Do you see the connections with *Daughters of the Dust*?" And I actually said, no. At first, I said no. But what I saw was something like this: A forty-minute multiple video music video extravaganza. This is something new! This is something wonderful! And then people asked, "But didn't you see the people in the tree?" [*Laughs*]

Martin: Straight to the point!

Dash: And I said, "Well, yeeeeah." And people said, "Well, how did that make you feel?" It's just that I was not watching it from the perspective or point of view of recognizing anything that I had done. I was recognizing it for what it was, and it was *extraordinary*! It was invigorating and I wanted to know, "What's this editing technique they were using?" I was looking at it technically—they were changing the shutter speed and all these wonderful things. Each piece flowed and segued into one another. And then she was singing in this dress, and she sounded like a cowboy [talking] about my daddy and a shot gun. All I could say was it was exciting. I've had a lot of people ask me about it. I wanted to know who did the costumes and the mise-en-scène and all that kind of stuff. Melina [Matsoukas]? I know Melina! This is great. It was a wonderful thing. No one owns an image; you know what I mean? I've certainly been inspired by other filmmakers. Bill Gunn's *Ganja and Hess* (1973), for instance, which you know, was promoted as a vampire horror movie. But I just remember this one scene. This guy was standing in front of a tree and the other guy, you only see him from his legs down, [and he's] kicking and he's talking to this guy. And I use that framing in *Daughters of the Dust* where you see Trula's legs just kind of hanging, and Barbara is having a conversation with her. And then I remember Isaac Julien did a film called *Looking for Langston*. It was a short. It's just so beautifully done, sensuously beautiful.

I use that as inspiration for some of the scenes in *Daughters*. I'm saying all that to say I loved watching *Lemonade*. I love interacting with it. It was like Toni Morrison visuals. It was Toni Cade Bambara. It was Alice Walker. It was all of that, and I felt at peace. I felt at home, and I felt invigorated. I let other people break down the shots and the terms of what was what but yeah, this is good stuff.

Martin: You're absolutely right. There are several influences that are easily identifiable in the film. The collaborators did an amazing job of putting it together and blending all of those influences. But we, the viewers, we who've grown up admiring Julie Dash and *Daughters of the Dust*, we *immediately* knew the references. And I think what's beautiful about it is that it has introduced a whole new generation who may not have engaged *Daughters* directly, they now know about *Daughters of the Dust*. They now know who Julie Dash is, and I think I think that's a beautiful thing.

Dash: I have to say one thing about Solange. After *Lemonade* and everything had launched, Solange Knowles invited both AJ [Arthur Jafa, the cinematographer for *Daughters*] and myself down to New Orleans. She had a town hall meeting in a wide, open church space, and it was wonderful. Where people could question us about *Daughters of the Dust* and *Lemonade*. All of that, and my students at Howard were really impressed because I was going to see Solange! [*Laughs*]

Martin: Oh, you have street cred!

Dash: Yeah, exactly! Street cred! Then she sent me a beautiful calendar, and I had it up in my office there. So when I think of Beyoncé and *Lemonade*, I also think of Solange and her salons. It's all woven together, these wonderful, courageous, bleeding-edge bites of magical reality. If that makes any sense?

Martin: What has surprised you most about the intergenerational impact that *Daughters of the Dust* has had?

Dash: Okay, intergenerational? Well. Hmm. I know a lot of people said they've seen it multiple times. Back in the 1990s people were saying . . . well, *some* people were saying, not *all* people. Some people were saying, mostly males, "Why don't you just make a linear story? Tell me what the hell is going on!" [*Laughs*] Well, to me it's linear! I came up watching foreign films, and so I have a whole different eye and patience and rhythm and tone and tempo when I'm watching a film. Especially the films that eventually live with you . . . you know, live inside of your head forever [as] images. So *Daughters* came out at a time where a lot of the urban films were coming out. And I remember *The New York Times Magazine* had a cover story called "Hollywood's Gotta Have Them," and they didn't have any women on that cover. They didn't have Euzhan [Palcy]. They didn't have Kasi [Lemmons]. They didn't have me. They didn't have Neema Barnett, and we all had the same entertainment attorneys and agents. And [the story] was written by a Black woman. And I remember she said that my movie was a "television movie."

I was stunned because the budget from American Playhouse Theatrical was the same as Maddie Rich's movie, *Straight Out of Brooklyn*. It was the same initiative. They did about four theatrical films, and *Daughters* was one. She never interviewed me. She just determined that it was a television movie. I never had a chance to speak to her, but after that the people were saying it wasn't a theatrical film. It was misinformation, and it was strange. That's all I will say . . . it was strange. *Daughters* played in the New York Villages Theatre for thirty-two consecutive weeks. But she said it was a "television movie." I realized that around that time that there were certain people who were trying to curate Black culture. [Trying] to determine who was doing what and how well they were doing it. [Defining] was hip and what was cool; what was Black and what was *not*. I don't know who they were, and I just don't want to say, "Hollywood," because that's just so broad. But there were certain people who tried to curate and tell the general public what was Black enough for you and what was not. I actually had an Asian distributor. And I don't know whether it's because of his accent or comprehension of English, but he [even] told me it really wasn't a Black film! [*Laughs*]

Martin: [*Laughs*] If it's not a Black film, what kind of film is it?

Dash: Then *Daily Variety* did their thing . . . saying it looked like an hour-long Laura Ashley commercial. This [criticism] all came from [expectations about] Black people [in film]. If you were [Black] in a historical film, you [were expected] to be within an agrarian situation, laboring. You were not "allowed" to have on a white dress. [Critics questioned], "Where did they get those white dresses from?"

[If they cared to notice], those were Gibson Girl dresses from twenty years *prior* to the turn of the century date [of the film]. And so they were old. [The dresses] were discarded clothing that these women were repairing for mainland people, or keeping, rather. We made sure everything was aged appropriately. Some of the lace was like hanging and dragging [to convey its age and condition]. Why can't we have a story about a family's last supper? Why did they have to be working? [Another expectations was] you have to see them [Black people] digging in the fields, too. "Why weren't they working?" There were weird things, weird questions [such as that], which were asked in print.

Martin: Hmm. That's interesting to learn. I remember being in college and my professors were hoarding the VHS copy of *Daughters*. They wouldn't take it back to the library because they were afraid someone was going to lose it, damage it, and it wouldn't get replaced. But I remember watching it in class—in the deepest context of it being a Black film. I can appreciate watching this film evolve within academia over the course of my career. I remember conversations moving from *Daughters* feeling like a foreign film to really homing in on the very specific ways you went about representing Black women in intentionally different ways.

Dash: And that's exactly why it *was* a foreign film. Because what we usually see is not real. And so when you show something that's just real, that's evolving, then it [causes you to question], what country is that?

Martin: It was beautiful, it was beautiful! And it has had such a lasting impact. And I think now, when I teach it, and I'm engaging students with the film . . . thankfully, they have to be taught about the stereotypes of Black women and what used to exist. Well, maybe not "used to," but what were more traditional stereotypes in the way that Black women were represented. They don't know that history right away, and I think that's a beautiful thing. And I think that your film has been part of the change to move away from certain derogatory representations of Black women. They know *Daughters*, but they don't know Sapphire [from the *Amos 'n' Andy* radio and television shows]. So [your depictions] have been impactful in that way as well.

Dash: Good.

Martin: When considering the breadth of your work, one would note that you have a diverse portfolio of projects and credits. This includes music videos, documentary film series, writing credits, sound, and commercials. Not just directing. Why was it important for you to dabble in all these different areas of filmmaking?

Dash: Well, when an opportunity presents itself to go up to Canada and shoot a car commercial on the side of a mountain . . . well, yeah, I'll do it! Because it's all about the images, the images. Are we're going to have a Black couple getting into the car? So I guess it's the geek in me. [*Laughs*] What else can I say?

Martin: I am glad to hear that because my assumption is that you are just *that* intrigued and engaged in the industry that you want to know and work in sound and production and editing all these different things, because it's part of what you love. It's why you are so passionate about filmmaking. That makes perfect sense to me.

Dash: It's story telling in a different way, in a way that we are not used to seeing. You know, that was great. Music videos were like that, too. It was great.

Martin: Let's go back to that moment when you took the photography course at the Studio Museum in Harlem as an adolescent. You say that you knew then that you wanted to make film, even if you weren't sure how that would happen . . . that was the moment that you knew this is what you wanted to do for a living. What do you say to that version of Julie Dash now? If you could go back, what would you say to her? Are you satisfied with the journey? Do you question any decisions you have made? Are there any discernible regrets or triumphs that you would share with her?

Dash: Well, I knew that I wanted to tell stories, but it's a lot easier today than it was then. Because back then, when we were working chemical filmmaking with celluloid film that you had to load into the camera—there was no memory card—so you had to load into the camera. First, you had to buy it. It's *real* expensive. Two minutes was like a hundred dollars. You had to load it into the camera without scratching it. And then, if you want to do sound—this was before crystal sync sounds so the sound person was tethered to the camera, meaning you had a plug you had to connect to the camera. The sound person and the camera person were running at the same time. You could hear the spool going. You only have two minutes, and there's no running around or whatever you're shooting with the little Bolex spring-driven camera that we had at the Studio Museum of Harlem.

Then once [the scene is] shot, then you have to send it off to get developed. And then there's the work print. That's more money. Then you get the work print that you start editing on, and I think it was especially doing the editing process when—I feel so terrible. I can't remember her name, but a Black woman editor came from the newsroom once and was teaching us how to edit documentary films. And she was basically telling us, which would be proven time and time again, with any given hundred feet of film, you could edit it into anything you want. You can make it into a comedy, a serious film, a horror film, whatever. And that proved to be true. When we got to UCLA, they had a editing class called "Gun Smoke," that gave everybody the same ten minute piece of film reel, and you would have to edit it into something. Everyone's edit would be different depending on what sound effects and what music you attach to it. I knew I wanted to be a filmmaker because it was hella fun and technical, and it was challenging. The technical aspects of filmmaking back then were so much more challenging.

And I liked to be able to do everything that that the guys were doing. I could load. I could edit. I could load the movie without scratching the film and all of these things. When you are young, you're never really thinking that's what you have do to pay your rent. You have to make money in this industry to pay your rent—that never factored in [for me]. I thought, "I'm going to go to college and major in this, too." The first year of college was not [as a] film major. You could not get there until your sophomore or junior year. But I got to be in all these special film programs like at City College because it was the David Picker Film Institute. No one was interested, and when I graduated and went out to the American Film Institute, I just got in to AFI [without a lot of competition] because no one was interested! There were only like eighteen people in my class. And then, even when I finished the AFI, I went to UCLA. Just breezed through. You can't do that any longer . . . because film began trending, and now there is so much competition. And it's so expensive. But they were giving us the film then. When I was an undergrad [faculty] gave us a shopping bag full of film and said, "Go home and make these films. Do this, do that to the other one." I was like, "Yes, sir!" It's a whole different world. I didn't feel any competition. I didn't feel any competition while I was at AFI. I knew I was never going to make a film there because I was in the producing-writing fellowship department because everyone was all parceled out. I wasn't in the directing category. Amy Heckerling was there. She was in the directing category. Mimi Leder was there. She was in the cinematography category. Now she's a great director, and Amy has directed quite a few films. It was really about learning and being on film sets and learning how to do different things. There was no competition.

And now what I hear from *my* students is, "I gotta do a film. It's gotta be *great*. It's gotta do *this*, and I have to do it like *this*." Oh, my god! What about the story? And then, as soon as they make the film, they post it on YouTube so they can get likes. [They don't realize] if you post it on YouTube, then you can't get into film festivals. [Their approach is]: "I don't care about film festivals. I just want people to see it, because then I'll get discovered like" fill in the blank.

Everything is real immediate [for this generation]. They're going to upload it to TikTok. They're going to upload it to the Instagram. It's like, "Don't you want to travel the world with your films?"

Martin: Yeah, yeah, absolutely. Not many do, do they?

Dash: We didn't have the whole online situation. So that's different. I can't really comment on that or critique that. But I do know that it's going to limit you from various film festivals. In the same vein they don't care about film festivals. It's a whole different world.

Martin: Instant gratification versus more traditional or conventional routes, right? You want students to engage in the film festivals because that's where your work is evaluated by other professionals in the industry. That seems to have some merit, no?

Dash: And being there with all of these people who have been making films for many years. And you get to learn. There's a lot more to being discovered than just simply uploading your film. People might call it a discovery, but you need people to write about it, to analyze [and] critique it, to see it. Not just copy it. But that's a real contemporary issue. And then people say, "Well, I just want people to see it." *What* people? We all want people to see our films. What are you really looking for . . . a career? Or someone getting a thousand likes?

Martin: Well, that was a mouthful. Let's talk a little bit about some of the projects you've mentioned in past interviews. I think of *The Colored Conjurers*, for instance. You've mentioned that in earlier interviews. Also, the documentary on Vertamae Smart-Grosvenor Where did those projects stand?

Dash: Well, *Vertamae* is shot. Between school and my different projects I'm doing outside of Spelman, I can't edit two things. I can't edit two projects simultaneously. The *Seeking* project for the International African American Museum just ended last week. *The Colored Conjurers*, I've been pitching that for many, many years. Eleanor Roosevelt's battalion about the Sixth Triple Eight Postal Battalion is a limited series that I wrote, and I've been pitching that for years. I went to Belgium to scout locations for it, and all these wonderful things. And then, I think it was last month, it was just announced that Netflix is doing a film about the Six Triple Eight Postal Battalion. They're doing it with Tyler Perry. So I'll have to wait. Let him do his film. It doesn't mean that I'll never do it, but it's been eleven years that I've been pitching that at every major movie studio, streaming network, everywhere. I've come to realize over the years, it's not the story you want to tell. It's who financiers and venture capitalists and the studio want to work with.

It comes down to that. Who do they want to be aligned with? What kind of story are you going to tell that they would be comfortable with? But that was a long haul. That was eleven years that I was working with Sandra Evers-Manly. We optioned a book for eleven years on Charity Adams Early, who was a twenty-four-year-old major and who commanded 850 African American women in England and France. And that I pitch that story from the point of the studio executives saying they never heard of that story. We had a beautiful deck made where they could see the actual photographs from the era. And they always tell you [that] it's always good to have a book that you can option. So we had the book. And we'll probably lose it now, because it's been eleven years. The other film that's being made is based upon a newspaper article about these 850 African

American women. We did everything we were supposed to do. We even went to the Congressional Black Caucus with it. We needed help with this, and they were accommodating and all of that. We had so much support behind us. But no, [the studios] just would not do it with us.

There are the other screenplays that I have written, including *Enemy of the Sun*, another one called *Cypher*, an encryption thriller. There are multiple, multiple, multiple stories that I'd like to tell, and not one of them in the last thirty-two years has been financed. I have to look at the big picture, and the big picture is that people work with who they want to work with, basically, and they are going to tell the story that they want told.

Martin: It's unfortunate. Yet, you've done a lot in your career: television, film, commercials, music videos. What is left for Julie Dash to experiment in with film? What have you not yet explored in your work?

Dash: Virtual reality and gaming.

Martin: Ha! Say more.

Dash: Very interested in that. Well, doing those two rooms at the Metropolitan Museum . . . that was something different. I didn't even understand what I was supposed to do when I agreed to do it! Just design these rooms. It was like, "Okay. I'll try it!"

Martin: You are at a point in a very storied career (that is still evolving) . . .

Dash: I forgot to talk about the projects that other people have written that I'm attached to! Have you ever heard of Ernest Withers, the photographer? He worked for Martin Luther King Jr., and he also worked for the FBI.

Martin: Now that's a story!

Dash: It's a story that's being told by Andre Holland, the actor. His company is doing it as a limited series, and it's very complicated. The details are just extraordinary, all based upon Ernest Withers. Another one is Anne Lowe, the designer. I had the opportunity to honor her designs and her persona inside of the Metropolitan Museum of Art. And so there's a feature film that's being written about her. And it's like, yeah, I'd like to do that.

Martin: And you were attached to do the biopic on Angela Davis. Is that still moving forward?

Dash: Not with me.

Martin: What would you like for the name Julie Dash to connote? If we think about your legacy and how your career will move forward from this point, what do you want your name to connote to the film-watching world?

Dash: That I made meaningful films, short and long, domestic and abroad. [I made] films that made you think. Films that help to make the world better, maybe in some small way, because they were courageous in their own way. Meaningful is the most important thing.

I don't want to do things that—unless they are like a commercial—aren't meaningful to someone. I love creating. I love creating visual metaphors. How do you tell a story visually? It's just like, "Oh, that's a challenge." And I love a good challenge.

Martin: I can't say enough what a treasure you are to the world. It has been my immense pleasure to edit this collection and to honor your work in this way. Thank you!

Dash: I mean, wonderful questions! It's all been so good. Thank you!

Additional Sources

Articles

Amine, Laila. 2004. "Julie Dash's Aesthetic Vision." *Black Camera* 19, no. 2: 3–4.

Backstein, Karen. 1993. "The Cinematic Jazz of Julie Dash." *Cinéaste* 19, no. 4: 88.

Brody, Richard. 2016. "The Return of Julie Dash's Historic 'Daughters of the Dust.'" *The New Yorker*, November 18.

Brouwer, Joel. 1995. "Repositioning: Center and Margin in Julie Dash's *Daughters of the Dust*." *African American Review* 29, no. 1: 5–16.

Buckley, Cara. 2016. "Julie Dash Made a Movie. Then Hollywood Shut Her Out." *The New York Times*, November 18.

Burton, Rachal. 2023. "Filming Social Death and the Fixed Position of Blackness: On L.A. Rebellion Director Julie Dash's *Four Women*." *Black Camera* 14, no. 2: 49–70.

Cade, Maya S. 2024. "How Julie Dash Became the First Black Woman to Helm a Theatrically Distributed Movie." *WeScreenplay*, March 1. https://www.wescreenplay.com/blog/how-julie-dash-became-the-first-black-woman-to-helm-a-theatrically-distributed-movie/.

Dash, Julie. 2019. "Julie Dash: 'Queen & Slim' Director Melina Matsoukas Knows How to Evoke 'the Danger of Our Times.'" *Variety*, December 18.

Davis, Cienna. 2017. "From Colorism to Conjurings: Tracing the Dust in Beyoncé's Lemonade." *Taboo* 16, no. 2: 7–28.

Davis, Nick. 2014. "The Face Is a Politics: A Close-Up View of Julie Dash's Illusions." *Camera Obscura* 29, no. 2: 149–83.

Erhart, Julia. 1996. "Picturing What If: Julie Dash's Speculative Fiction''." *Camera Obscura* 13, no. 2: 116–31.

Felton, Wes. 2009. "Rewriting Hollywood History in Julie Dash's *Illusions*." *Senses of Cinema* 49. https://www.sensesofcinema.com/2009/feature-articles/illusions-julie-dash/.

Francis, Terri. 2020. "Julie Dash: Challenging the Paradigm." *Post Script* 39, nos. 2–3: 50–65, 133.

Gaither, Laura. 1996. "Close-Up and Slow Motion in Julie Dash's *Daughters of the Dust*." *Howard Journal of Communications* 7, no. 2: 103–12.

Gourdine, Angeletta K. M. 2004. "Fashioning the Body [as] Politic in Julie Dash's 'Daughters of the Dust.'" *African American Review* 38, no. 3: 499–511.

Hall, Aimee. 1996. "Julie Dash: Filmmaking Within a Culture of Women." *Black Camera: The Newsletter of the Black Film Center/Archives* 11, no. 2: 2–4.

Hartman, S. V., and Farah Jasmine Griffin. 1991. "Are You as Colored as That Negro?: The Politics of Being Seen in Julie Dash's *Illusions*." *Black American Literature Forum* 25, no. 2: 361–73.

Heller, Daniel A. 1998. "Julie Dash." *English Journal* 87, no. 4: 90.

King, Jeannine. 2010. "Memory and the Phantom South in African American Migration Film." *Mississippi Quarterly* 63, no. 3: 477–91.

King, Tiffany Lethabo. 2016. "The Labor of (Re)Reading Plantation Landscapes Fungible(ly)." *Antipode* 48, no. 4: 1022–39.

Letort, Delphine. 2008. "Daughters of the Dust (Julie Dash, 1991), le récit d'esclave revisité." *Amnis* 8.

Lewis, Mel, and Melissa L. Cooper. 2020. "The Saviors of Gullah Identity: Teaching *Daughters of the Dust* and the 'Classics' of Black Women Writers." *Feminist Formations* 32, no. 1: 216–25.

Machiorlatti, Jennifer A. 2005. "Revisiting Julie Dash's 'Daughters of the Dust': Black Feminist Narrative and Diasporic Recollection." *South Atlantic Review* 70, no. 1: 97–116.

M'Baye, Babacar. 2016. "African Influences in Atlantic World Culture: Julie Dash's *Daughters of the Dust.*" *Literature Compass* 13, no. 5: 277–87.

McHugh, Kathleen. 2021. "Prolegomenon: Anger, Aesthetics, and Affective Witness in Contemporary Feminist Cinema." *Film Quarterly* 75, no. 1: 10–22.

McKoy, Sheila Smith. 1999. "Limbo: Diaspora Temporality and Its Reflection in *Praisesong for the Widow* and *Daughters of the Dust.*" *Callaloo* 22, no. 1: 208–22.

Mellencamp, Patricia. 1993. "Haunted History: Tracey Moffatt and Julie Dash." *Discourse* 16, no. 2: 127–63.

Mellencamp, Patricia. 1994. "Making History: Julie Dash." *Frontiers: A Journal of Women Studies* 15, no. 1: 76–101.

Nordine, Michael. 2019. "'Daughters of the Dust' Director Julie Dash Is Finally Making Her Second Film." *IndieWire.com*, January 28. https://www.indiewire.com/features/general/julie-dash-angela-davis-biopic-lionsgate-1202039205/

Ogunleye, Foluke. 2007. "Transcending the 'Dust': African American Filmmakers Preserving the 'Glimpse Of the Eternal.'" *College Literature* 34, no. 1: 156–73.

Papagianni, Chrysavgi. 2022. "The Affectivity of Things in Julie Dash's *Daughters of the Dust.*" *Quarterly Review of Film and Video* 39, no. 2: 272–88.

Platas Alonso, María. 2023. "La narrativa biográfica como contradiscurso feminista en *The Rosa Parks Story* (2002) de Julie Dash." *Asparkía: investigación feminista* 43: 143–61.

Pozo, Diana. 2013. "Water Color: Radical Color Aesthetics in Julie Dash's *Daughters of the Dust.*" *New Review of Film and Television Studies* 11, no. 4: 424–37.

Richardson, Judy. 2003. Review of *The Rosa Parks Story*. *The Public Historian* 25, no. 3: 142–47.

Richardson, Riché. 2013. "Framing Rosa Parks in Reel Time." *Southern Quarterly* 50, no. 3: 54–65.

Rogers, Jamie Ann. 2020. "Diasporic Communion and Textual Exchange in Beyoncé's *Lemonade* and Julie Dash's *Daughters of the Dust.*" *Black Camera* 11, no. 2: 130–57.

Ruth. 2024. "Julie Dash: Reinventing the Language of Film for Black Cinema." Fountaindale Public Library, February 2. https://www.fountaindale.org/julie-dash-reinventing-the-language-of-film-for-black-cinema/

Ryan, Judylyn S. 2004. "Outing the Black Feminist Filmmaker in Julie Dash's *Illusions*." *Signs* 30, no. 1: 1319–44.

Sabir, Wanda Ali Batin. 2018. "Sweeping Conversations: Julie Dash's *Daughters*." *Journal of Pan African Studies* 11, no. 6: 231–46.

Streeter, Caroline A. 2004. "Was Your Mama Mulatto? Notes Toward a Theory of Racialized Sexuality in Gayl Jones's *'Corregidora'* and Julie Dash's *'Daughters of the Dust.'*" *Callaloo* 27, no. 3: 768–87.

Sudhinaraset, Pacharee. 2018. "'We Are Not an Organically City People': Black Modernity and the Afterimages of Julie Dash's *Daughters of the Dust*." *Black Scholar* 48, no. 3: 46–60.

Troutman, Stephanie, and Brenna Johnson. 2018. "Dark Water: Rememory, Biopower, and Black Feminist Art." *Taboo* 17, no. 3: 73–84.

Ugwu, Reggie. 2019. "'They Set Us Up to Fail': Black Directors of the '90s Speak Out." *The New York Times*, July 3.

White, Marilyn M. 2021. Review of "*Daughters of the Dust* by Julie Dash." *Journal of American Folklore* 134, no. 54: 532–33.

Books

Aldama, Frederick Luis. 2003. *Postethnic Narrative Criticism: Magicorealism in Oscar "Zeta" Acosta, Ana Castillo, Julie Dash, Hanif Kureishi, and Salman Rushdie*. University of Texas Press.

Brooks, Tisha M. 2023. *Spirit Deep: Recovering the Sacred in Black Women's Travel*. University of Virginia Press.

Cummins, Kathleen. 2020. *Herstories on Screen: Feminist Subversions of Frontier Myths*. Wallflower Press of Columbia University Press.

Dash, Julie, with Toni Cade Bambara and bell hooks. 1992. *Daughters of the Dust: The Making of an African American Woman's Film*. The New Press.

Field, Allyson Nadia, Jan-Christopher Horak, and Jacqueline Najuma Stewart, eds. 2015. *L. A. Rebellion: Creating a New Black Cinema*. University of California Press.

hooks, bell. 1996. *Reel to Real: Race, Sex, and Class at the Movies*. Routledge.

Lessane, Patricia Williams, ed. 2020. *Teaching "Daughters of the Dust" as a Womanist Film and the Black Arts Aesthetic of Filmmaker Julie Dash*. Peter Lang.

Martin, Kameelah L. 2016. *Envisioning Black Feminist Voodoo Aesthetics: African Spirituality in American Cinema*. Lexington Books.

Patton, Venetria K. 2013. *The Grasp That Reaches Beyond the Grave: The Ancestral Call in Black Women's Texts*. State University of New York Press.

Raphael-Hernandez, Heike. 2008. *The Utopian Aesthetics of Three African American Women (Toni Morrison, Gloria Naylor, Julie Dash): The Principle of Hope*. Edwin Mellen Press.

Ryan, Judylyn S. 2005. *Spirituality as Ideology in Black Women's Film and Literature*. University of Virginia Press.

Thompson, Lisa B. 2009. *Beyond the Black Lady: Sexuality and the New African American Middle Class*. University of Illinois Press.

Book Chapters

Benton, Jacquelyn. 2000. "Grace Nicols' *I Is a Long Memoried Woman* and Julie Dash's *Daughters of the Dust*: Reversing the Middle Passage." In *Black Women Writers Across Cultures: An Analysis of Their Contribution*, edited by Valentine Udoh James, James S. Etim, Melanie Marshall James, and Ambe J. Njoh, 221–32. International Scholars Publications.

Diawara, Manthia. 1993. "Black American Cinema: The New Realism." In *Black American Cinema*, edited by Manthia Diawara, 3–25. Routledge.

Mayer, So. 2019. "'Being a Together Woman Is a Bitch': 'An African American Woman's Film' Genealogy of Julie Dash's *Four Women* (1975)." In *Women Artists, Feminism and the Moving Image: Contexts and Practices*, edited by Lucy Reynolds, 73–86. Bloomsbury Academic.

Weisenfeld, Judith. 2003. "'My Story Begins Before I Was Born': Myth, History, and Power in Julie Dash's *Daughters of the Dust*." In *Representing Religion in World Cinema: Filmmaking, Mythmaking, Culture Making*, edited by S. Brent Plate, 43–66. Palgrave Macmillan.

Digital Media

Byrd, Twinkie, host. 2020. "TCM Tea with AWD – Daughters of the Dust." Turner Classic Movies with Alliance of Women Directors, September 22. Video, 50 min., 23 sec. YouTube, https://www.youtube.com/watch?app=desktop&v=AuWosdQYB_g&t=2118s.

D., Mike. 2010. "Julie Dash: The Reelblack Interview." Posted by Reelblack One, February 24, 2014. Video, 7 min., 19 sec. YouTube, https://www.youtube.com/watch?v=EmI2HIhZqdU.

Dash, Julie, and Alex Haley. 1992. "Alex Haley Interviews Julie Dash, January 14, 1992." Posted February 26, 2013. Video, 6 min., 57 sec. Vimeo, https://vimeo.com/60593172/306b3c0188.

Dash, Julie, and Lindsay Law. 1993. "Julie Dash: American Playhouse Tribute." Dialogues and Film Retrospectives, June 11. Posted by Walker Art Center, April 28, 2020. Video, 1 hr., 35 min., 43 sec. YouTube, https://www.youtube.com/watch?v=g_7poDKTJEA.

Harris-Perry, Melissa, host. 2016. *The Takeaway*. "Director Julie Dash on Black Representation in Entertainment." WYNC Studios and PRX, December 5. Radio show, 7 minutes, 46 sec. https://www.wnycstudios.org/podcasts/takeaway/segments/director-julie-dash

Harris-Perry, Melissa. 2017. "Melissa Harris-Perry is live now interviewing filmmaker, director, and author Julie Dash at the Wexner Center in Columbus, Ohio. Tonight is the world premiere of the new restoration of her 1991 film Daughters of the Dust. Watch and ask your questions below!" *Elle Magazine*, January 2. Facebook Live Video, 29 min., 3 sec. Facebook, https://www.facebook.com/watch/?v=10153543381581301.

Hockley, Rujeko, host. 2017. "We Wanted a Revolution: Black Radical Women, 1965–85: *Daughters of the*

Dust Panel Discussion." Brooklyn Museum, April 22. Posted by the Brooklyn Museum, May 5, 2017. Video, 1 hr., 3 min., 8 sec. YouTube, https://www.youtube.com/watch?v=ehoNb1i6vYo.

IUC Cinema. 2016. "Final Draft: Julie Dash on Film." Indiana University Cinema, April 19. Video, 8 min. YouTube, https://www.youtube.com/watch?v=vyidjfZMMhw.

Martin, Michael, host. 2016. *All Things Considered*. "'Daughters of the Dust' Re-Released Following Attention from Beyoncé." NPR, November 20. Radio show, 8 min. https://www.npr.org/2016/11/20/502797705/daughters-of-the-dust-re-released-following-attention-from-beyonc.

McCullough, Barbara, host. 1979. *The View*. "L. A. Rebellion: Julie Dash on UCLA's 'The View' (c. 1979)." Posted by UCLA Film & Television Archive, May 3, 2013. Video, 7 min., 16 sec. YouTube, https://www.youtube.com/watch?v=wq-9-bt5Ho8.

Oscars. 2020. "Ava DuVernay, Julie Dash & Euzhan Palcy: Academy Dialogues: Broadening the Aperture of Excellence." Academy Dialogues: Broadening the Aperture of Excellence, October 20. Video, 53 min., 12 sec. YouTube, https://www.youtube.com/watch?v=pz-8LoMzLbc.

Welbon, Yvonne, dir. 1992. *The Cinematic Jazz of Julie Dash*. Video, 26 min. Third World News Reel, https://film.twn.org/products/the-cinematic-jazz-of-julie-dash.

Yates, Courtney, dir. 2022. "Julie Dash Tells the Story Behind the Iconic Costumes From 'Daughters of the Dust.'" *Vogue*, April 26. Video, 11 min., 13 sec. YouTube, https://www.youtube.com/watch?v=wAYRchfBPzw.

Dissertations (selected)

Alao, Folashade. 2009. "Islands of Memory: The Sea Islands, Black Women Artists, and the Promise of Home." PhD diss., Emory University.

Brown-Hinds, Paulette. 1998. "'Long-Memoried' Women: Memory and Migration in Twentieth Century Black Women's Narrative." PhD diss., University of California, Riverside.

Combs, Rhea Lynn. 1984. "African American Independent Filmmaker, Julie Dash: Developing a Black Female Voice in *Daughters of the Dust*." PhD diss., Cornell University.

Davis, Nicholas Keeling. 2005. "The Desiring-Image: Gilles Deleuze, Film Theory, and Contemporary Queer Cinema." PhD diss., Cornell University.

Dozier, Judy Massey. 2000. "Conjure Woman: Cultural Performances of African American Women Writers." PhD diss., Loyola University Chicago.

Dube, Zama. 2024. "Visualizing the Wake: A Black Feminist Grammar for Visual Dissent in the African Diaspora." PhD diss., University of California, Los Angeles.

Gauthier, Marni Jeanine. 2001. "Narrating America: Myth, History, and Countermemory in the Modern Nation." PhD diss., University of Colorado at Boulder.

Hewett, Heather Anne. 2001. "Diaspora's Daughters: Buchi Emecheta, Julie Dash, Edwidge Danticat and the Remapping of Mother Africa." PhD diss., University of Wisconsin–Madison.

Johnston, Jaime Elizabeth. 2024. "Death, Dreaming, and Diaspora: Achieving Orientation through Afro-Spirituality." PhD diss., Louisiana State University.

Machiorlatti, Jennifer Alyce. 1996. "Implications of a Feminist Narratology: Temporality, Focalization and Voice in the Films of Julie Dash, Mona Smith and Trinh T. Minh-Ha." PhD diss., Wayne State University.

Restovich, Catherine R. 2000. "Negotiating Identity in the Waters of the Atlantic: The Middle Passage Trope in African-American and Afro-Caribbean Women's Writing." PhD diss., Saint Louis University.

Sempreora, Margot Sahrbeck. 1997. "Translating Women: The Short Fiction of Kate Chopin and Alice Dunbar-Nelson and the Films of Julie Dash." PhD diss., Tufts University.

Sharpe, Christina Elizabeth. 1999. "The Work of Re-Membering: Reading Gertrude Stein, Gayl Jones, Julie Dash, Cherrie Moraga, and Bessie Head." PhD diss., Cornell University.

Sivak, Nadine. 2000. "'Howwe Gonna Find My Me?': Postcolonial Identities in Contemporary North American Drama and Film." PhD diss., University of Toronto.

Smith, John. 2020. "Social Death in the Work of Julie Dash." PhD diss., Emory University.

Streeter, Caroline Anne. 2000. "Ambiguous Bodies, Ambivalent Desires: The Morphing Mullata Body in United States Culture, 1965–1999." PhD diss., University of California, Berkeley.

Welbon, Yvonne Lynn. 2001. "Sisters in Cinema: Case Studies of Three First-Time Achievements Made by African American Women Feature Film Directors in the 1990s." PhD diss., Northwestern University.

Interviews

Dash, Julie. 1992. "Dialogue Between bell hooks and Julie Dash." Interview by bell hooks. In *Daughters of the Dust: Making an African American Women's Film*, Julie Dash with Toni Cade Bambara and bell hooks. The New Press.

Dash, Julie. 1993. Interview by Valerie Smith. Hatch-Billops Oral History of Black Culture. City College of New York Archives, CCNY, New York, NY.

Dash, Julie. 2003. "Interview: Julie Dash on Her Nomination for a Directors Guild of America Award." Interview by Toni Cox. *The Tavis Smiley Show*, NPR, February 2.

Dash, Julie. 2004. "A Splash of Julie Dash; The 'Sisters in Cinema.'" Interview by Kam Williams. *Afro-American*, February 13.

Dash, Julie. 2015. "'There's a Movement Here': Pioneering Director Julie Dash on the LA Rebellion, Black Lives Matter, and the New Generation of African-American Women in Film." Interview by Allison Nastasi. *Flavorwire*, October 21. https://www.flavorwire.com/543984/theres-a-movement-here-pioneering-director-julie-dash-on-the-la-rebellion-black-lives-matter-and-the-new-generation-of-african-american-women-in-film

Dash, Julie. 2016a. "Julie Dash Talks 'Daughters of the Dust.'" Interview by Jerry Nunn. *Windy City Times*, November 16.

Dash, Julie. 2016b. "Director Julie Dash on *Daughters of the Dust*, Beyoncé, and Why We Need Film Now More Than Ever." Interview by Julia Falsenthal. *Vogue*, November 18.

DuVernay, Ava. 2014. "Conversations with Ava DuVernay: 'A Call to Action': Organizing Principles of an Activist Cinematic Practice." Interview with Michael T. Martin. *Black Camera* 6, no. 1: 57–9.

Index

Abbott, Randy, vii, xvii, 36, 111. *See also* Mubarak, Omar (Randy Abbott)
abortion, 65
Academy of Motion Picture Arts, xiv
aesthetic sensibilities, 35, 91
aesthetics, viii, 19, 94, 97
African American culture, x, 65, 68
African American Film Critics Association, 49
African American history/identity, xi, 45, 50, 128; historical drama, 54, 66, 105, 135, 150, 156
African Americana, 95
African diaspora, vii, xii–xiii, 51, 52, 54, 105, 163
African griots, 14
Africanisms in the Gullah Dialect (Turner), 100
Afrocentrism, 9, 10, 19
Afrofuturists, 84, 125, 131, 145
Agfa-Gevaert film, 8, 89
Amelia (character), 123, 157
American Film Institute (AFI), viii, 3, 5, 18, 19, 28, 46, 47, 58, 69, 85, 91, 95, 101, 120, 144, 155, 173; Conservatory Fellowship Program in Producing and Writing, viii, xvii, 18, 91, 144
American Playhouse, 5, 6, 10, 42, 170
answer print, 60, 74, 80, 89, 97
auteur films, 39, 40
Autobiography of Miss Jane Pittman, The (Korty), 55

awards: Best Film of the Decade, ix, xvii, xviii, 3; Best Film by a Woman, viii, ix, xvii; Black Filmmaker Foundation, ix, 3, 117; Black Filmmakers Hall of Fame Award, 29; Director's Guild of America Award, viii, ix, xvii, xviii, xix, xx, 3, 29, 45, 117, 126; Excellence in Cinematography Award, 46; Golden Lion Award, 136; Joseph R. Biden President's Lifetime Achievement Award, xxi; MTV Music Video Award, xviii, 29

Back Inside Herself (Sharp), 6
Baker, Houston A., Jr., 13–27, 41, 42
Bambara, Toni Cade, ix, x, xiii, xviii, 13, 14, 23, 28, 37, 81, 95, 124, 144, 155, 169
Baraka, Amiri, 13, 104
Barnes, John, 76, 82, 90, 136
Barnette, Neema, 32, 163, 170
Bassett, Angela, 29, 30, 39, 45, 71, 146, 167
Believer, The, vii, 121–32
Beloved (Morrison), 37, 48, 60, 155
Bergman, Ingmar, 145
Bessie (Rees), 102
Beyoncé, vii, xiv, xx, 74, 75, 79, 81, 88, 94, 96, 97, 106, 107, 121, 168, 169; Bey Hive, 94. *See also Lemonade* (Beyoncé)
Bicycle Thief, The (De Sica), 90
Billops, Camile, 20, 110
binary narrative, 52

Black aesthetic, 36, 97
Black American Cinema (Diawara), xiii
Black anti-Hollywood Movement, 133
Black Arts Movement, viii, 15, 29, 61, 104, 110, 114; "postsoul," viii
Black Cinema Movement, 61
Black Empire (Schuyler), 125
Black exploitation/Blaxploitation films, 10, 22, 41
Black feminist narrative, xiii, 154, 163
Black Film Review, 3–12
Black Filmmaker Foundation, ix, 3, 117
Black History Month, 55, 134
Black independent cinema, ix, vii, xii, xiii, 6
"Black insurgents," 28
Black Lives Matter, 71, 79, 137, 138, 142, 149
Black magicians, xii, 151
Black men, 24, 55; tenderness, 107
Black narrative traditions, ix
Black Nationalism, 10
Black Power Movement, 49, 104
Black romantic comedies, 32
Black Star Film Festival, 69, 100
Black women: artists, 21; in cinema and film, vii, xii, xiii, xiv, 12, 64, 163; film executives, 55; film technicians, 7; hair, x, 9, 95; intragroup relationships, 4; literary tradition, x, 157; in media, xiv, xv; narrative, ix, xiv; stories, ix; womanist utopia, 121; writing, xiii, 154, 156
#BlackGirlMagic, vii
Bless Their Little Hearts (Woodberry), 6, 22, 29, 80, 165
blue hands, 26, 53, 76, 82. *See also* indigo-handed people
Bluest Eye, The (Morrison), 37
Bogle, Donald, 20
Bolex cameras, xvii, 114, 172
bottle trees, x, 95, 131

Bourne, St. Clair, viii, xvii, 16, 36, 37, 110; Chamba Productions, 110
Bowe, Nandi, 7
Boyz n the Hood (Singleton), 22
Breaking the Silence (Dash), ix, xviii; National Black Women's Health Project, ix, xviii, 9
Brothers of the Borderland (Dash), xix, 29, 63, 66, 102, 134; National Underground Railroad Freedom Center Museum, xix, 29, 55, 63, 66, 102, 134
"brown paper bag" issue, 70
buddy films, 32
Burnett, Charles, viii, viii, xvii, xviii, 6, 7, 21, 22, 28, 29, 32, 36, 80, 85, 86, 102, 112, 135, 139, 140, 164, 165
Bush Mama (Gerima), 6, 80
Butler, Octavia, 84, 105, 154, 155

Calendar, Eugene S., 16
Campbell, Veda, 7
Cannes International Film Festival, viii, xviii, 83, 96, 161
CBS (Columbia Broadcasting System), 29, 30, 142
Chamba Brothers, 16, 37; Chamba Productions, 16, 37, 110, 111; Charles Hopson, 16, 37; St. Clair Bourne, 16, 110; Stan Lathan, 37; Stan Wakeman, 16, 37
Chapman, Tracy, xviii, 29, 45, 148
Chase, Andrea, 57–62
Che-Lumumba Club (Communist Party), 129, 137
chemical filmmaking, 172
Chenzira, Ayoka, 109–19
Chicago International Film Festival, 74
cinema, vii, ix, xii, xiii, xiv, xix, xviii, 29, 51, 52, 54, 61, 67, 76, 79, 80, 81, 88, 97, 98, 104, 111, 116, 120, 135, 149, 150, 162; representation in, xiii

cinéma verité, 135, 162
ciphers, 35, 121, 131
Clarke, Larry, viii, xvii, xviii, 18, 29, 36, 85, 95, 102
code switching, 90, 128
Cohen Media Group, 51, 59, 75, 89, 90, 94, 121
Colored Conjurers, The (Dash), 32, 33, 148, 150, 151, 174
College of Charleston, xx, 45, 47, 160; Avery Research Center, xx, 45, 47, 48; Dash's faculty position, 47, 160; Patricia Williams Lessane, xxi, 46
Collins, Kathleen, 16, 37, 80, 101, 110, 119
"Comet, The" (Du Bois), 125
commercial viability, 10
competition, 21, 41, 42, 126, 139, 167, 173
conjure woman (archetype), xiii
Corporation for Public Broadcasting (CPB), 5
costumes/outfits, 7, 52, 61, 68, 77, 78, 104, 169
cotton, xi, 53, 54, 76, 82, 83, 92, 138
Creative Artists Agency (CAA), 140
Creel, Margaret Washington, 5, 6, 98
crowdfunding, 48, 66
Cruz Brothers and Mrs. Malloy, The (Collins), 101, 112
Cry Freedom (Bowe), 7
Cypher (Dash), 131, 132, 140, 175. See also *Digital Diva* (Dash)

Da Cota, Cassie, 50–56
Daily Variety, 68, 138, 170
Dark Exodus (White), 6
Darling, Nola, 22–23
Dash, Charlene (sister), 45–56, 47
Dash, Charles Edward (father), vii, xvii
Dash, Emma (great-grandmother), 99

Dash, Julian (uncle), 46, 165
Dash, Julius (uncle), 99
Dash, N'Zinga (daughter), 63, 64
Dash, Rosie (great-great-great grandmother), 99
Dash, Saint Julian (uncle), 46, 99, 165
Daughters of the Dusk (Dash), ix–xi, xii, xiii–xiv, xviii–xix, xx, 3–4, 9–11, 13–14, 25–27, 29–30, 33, 34, 41–42, 45–48, 50–55, 57–62, 63–66, 67–71, 74–75, 77, 79–84, 86–87, 88–91, 93–94, 95–97, 100, 101–3, 106–8, 109, 112, 121–23, 125, 127–28, 130–31, 133–36, 138, 141, 142, 145, 147, 150, 152, 154–55, 156–58, 164–65, 166–71
Davis, Zeinabu irene, 3–12, 97
del Valle Schorske, Carina, ix, 120–32
Denise LaMarge (character), 34
DeSica, Vittorio, 36, 90
Diary of an African Nun (Dash), ix, xvii, 3, 6, 29, 95, 109, 124, 133, 154
"Diary of an African Nun" (Walker), ix, 3, 120
Dickerson, Ernest, 105, 138
Different Image, A (Larkin), viii, xviii, 6, 102
Digital Diva (Dash), 31, 32, 33, 35, 108, 131, 140
digital remastering, xiv, 59, 60, 80
directing work, ix, xii, 29, 31, 86, 96, 107, 121, 125, 136, 144, 173
Disappearing Acts (Prince-Bythewood), 102
diversity, ix, xiii; lack of, ix
documentary film work, 16, 109, 111, 161, 162
documentary form, 14, 113, 129
Dry Bones (Dash), 148
Du Bois, W. E. B., 4, 35, 90, 125; "double consciousness," 35, 90

Due, Tananarive, 84, 105
Dupree, Mignon, 122, 131, 146
DuVernay, Ava, xiv, xx, 49, 55, 85, 86, 87, 101, 107, 108, 118, 134, 140, 151, 163

Early, Charity Adams, 174
Ebiri, Bilge, 67–73
Eisenstein, Sergei M., 69, 124
Eliott, Delores, 16
Emanuel Nine, 99
Enemy of the Sun (Dash), 33, 175
Esther Jeter (character), 124, 147
Eve's Bayou (Lemmons), vii
Evers-Manly, Sandra, 174
experimental film, 75, 87, 91, 98, 101, 109, 114

Farmer-Paellmann, Deadria, 148
Ferris, Amy Schor, 70
film, as propaganda, 146, 166
film industry credits: cable television films, 96; commercials, 52, 63, 64, 66, 93, 96, 121, 171, 175; documentary films, xi, 165, 171, 172; editing, 172; film exhibit, 134; movies of the week, 84, 93, 102, 136; museum films, 93; music videos, xi, xviii, 29, 34, 64, 84, 93, 96, 121, 136, 147, 171, 172, 175; production, 172; screenplays, xii, 23, 28, 53, 175; short films, x, xi, 8, 73, 84, 109, 120, 133, 134; sound, 171, 172; television advertisements, xi; television films, xi, 96; television serial episodes, xi, xii; webisodes, xi; writing credits, 171
FilmEx, 88, 94
films, x, xi, 8, 11, 39, 40, 61, 73, 81, 84, 109, 120, 133, 134, 149; auteur, 11, 39, 40; feature, 61, 81, 84, 149; short, x, xi, 8, 73, 84, 109, 120, 133, 134; signature, 39
Finding Christa (Billops), 20
Flash and the Spirit (Thompson), 3
Floyd, George, 134, 138

folklore, ix, 6, 87, 98; studies, xiii
foreign films aesthetic, x, 40, 52, 54, 93, 124, 134, 143, 145, 170
Forster, Nick, 112
"four hundred questions," 35, 40
Four Women (Dash), viii, ix, x, xvii, 3, 17, 19, 69, 87, 95, 109, 113, 114, 120, 130, 154
Freeman, Monica, 116
funding, xii, 5, 31, 29, 32, 80, 83, 96, 102, 114, 175
Funny Valentines (Dash), xii, xix, 30, 54, 61, 63, 70, 71, 72, 96, 102, 121, 134, 136, 167

Ganja and Hess (Gunn), 97, 112, 113, 169
Geechee Girls Productions, 159
"Geechee Recollections" (Dash), 156
gender issues, 16, 17, 55, 59, 61, 164
Georgia/South Carolina Sea Islands, vii, ix, 3, 5, 6, 13, 25, 95, 99, 130, 131, 158, 167
Gerima, Haile, viii, xvii, 6, 21, 28, 29, 36, 80, 85, 86, 102, 112, 161
Gibson Girl dresses, 68, 77, 171
Girls Who Wore Black (Grace), 48
Ginsberg, Allen, 48, 61, 104
Giovanni, Nikki, 81
"Give Me One Reason" (Chapman), xviii, 29, 45
Glover, Danny, 31, 45, 48, 104
Gómez, Sara, 81, 101, 124
Gone with the Wind (Fleming), 53, 54, 77, 82, 83, 91, 93
Gorilla, My Love (Bambara), 14, 155
graveyard ornaments, 27, 165
Great Migration, 75, 95, 100, 121
Green Book, The (Farrelly), 161
Grisby-Bates, Karin, 42
Grosvenor, Robert, 104
Guerrero, Ed, 96
Gullah Geechee, vii, viii, xi, xvii, 3, 28, 33, 45–49, 50, 51, 60, 61, 66, 77, 79, 82, 83,

88, 89, 98, 100, 103, 108, 121, 123, 127, 128, 133, 135, 143, 157, 158, 159; roots/culture, vii, 13, 157; tongue, vii
Gullah Gullah Island (Day), 103
Gunn, Bill, 97, 104, 110, 112, 169

Hair Piece (Chenzira), 117
Hammon, David, 7
Hans, Simran, 106–8
Harris-Perry, Melissa, 83
Heckerling, Amy, 85, 173
Henderson, Roni Nicole, xvii, 100
Henderson, Rhudine (mother), vii, xvii
Hentz, Madam Eta, 163
hippie culture, 47, 85
historical drama, 54, 58, 66, 105, 135, 150, 156, 170
historical events/issues, 4, 25, 31, 72, 76
historical films, 53, 55, 135, 170
Holland, Andre, 175
Hollywood, viii, xii, 10, 19, 22, 28, 29, 30, 32, 33, 34, 38, 39, 40, 41, 42, 45, 46, 53, 56, 67, 72, 80, 82, 83, 85, 87, 91, 100, 103, 112, 121, 126, 132, 133, 134, 135, 140, 145, 146, 152, 158, 161, 165, 170
Holmes, Karmel Maori, 95–105
Holst, Lynn, 5
"hood" films, 34
hooks, bell, x, xiii, xviii, 51, 55, 130, 154, 155
Hopkinson, Nalo, 84, 105
Horak, Chris, 51
horror movies, 38, 158, 169, 172
Hoosier, Trula, 6, 169
Houston-Jones, Ishmael, ix, xviii, 9
How to Become a Union Camerawoman (Maple), 115
Howard University, xx, 160, 161, 169; Dash's faculty position, xx, 160, 161
Hudlin brothers, 22, 42; Warrington, 117
Hudson, William, 7

Hughes, Langston, 24, 25
Hunt, A. E., 133–41
Hunt, Stephanie, 45–49
Hurricane Hugo, 46, 57
Hurricane Katrina, 42, 43
Hurston, Zora Neale, xi, xix, 122, 123, 157

I and I (Caldwell), 165
Ibo Landing, x, 26; Eula's monologue, x
Igbo language, 31, 79
Ikiru (Kurosawa), 90
Illusionist, The (Burger), 33
Illusions (Dash), ix, x, xiii, xviii, xix, 3, 4, 5, 29, 32, 37, 53, 67, 68, 80, 87, 95, 101, 109, 120, 122, 124, 131, 133, 138, 146, 164, 165
Imitation of Life (Sirk), ix, 53
improvisation, 52, 68, 122
Incognito (Dash), 61, 70, 72, 96
independent Black films, viii, 6, 10, 11, 30, 42, 163
Indianapolis Museum of Art, xix, 30, 72; "Film with Artist Talk Program," 30
indigo fields, 53, 76, 83, 92
indigo-handed people, 25, 26, 50, 53, 76, 82; dyeing mounds, 52; scars of slavery, 25
Industrial Revolution, 65, 75, 76
Inside Man (Lee), 43
integrity, xiii, 9, 25, 31, 34, 39
"interiority" of Black lives, 157
International African American Museum, xxi, xxii, 158, 167, 174; *Seeking* project, xxi, 174
Iona (character), xi, 157

Jackson, Pam, 7
Jafa, Arthur (AJ), 50, 51, 52, 59, 60, 64, 74, 89, 92, 94, 107, 130, 136, 169
Jarvis, Martha Jones, 7
Jenkins, Barry, 107, 136
Jewison, Norman, 23, 77

188 INDEX

Jones, Steven, 7
Juan (character), 126
Jules and Jim (Truffaut), 69, 90
Julien, Isaac, 24, 169
Juneteenth, 134

Kai, N'gai, 6
Killer of Sheep (Burnett), 6, 22, 29, 79–80, 139, 165
Kindred (Butler), 105
Kino International Films, 89
Knowles, Solange, 81, 94, 107, 169; "Cranes in the Sky," 94; "Don't Touch My Hair," 94; Saint Heron, 94
Krim, Don, 89
Kubler-Ross, Elizabeth, 96
Kurosawa, Akira, 36, 90, 124
Kwanzaa, 115

La Lectrice (Deville), 34
LA Rebellion, viii, xv, xvii, 18, 28, 63, 69, 79, 84, 85, 86, 95, 97, 101, 106, 118, 120, 133, 139, 161, 163, 165; Barbara McCullough, viii, xv, xvii; Billy Woodberry, viii, xvii, 28, 165; Charles Burnett, viii, xvii, 28, 85, 86, 139, 165; Haile Gerima, viii, xvii, 28, 85, 86, 161; LA School of Black Filmmakers, viii, xvii; Larry Clark, viii, xvii, 85, 95
Lanza, Tim, 59, 75, 94
Larkin, Alile Sharon, viii, xviii, 6, 102
Larsen, Nella, ix
Last Samurai, The (Zwick), 85
Latin American Cinema Movement, 29
Lee, Spike, 22, 23, 30, 37, 42, 43, 45, 85, 86, 102
legacy, x, xii, xiv, 50, 51, 61, 96, 108, 121, 137, 150, 154, 160, 166, 175
Lemmons, Kasi, vii, 170

Lemonade (Beyoncé), vii, xiv, xx, 74, 75, 79, 80, 81, 88, 93, 94, 96, 97, 106, 119, 121, 168, 169
Lessane, Patricia Williams, xxi, 46, 47, 48, 49
Let the Church Say Amen! (Charles), 110
LGBTQ+ issues, 126
Libatique, Matthew, 152
Library of Congress, xi, 29, 46, 63, 96, 121, 156; National Registry of Films, xi, 29, 46, 63, 96, 121, 166
Like It Is (Noble), 110, 113
"locus of creativity," 36
London Film Festival, 63, 83, 126
Looking for Langston (Julien), 24, 25, 169
Los Angeles Film Exposition, ix, xvii
Los Angeles Film School, 28, 36
Losing Ground (Collins), 80, 101, 112
Love Boat, The (Lange), 18
Love Song (Dash), xix, 29, 51, 54, 55, 61, 63, 66, 69, 72, 96, 102, 121, 134, 136, 147
Lowe, Anne, 163, 175
Luciano, Felipe, "The Last Poets," 115
Luckett, Josslyn, 69
Lynch, David, 91
lynching, 71, 95, 138

Malcolm X, 23, 84, 114, 155
male Western narrative, 14, 41
Mama Day (Naylor), ix, 8
Mammy, 54, 78, 83
Man Who Cried I Am, The (Williams), 32
Manoogian, Haig, 111
Maple, Jessie, 37, 101, 115
Maple, Leroy, 116
Marshall, Carrie, 27
Marshall, Kerry James, 7, 52, 91
Marshall, Paule, x, 26, 124, 154
Martin, Kameelah L., 154–76
Martin, Michael T., 28–44

Masakela, Hugh, 45, 48, 104
Masilela, Ntongela, 29, 43n2
Massiah, Louis, 100
Mayer, So, 63–66
Maynard, Valerie, 116
McCullough, Barbara, viii, xvii, xviii, 85, 101, 102
Melayne, Deirdre, 157
memory, 4, 13, 60, 97
metaphor, 40, 54, 58, 71, 76, 83, 92, 166, 176
Metropolitan Museum of Art, xxi, 163, 175
Miami International Film Festival, viii, ix
Middle Passage, 76, 82
Mignon Dupree (character), 122, 131, 146
misogyny/misogynoir, xii
Mobley, Mamie Till, 163
Morehouse College, xx, 51, 160, 161, 163
Moonlight (Jenkins), 107, 126, 135, 136
Moore, Kaycee, 6
Morris, Butch, 7
Morrison, Toni, ix, 13, 14, 23, 37, 52, 81, 92, 117, 123, 137, 144, 155, 157, 169
Morton, Tina, 100
Mother Bethel AME Church, 99, 100
Mother Emanuel AME Church, 99, 100
Mubarak, Omar (Randy Abbott), vii, xvii
Murphy, Eddie, 23
My Brother's Wedding (Burnett), viii, xviii, 7, 80
"My Narrative: Experiences of a Filmmaker" (Dash), 30
Myth of the Negro Past, The (Herskovitz), 3

NAACP, xix, 71, 142, 146
Nair, Mira, 101, 163
Nana Peazant (character), 6, 46, 50, 95, 130, 133
narration, 20, 39, 41, 66, 123; literary modes, 39; visual modes, 39

narrative(s), ix, x, xii, xiv, xv, 35, 50, 89, 163; binary style, 52; features, 41, 89, 93, 124; fiction, 35, 53; film, 16, 17, 19, 35, 41, 96, 110, 111, 150, 161; style, xiii
National Black Women's Health Project, ix, xviii, 9
National Endowment for the Arts, ix, xviii, 5, 48
National Public Radio (NPR), 48, 60
National Underground Railroad Freedom Center Museum, xix, 29, 55, 63, 66, 102, 134
Navajo Code Talkers, 121, 131, 132
Naylor, Gloria, ix, 7, 92, 103, 154
New Black Cinema, 49
New York Scene, 109, 110
New York Times, The, 37, 42, 135, 170
New York Times Magazine, The, 170
Nigerians, codebreaking, 31
Nothing but a Man (Roemer), 29

Onassis, Jackie, 48, 104, 127
One Way or Another (DeCierta Manera) (Gómez), 101
#OscarsSoWhite, 106–8
Our Kind of People (Dash), xii, xxi, 163

Palcy, Euzhan, xiv, 35, 40, 51, 163, 170
Parable of the Sower (Butler), 105
Parajanov, Sergei, 81
Parasecoli, Fabio, 48
Paris Is Burning (Livingston), 24
Parks, Raymond, 39
Parks, Rosa, xii, xix, 30, 32, 39, 40, 51, 54, 61, 63, 71, 102, 107, 121, 122, 134, 136, 137, 142, 145, 167
Passing (Larsen), ix
passing for white, ix, 29, 53, 121, 147
Passing Through (Clark), viii, 95, 102
Peazant family (characters), xi, 79, 88, 157

Penn's Landing, 100
Perry, Tyler, 31, 38, 174
Picker, David V., 112; Picker Institute, 111, 112
Pierce-Baker, Charlotte, 24
Potemkin (Eisenstein), 69
Praise House (Dash), xiii, xviii, 8, 69, 87, 165
Praisesong for the Widow (Marshall), x, 26
Prettyman, Michele, 109–19
Prince-Bythewood, Gina, 38, 55, 101, 102, 163
psychology of colors, 69, 150, 166
Public Broadcasting Service (PBS), xviii, 5, 10
Pursuit of Happyness, The (Muccino), 31

Qualles, Paris, 39, 146
Queen Sugar (Dash), xii, xiii, xx, 87, 108, 118, 140, 142
Queensbridge Projects, vii, 28, 38, 84, 117, 120, 155

racism, xii, 28, 61; systemic, 55
rape, 26, 70, 95, 146
Reader, The (Dash), 34
reality, of film industry, xi, 68, 138; inside/outside the frame, 144
Reasonable Doubt (Dash), xii, xxi, xxii, 163, 167
Reel to Real (hooks), xiii
Rees, Dee, xiv, 55, 101, 102
Reeves, Dianne, 148
Relatives (Houston-Jones), xviii, 9
reparations, 150–51
restoration, xx, xxii, 51, 59, 74, 80, 88, 89, 96, 106
rice, 83, 92, 108, 158
Rich, Matty, 22, 42, 138, 170
Rize (LaChapelle), 35
Rogobodiyan, A. J., 6

Rosa Parks Story, The (Dash), xii, xix, 30, 32, 39, 40, 51, 54, 61, 63, 71, 72, 102, 107, 121, 122, 134, 136, 137, 142, 145, 167

Saito, Stephen, 88–94
Sanchez, Sonia, 14, 81, 98, 155
Santana, Al, 111
Sayles, John, 58, 59
School Daze (Lee), 6, 7
sci-fi, 84, 105, 108, 117, 135
screenplays, xii, 23, 28, 53, 175
Sea Islands, vii, x, 3, 6, 13, 25, 46, 88, 95, 99, 130, 131, 158, 167; Sullivan's Island, 99
Seeking (Dash), xxi, 174
Selma (DuVernay), 49, 107
sex, xiii, 22, 54, 152
sexual harassment, 126
Shaft (Parks), 41
She Hates Me (Lee), 43
She's Gotta Have It (Lee), 7, 22, 23, 42, 102
Shire, Warsan, 96
short films, x, xi, 8, 73, 84, 109, 120, 133, 134
Sidewalk Stories (Lane), 6
Simone, Nina, viii, xvii, 17, 19, 48, 87, 104, 105, 114, 120, 154
Singleton, John, 22, 86
Six Triple Eight Postal Battalion, xii, 148, 174
16th Street Baptist Church, 137
slave ships, 26, 76, 122; figurehead, 26, 27, 52, 130; *Wanderer*, 122
slavery/enslavement, xi, 5, 25, 26, 46, 50, 53, 54, 68, 76, 79, 80, 82, 83, 121, 135, 148; scars/stains of, 25, 26, 50, 53, 83; symbols of, xi. *See also* indigo-handed people
Smallwood, Stephanie, 121
Smart-Grosvenor, Vertamae, 45, 47–49, 60, 61, 63, 66, 89, 96, 103, 108, 127, 128, 174

Smith, Michael Glover, 74–78
Smith, Will, 31, 38
"smugglers," 72
"Smuggling Daydreams into Reality" program, 73
social media, 96, 102, 137
Soldier's Story, A (Fuller), 77, 105
Solomon, Frances-Anne, xiv, 142–53
Song of Solomon (Morrison), 37, 123
speculative fiction, x, 25, 84, 125, 145
Spelman College, xxi, 109, 119, 120, 126, 142, 160, 161, 162, 174; "Hollywood in History" class, 161
Spirits of Rebellion (Davis), 97
Spook Who Sat by the Door, The (Dixon), 32
St. Helena Islands, 46, 103, 128
Stand and Deliver (Menéndez), 42
Standing at the Scratch Line (Dash), xx, 98, 99
stereotypes, viii, xii, 8, 26, 76, 87, 171
storytelling, ix, x, xii, xiii, 23, 28, 36, 37, 66, 84, 115, 154, 156, 160, 162, 163
Straight Out of Brooklyn (Rich), 42, 138, 170
"street cred"/cultural cache, xiv
students, xii, xiii, xiv, xix, 17, 19, 24, 45, 49, 73, 85, 86, 93, 101, 109, 111, 120, 139, 160, 161, 162, 169, 171, 173, 174; projects, 162
Studio Museum of Harlem, vii, viii, xvii, 7, 15, 16, 17, 28, 37, 47, 69, 90, 109, 111, 113, 114, 116, 125, 144, 172
Subway Stories (Dash et al.), xix, 29, 58, 102
Sugar Cane Alley (Palcy), 35, 40
Sundance Film Festival, x, xviii, xx, 42, 46, 59, 83, 161
Sweet Sweetback's Baadasss Song (Van Peebles), 41

Talk of the Nation (Goodwin), 48
Tar Baby (Morrison), 37
Tarkovsky, Andrei, 81
Taylor, Betty Blayton, 116
Taylor, Clyde, 11, 24, 85
testosterone films, 37, 38, 42
They Dance to Her Drum (Chenzira), 109
Third World Newsreel, 111, 116
13th (Du Vernay), 107, 151
Thompson, Robert Farris, 3, 97
Toussaint (Glover), 31
Travel Notes of a Geechee Girl (Dash), xx, xxi, 48, 51, 66, 89, 103, 108, 127, 128
Truffaut, Francois, 90, 124
Trump, Donald, 108
Tupelo 77 (Dash), 72
Turpin, Bahni, xi, 157
Tyson, Cicely, 45, 71, 146

Unborn Child (character), 50, 58, 81, 93, 100, 121, 123, 125, 133
University of California, Los Angeles (UCLA), viii, ix, xviii, xx, xxi, 3, 5, 6, 18, 28, 36, 47, 51, 58, 69, 79, 84, 85, 86, 91, 95, 97, 98, 100, 101, 102, 106, 113, 114, 118, 122, 125, 133, 137, 144, 150, 161, 163, 164, 172, 173; Film and Television Archive, 51; "Gun Smoke" class, 172
Urban Bush Women (Zollar), xviii, 8

Valladares, Carlos, 79–87
Vibration Cooking (Smart-Grosvenor), 47, 60, 108
Vidato, Yolanda, 101
visibility, vii, xii, 65
Voodoo, 78
Vorkapich, Slavko, 18

Waiting to Exhale (Whitaker), 39
Wakeman, Stan, 16, 37

Wali, Monona, 69, 85
Walker, Alice, ix, 3, 29, 81, 92, 120, 124, 144, 154, 155, 169
Washington, Kerry, 167
Water Ritual #1 (McCullough), 101
Wayne State University, xx, 160
Webb, Floyd, 7
Western linear narrative, x, 14
When the Levees Broke (Lee), 43
White Album, The (Jafa), 136
white fragility, 138
white privilege, 135
Whole Earth Catalog, 122
Why the Sun and the Moon Live in the Sky (Dash), xxi
Will (Maple), 37, 101, 115
Williams, John A., 13, 32
Williams, Michael Kelly, 7, 27, 52, 92, 130
Wilson, Nancy, "Now I'm a Woman," 43
Winfrey, Oprah, xix, 66, 87, 118
Withers, Ernest, 175
Wizard of Oz, The (Fleming), 33
"womanist vision," 139

Women of Brewster Place, The (Naylor), ix, 92
Women of Brewster Street (Naylor), ix
Women of the Movement (Dash et al.), 163
Women: Stories of Passion (Dash et al.), xix
Woodard, Alfre, 30, 70, 167
Woodberry, Billy, viii, xvii, 6, 21, 22, 28, 29, 85, 135, 165
Working Models for Success (Dash), viii
World War II, xii, 29, 31, 77, 131, 146, 148, 152

Yellow Mary, 6, 65
Yoruba aesthetics, 97–98
Young, Bradford, 167
Young Lords, 115
Young Soul Rebels (Julien), 24, 25
young "urban male" films, 38

Zajota and the Boogie Spirit (Chenzira), 109
Zollar, Jawole Willa, xviii, 8
Zwick, Ed, 85

About the Editor

Kameelah L. Martin is professor of African American studies and English at the College of Charleston in Charleston, South Carolina. She is the author of *Envisioning Black Feminist Voodoo Aesthetics: African Spirituality in American Cinema* (2016), in which she writes extensively about Julie Dash's iconic feature film *Daughters of the Dust*.

www.ingramcontent.com/pod-product-compliance
Lightning Source LLC
Chambersburg PA
CBHW030108170426
43198CB00009B/534